CHO HUN-HYUN'S LECTURES ON THE OPENING VOLUME 1

Published by Yutopian Enterprises
2255 29th Street, Suite #3
Santa Monica, CA 90405
1-800-YUTOGO-3
yutopian@netcom.com, yutopian@aol.com
http://www.webwind.com/go

Volume ISBN: 1-889554-60-X

Translated by
Seong-June Kim

Editing, Diagrams, and Layout by Craig R. Hutchinson

Proof Assistance by
Anthony Blagrove, Charles Matthews

Originally Published in Korea by Baduk Seodang

First English Printing July 2005
Printed in America

INTRODUCTION

There is something inexhaustible about go. There have been many games played, but no two games have been the same. Those who wish to improve rapidly at go may find this a disadvantage. If you are familiar with a certain formation, your confidence in maneuvering in it increases. But if a position is unfamiliar, you may be confused as to whether your tactics are good or not. In an important game, it is normal to stay with well-known plays. However you will often meet novel shapes in real games. Then your true level of play is tested. One of the best ways to improve is to experiment with new plays in games. This is time-consuming, and the benefit you gain from it does depend on your innate talent.

The very best way is to concentrate on study of the fundamentals and common shapes. In this book standard patterns are treated, in problem style. It is for amateurs, not professionals, and their needs are considered throughout. I hope this book will help you to improve your own level.

Cho Hun-Hyun

EDITOR'S NOTES

The traditional Japanese word "nirensei" will be used to identify the occupation of two corner star points on one side of the board.

The traditional Japanese word "sanrensei" will be used to identify the occupation of three star points on one side of the board.

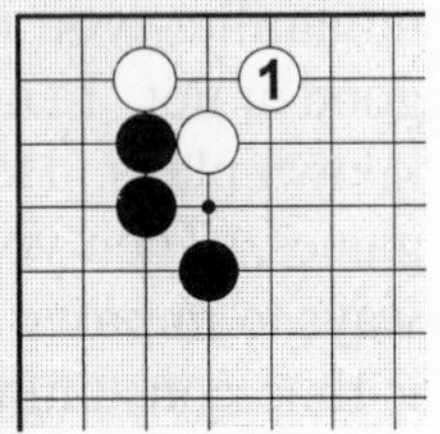

I call White's three stone shape a tiger and write "White plays a tiger link at 1" or "White plays a tiger attack" instead of "White connects with a tiger's mouth play at 1" or "White connects with a hanging connection at 1".

I take full responsibility for the final result. Please send any comments or suggestions to Yutopian Enterprises. Your critique will be much appreciated. Enjoy!

Craig R. Hutchinson

Lectures on the Openings
Table of Contents and Index

SECTION 1

FUNDAMENTAL CONCEPTS IN THE OPENING

Chapter 1: Territory and Framework

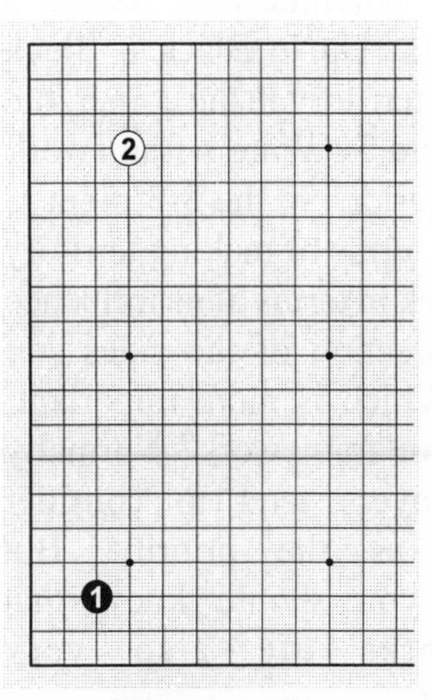

Diagram 1

Diagram 1 - Black 1 occupies the 3-3 point - the intersection between the third lines. From this point it is easy to make territory in the corner (normally we call the third line the territorial line and the fourth line the line of framework). This point, however, has weak influence towards the center and sides. Opposite it White 2 is a star point (4-4 point). It is the crossing point of the fourth lines and has an influence towards the center and sides. Starting at this point it is difficult to make secure territory either in the corner or on the sides.

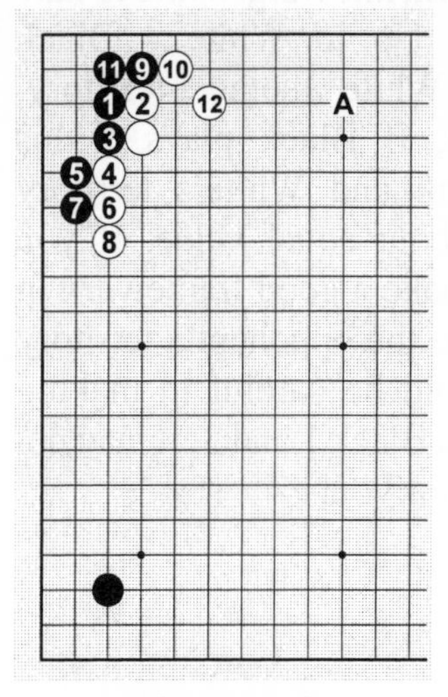

Diagram 2

Diagram 2 - Suppose Black invades at 1. Up to White 12 the ownership of the corner changes in favor of Black. However, from this position White has strong influence towards the center and the sides (especially towards **A**). This framework is good enough to balance the loss of territory in the corner.

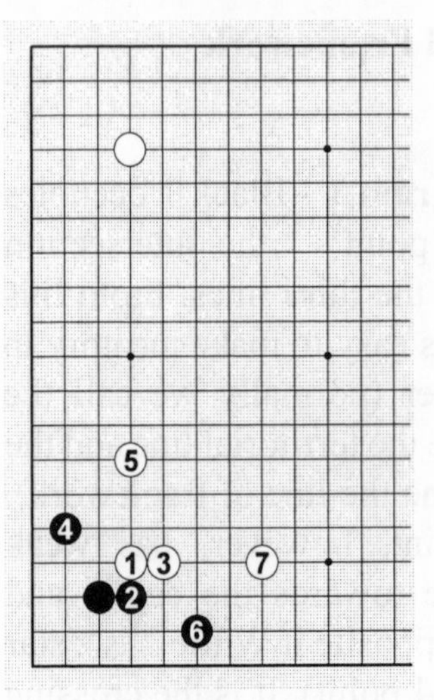

Diagram 3

Diagram 3 - White 1 is a play at a key point, limiting Black's territorial potential and making a framework. Up to Black 6 Black has good territory in the corner, but after White 7, White's framework is not inferior. So the 3-3 point is strong in terms of making territory but is weak in terms of its influence in the direction of the sides and center. Which is more important: territory or framework? Normally weak players tend to consider territory as the priority. But actually you should know that frameworks are also very important.

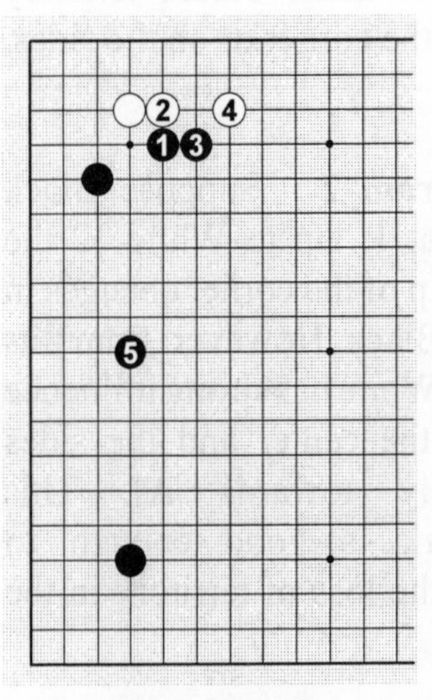

Diagram 4

Diagram 4 - Black 1 is a common play to make a framework, allowing White to take territory. Up to White 4 Black allows White some territory. However, if Black plays 5 this framework and White's territory are of about equal value. If you cannot make a good framework in answer to the opponent's territory you should be careful in making plays like Black 1 and 3; it may not be good for you.

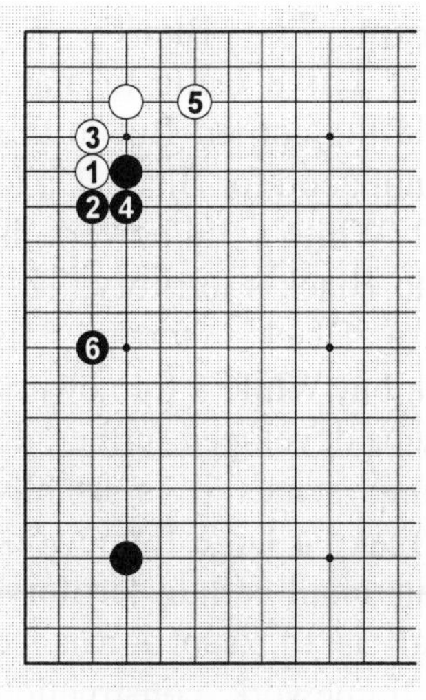

Diagram 5

Diagram 5 - White 1 is a common play to make territory. Up to White 5, White takes a considerable territory in the corner, but you should be aware that you allow Black to make a good framework. Up to Black 6, Black's framework is enough to rival White's territory. In this position Black's framework and White's territory are equally balanced. In the opening it can be of as much importance to make a framework as territory.

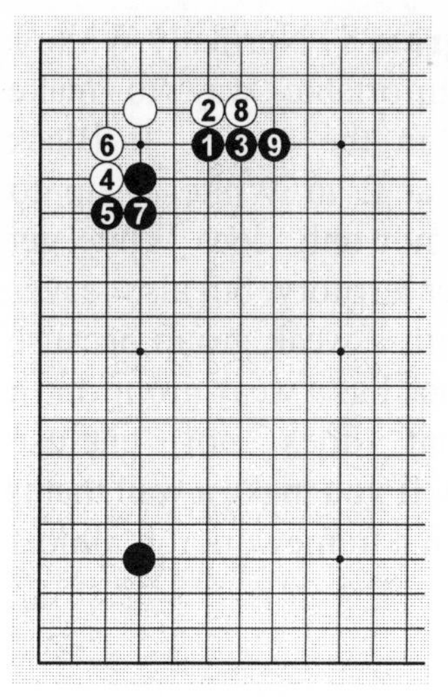

Diagram 6

Diagram 6 - Black's knight's shape at 1 is a common play to make a framework. Up to Black 9, its aim of making a good wall towards the center and sides is successful; now Black has strong influence towards center and sides. But allowing White some territory is inevitable. How you apply the framework concept is the key, and may decide the outcome of the game.

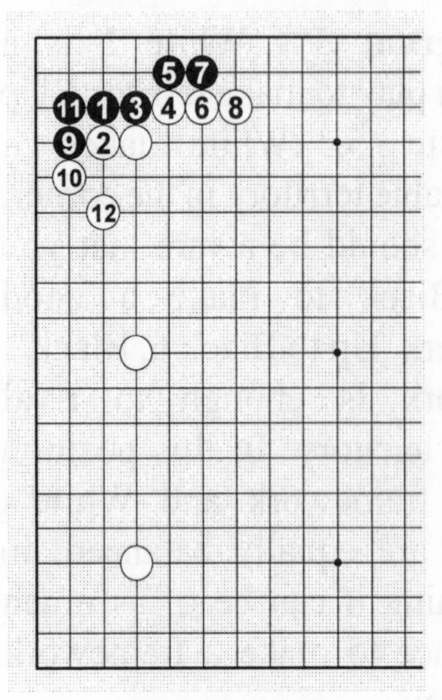

Diagram 7

Diagram 7 - Black's 3-3 invasion at 1 is a tactic to make territory in the corner. But in this case it is not good for Black. Up to White 12 White's framework is superior to Black's territory. This is because Black's territory is contained, but White's framework can easily be developed further. In the opening stages it is usually better to make a large framework rather than small certain territory. Best of all is to keep a balance between framework construction and the taking of definite territory.

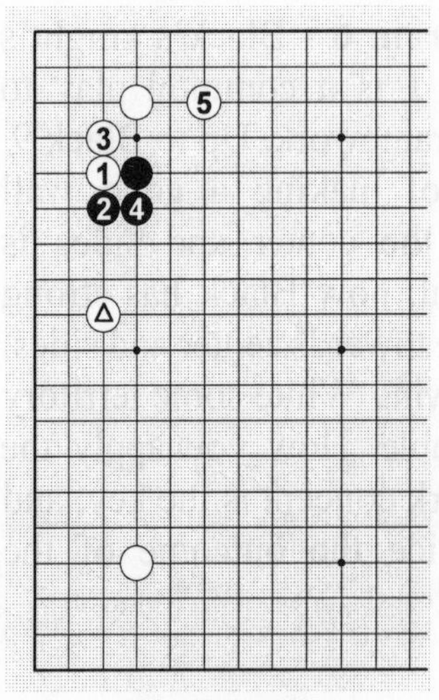

Diagram 8

Diagram 8 - Normally White 1 is a comfortable way to make territory in the corner. If Black answers at 2 to White 1, up to White 5 not only does White get the corner territory, but also leaves Black with a weak group because of Δ; Black has a weak group and a wall that does not enclose anything. If you make a wall that is not part of a framework it is almost useless.

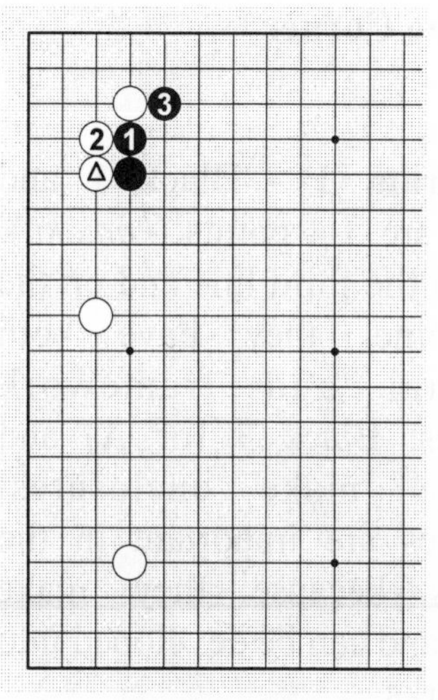

Diagram 9

Diagram 9 - Successful opening strategy is to keep the balance between territory and framework, so you must learn how to make frameworks too. In this situation when White attacks at Δ, Black 1 and 3 are correct. The crucial thing is to make a wall facing in an open direction (in this case the upper side). It is very important to make full use of a wall.

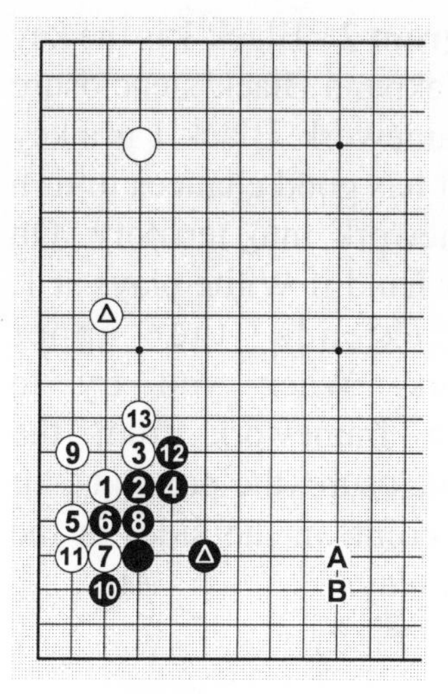

Diagram 10

Diagram 10 - Black 2 is a standard play to build a wall. But in this case up to White 13 the result is not good for Black; Black ▲ is too close to the wall. On the other hand Δ is properly placed. If Black ▲ were at **A** or **B**, Black would be satisfied with the result.

Chapter 2: Around The Corner

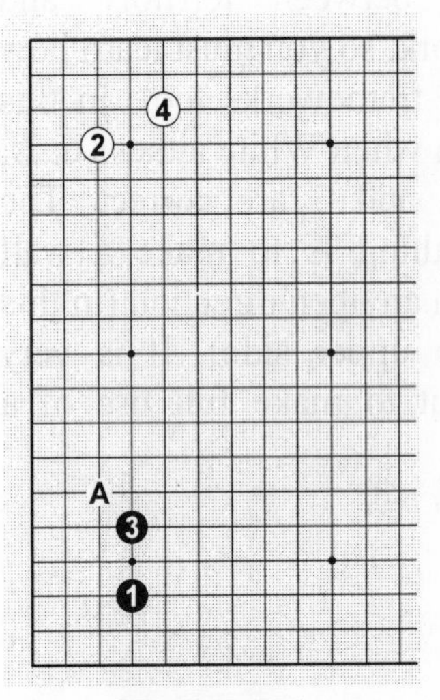

Diagram 1

Diagram 1 - Black 1 and White 2 are 3-4 points (*komoku*). Being on the third line and on the fourth line, they have both territorial and framework properties. Black 3 (or **A**) and White 4 make enclosures. Enclosures are important in the openings because they make territory and can be developed into frameworks.

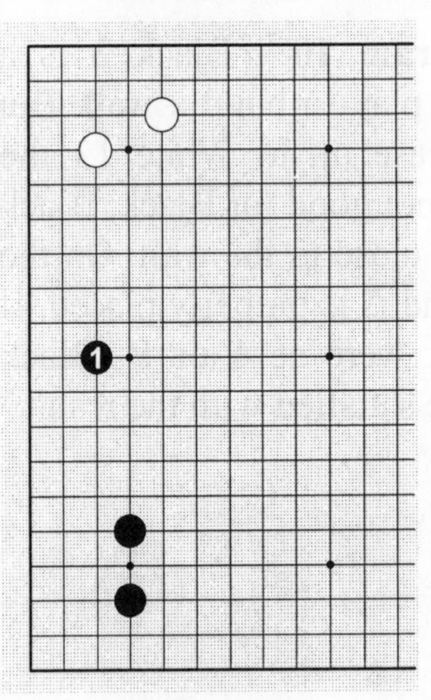

Diagram 2

Diagram 2 - Black 1 is the key point to expand Black's enclosure into a framework. Black 1 is a key play as it has good chances to turn the framework into territory. On the other hand if White plays at 1, White extends the upper framework. When you try to extend a framework from the corner enclosure, the point at 1 or the star point on the sides is the common play.

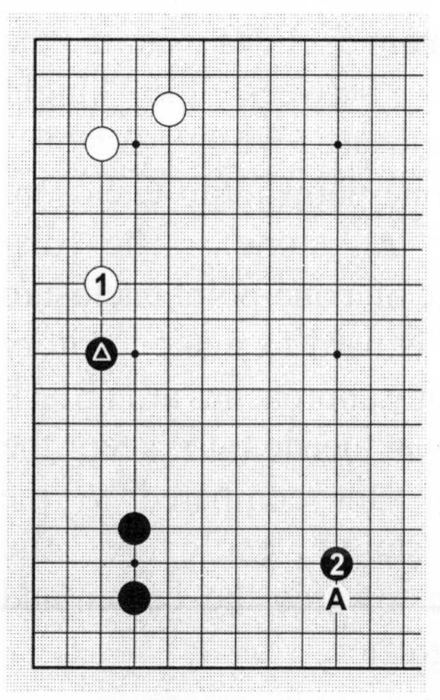

Diagram 3

Diagram 3 - White 1 against ▲ is a play to extend the framework, stopping Black's further extension on the left side. But after Black 2 (or **A**), Black's framework is almost perfect. In general it is not a good idea to allow your opponent to make a double-wing framework in the opening. White 1 at **A** is common, to stop Black's double-wing framework.

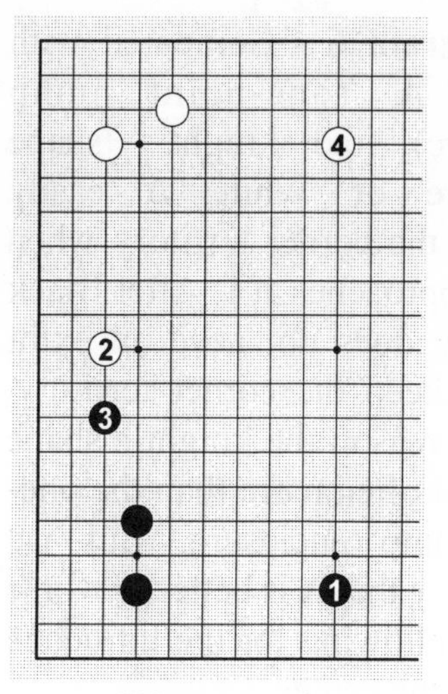

Diagram 4

Diagram 4 - Black 1 is a big play, but it is important for White to play at 2. This is an urgent point for both; not only do they extend their framework, but also restrict the opponent's influence. Up to White 4 White's framework is superior to Black's. This result is a success for White.

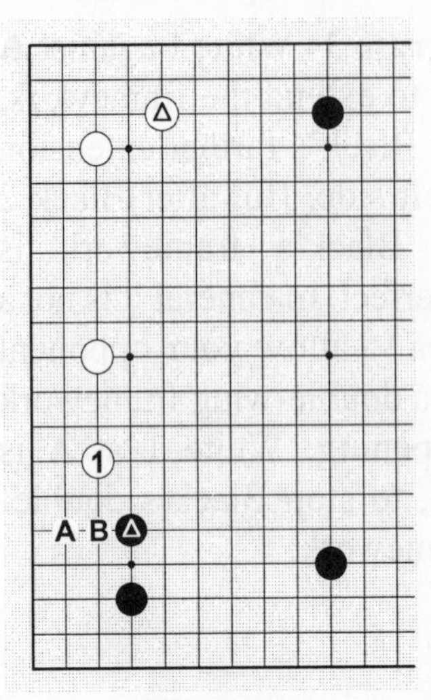

Diagram 5

Diagram 5 - Let's examine the difference between the knight shape enclosure (White's Δ stone) and the one-point jump enclosure (Black's ▲ stone). The disadvantage of a one-point enclosure is that it is hard to make territory when White approaches at 1 (Black **A** or **B** is needed to keep the territory). But compared to the knight shape enclosure the influence towards the center and sides is greater.

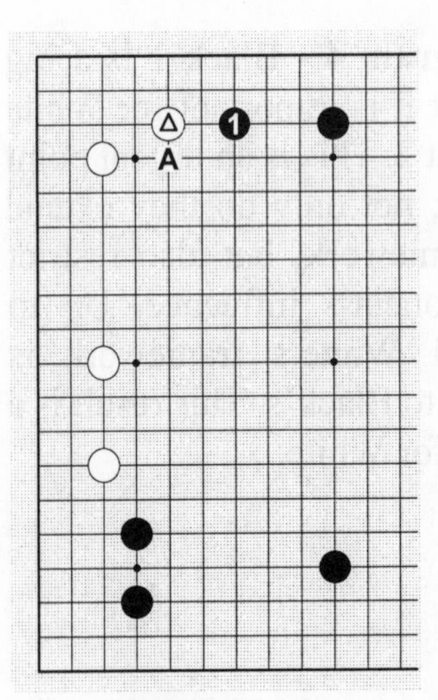

Diagram 6

Diagram 6 - Compared with White **A** (one-point jump enclosure), the knight's shape enclosure of White Δ easily defends the corner territory when Black approaches at 1. After Black 1, White does not need an extra play to keep the corner territory. For this reason the knight's shape is played often more than the one-point jump enclosure. But we cannot say that **A** is better or worse than Δ, allowing for the influence towards the center.

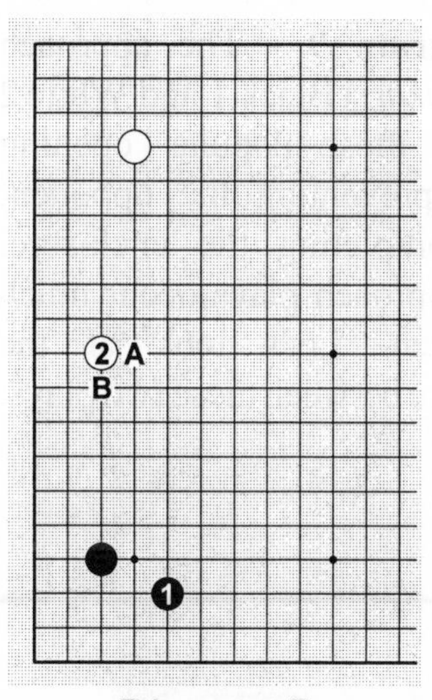

Diagram 7

Diagram 7 - In this situation Black's enclosure at 1 is the usual play. Usually it is hard to make territory by direct extension from the 3-4 point because it is not a wall. Black 1 takes solid territory in the corner and aims to extend the influence towards the sides later. On the other hand White's play is correct, as the star point has the makings of a wall. What about Black's direct extension at 2 (or **A** or **B**)? In general in the opening, first enclose the corner, then extend along the sides, and finally go towards the center. If your stone is already at the star point, you can extend directly on the sides.

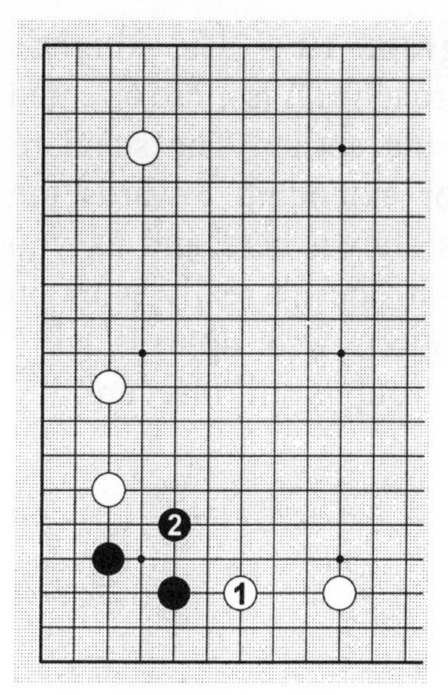

Diagram 8

Diagram 8 - If Black allows White to play at 1, Black can't extend towards either side. So Black's one-point jump towards the center is inevitable. If Black omits 2, White plays at 2. This blocks Black's access to the center and also threatens the corner group. Usually, if you cannot extend towards either side from the enclosure, this is not good.

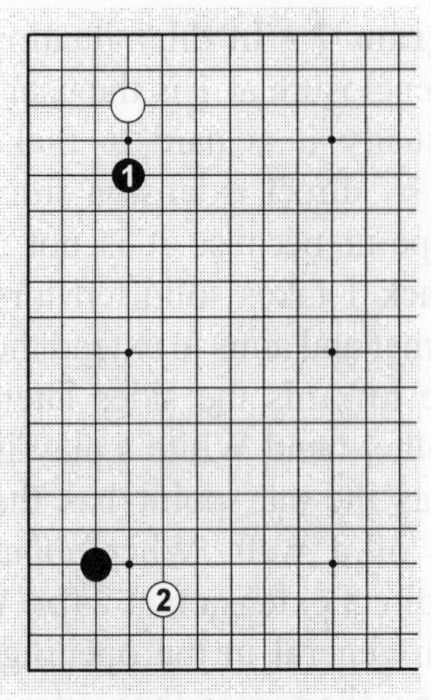

Diagram 9

Diagram 9 - The approach plays (*kakari*) Black 1 and White 2 are the most popular opening tactics, preventing the opponent from completing the enclosure. Other approach plays occur much less often. Let's look at the difference between these two plays.

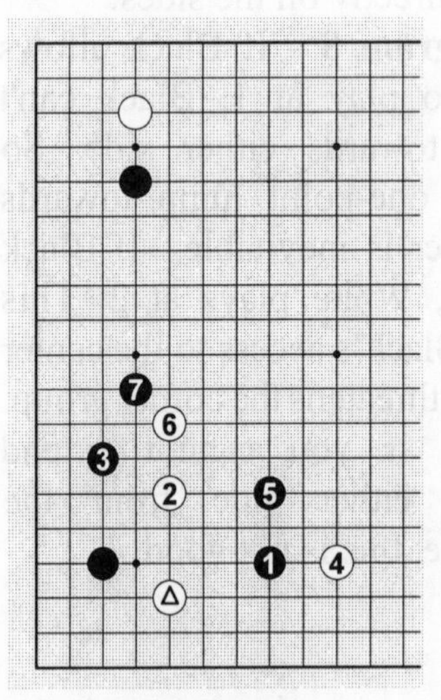

Diagram 10

Diagram 10 - The knight's play approach at Δ is more oriented towards the corner. The standard *joseki* for extending towards the center is shown here and as you can see, it doesn't really work in this situation. Also, up to Black 7 White's group is still insecure.

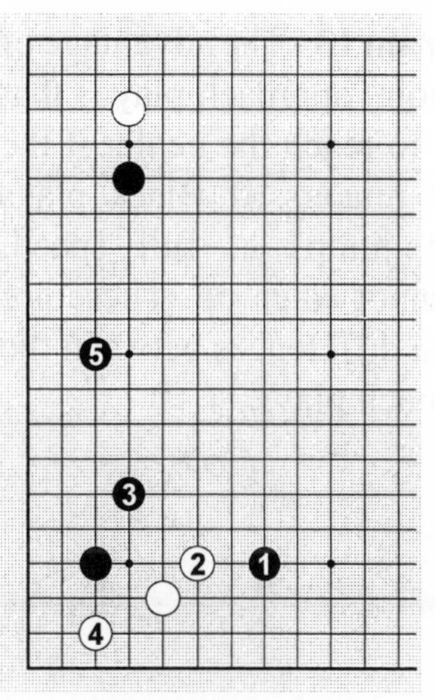

Diagram 11

Diagram 11 - On the other hand the knight's play approach can often easily give White a base in the corner. Up to Black 5 is a fundamental *joseki*. Now White has settled comfortably in the corner. There are no threatening plays for Black to make. If your style emphasizes territory, this is the maneuver for you.

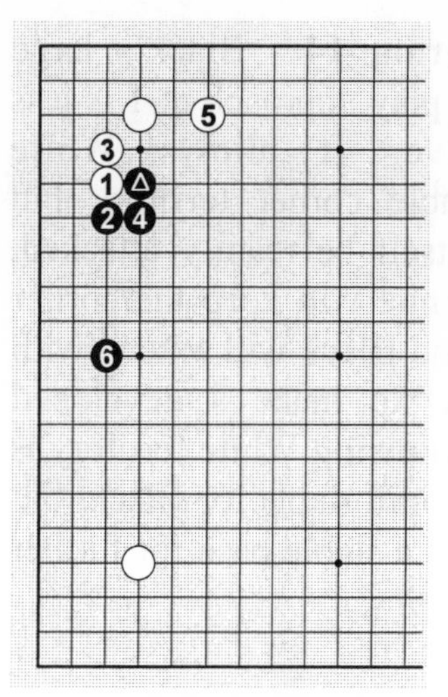

Diagram 12

Diagram 12 - Black's one-point approach at ▲, on the other hand, is more oriented towards walls and framework. Its disadvantage is that it allows White to take the corner territory easily with White 1. Up to Black 6 is a common *joseki*. White takes the corner territory, in *sente*.

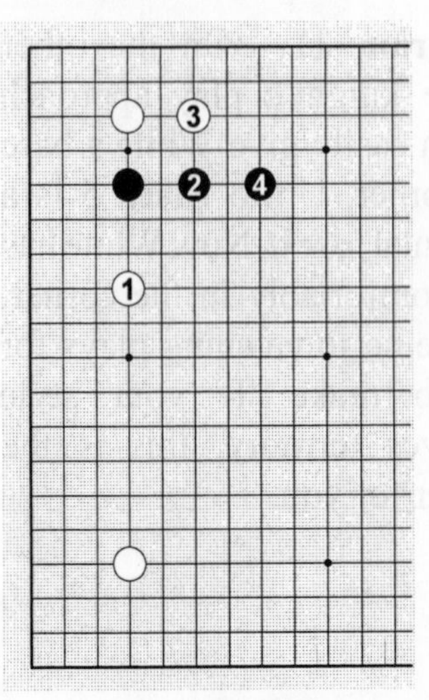

Diagram 13

Diagram 13 - The advantage of the one-point approach play is that it is easy to reach the center if the opponent pincers. If Black plays one-point jumps at full speed, White cannot catch up. These are the crucial differences between the two approach plays.

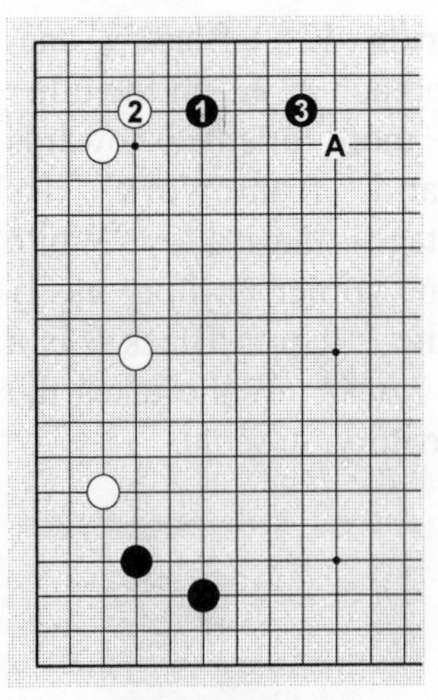

Diagram 14

Diagram 14 - Black's large knight's play approach at 1 is less aggressive. It allows White comfortable corner territory but cannot itself be readily attacked. Often White will keep the corner with 2 and Black will extend with 3 (or **A**) to make a developed group. Allowing White territory is a bit uncomfortable for Black, but Black has a stable base for further expansion.

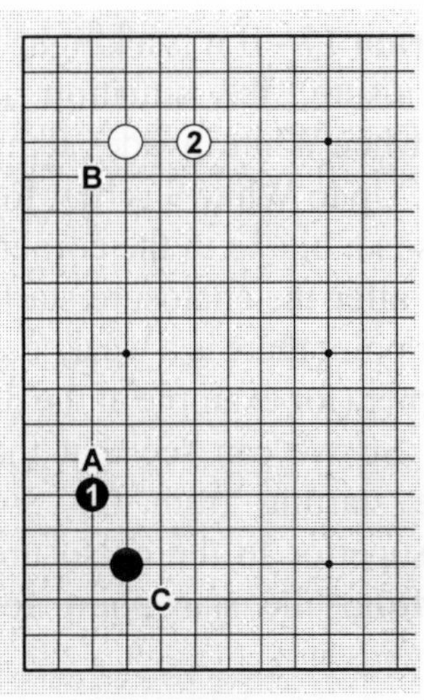

Diagram 15

Diagram 15 - Black 1 (or **A**) and White 2 are the most popular attempts to make an enclosure starting from the star point. Compared to enclosures starting at the 3-4 point, the corner territory is incomplete. To complete the territory a further play at **B** and **C** is required. Star points are oriented towards walls and framework and it is usually better to extend down the sides rather than to make an enclosure.

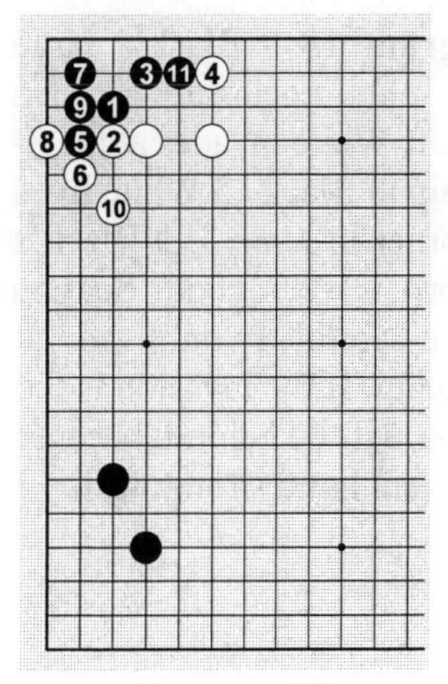

Diagram 16

Diagram 16 - One-point enclosures have the usual weakness at the 3-3 point. Up to Black 11 Black lives fairly easily in the corner, but White has strong influence outside. White may prefer to play to make territory more secure.

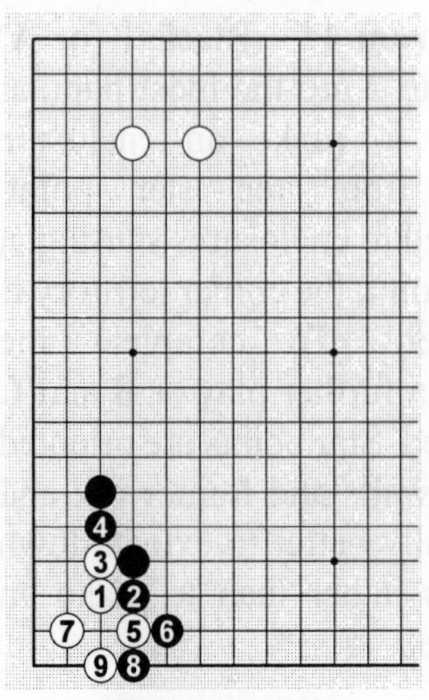

Diagram 17

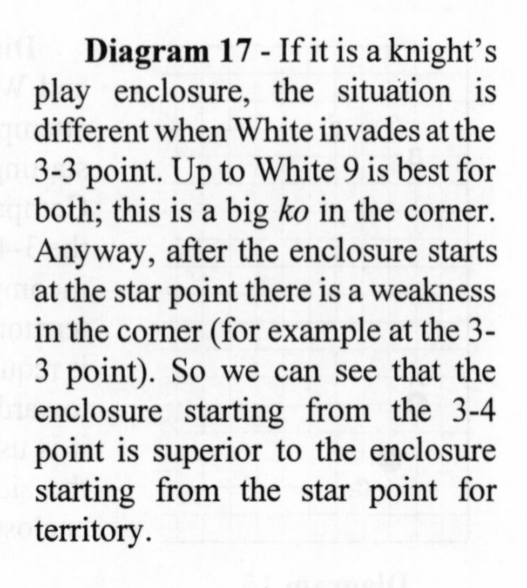

Diagram 17 - If it is a knight's play enclosure, the situation is different when White invades at the 3-3 point. Up to White 9 is best for both; this is a big *ko* in the corner. Anyway, after the enclosure starts at the star point there is a weakness in the corner (for example at the 3-3 point). So we can see that the enclosure starting from the 3-4 point is superior to the enclosure starting from the star point for territory.

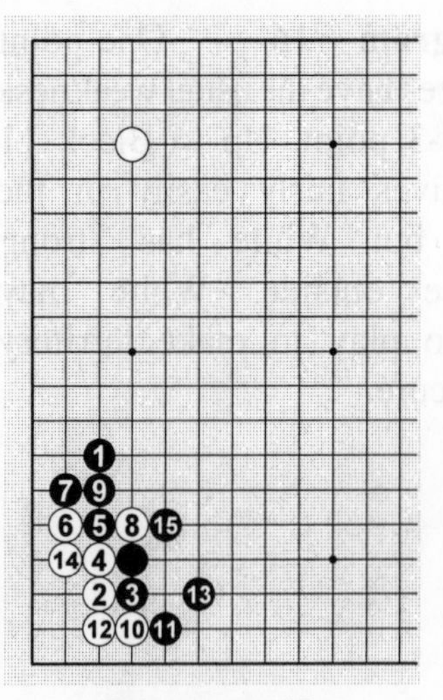

Diagram 18

Diagram 18 - Black's large knight's play enclosure is also possible. If White invades at the 3-3 point, up to Black 15 White lives in the corner in *sente*. But Black's framework is very good. So you should be careful if you invade at the 3-3 point. If the invasion is too early, you will be behind, because the opponent has a strong wall.

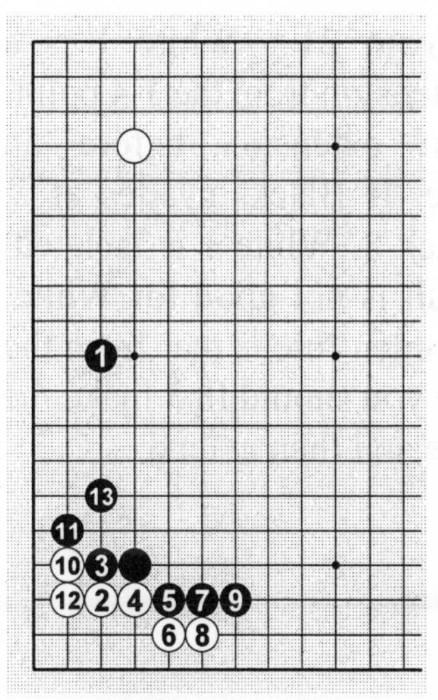

Diagram 19

Diagram 19 - Black 1 is a play to extend the influence from the corner. Extension from the star point has priority over the enclosure in the corner. White's invasion at 2 is not good. Up to Black 13, White has lived in the corner with some territory, but Black has a very strong framework indeed. This result is good for Black.

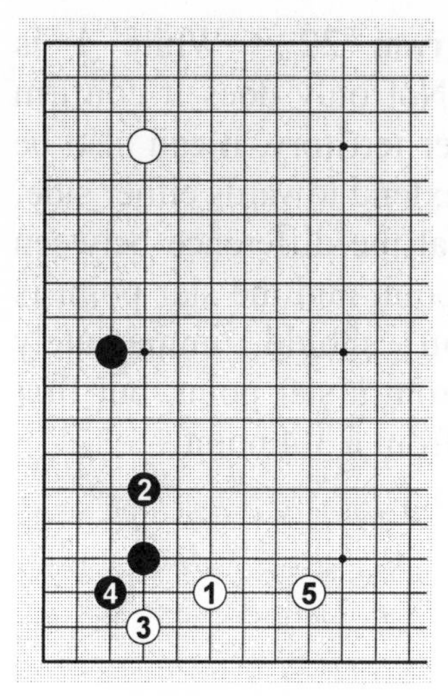

Diagram 20

Diagram 20 - White's approach at 1 is the correct direction to prevent Black from making influence towards the right side. Up to White 5 this is the most popular *joseki*. Black has got a good territory on the left side, while White's group settles on the lower side. Both players will be happy with this result. The important thing is that you should approach from the open side, so that you have got enough space to extend and settle the group/shape.

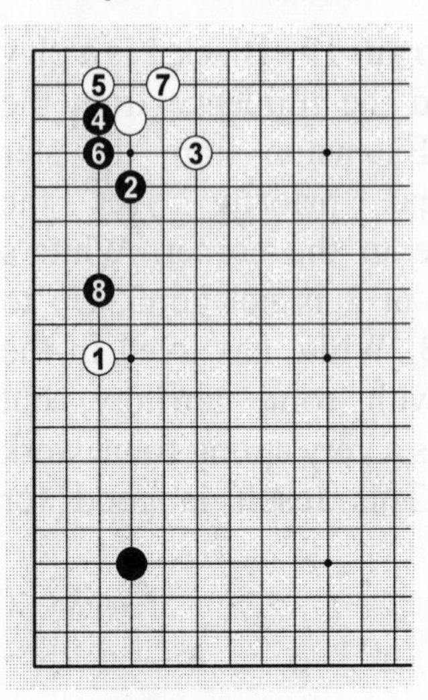

Diagram 21

Diagram 21 - White 1 is a direct extension from the 3-4 point. It is an extension before an enclosure. If Black invades at 2, after Black 8, White 1 is isolated. This result is not good for White. So the golden rule is that from the 3-4 point you should first make the enclosure and then extend.

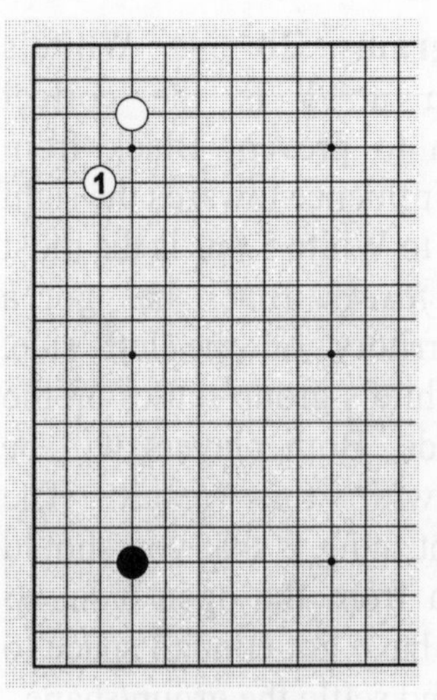

Diagram 22

Diagram 22 - White 1 is correct. Not only does it confirm the corner territory, it can also be used to extend towards either side. In general the difference between the 3-4 point and the star point is that you should immediately extend from a star point, but first enclose from a 3-4 point.

Chapter 3: Extensions

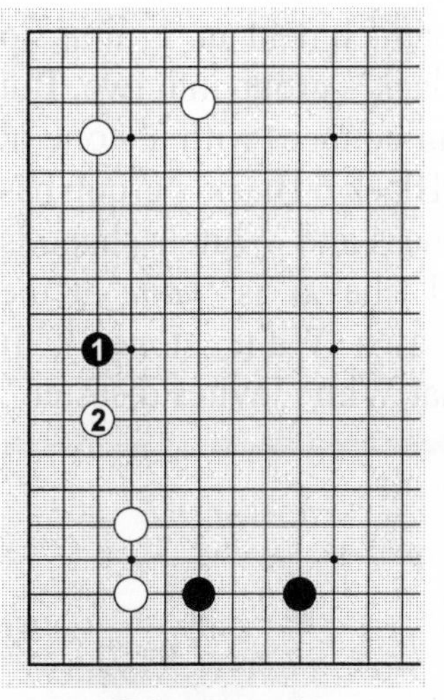

Diagram 1

Diagram 1 - In this situation Black's wedge at 1 is a standard intervention tactic. White 2 is the correct direction to shut off the lower corner, attacking Black 1. Now what is the best maneuver for Black? The best way for Black is to settle down on the side with some territory. Otherwise Black will have a bad result.

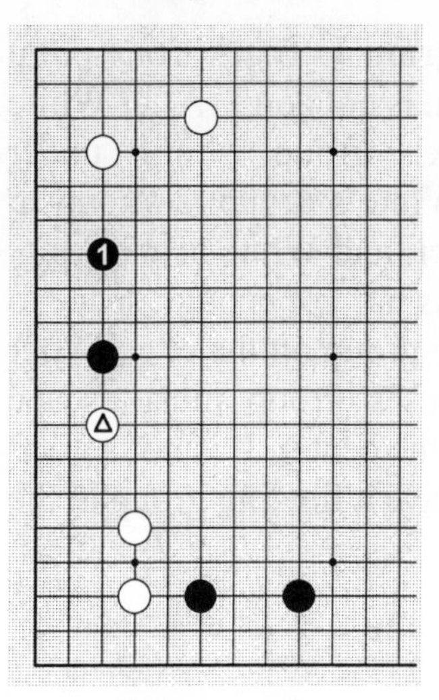

Diagram 2

Diagram 2 - Black 1 against White's approach at the Δ is best. You had better remember that if you have a two-point extension inside the opponent's framework, your group is almost safe. In this situation Black 1 – the two-point extension on the third line – is the fundamental extension to settle your group on the side.

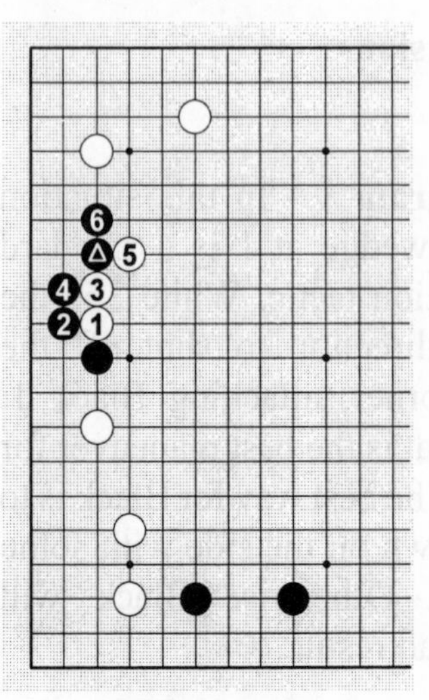

Diagram 3

Diagram 3 - In this position you can easily understand why two-point extensions are safe. White's attachment at 1 aims to divide Black's group into two. But Black can connect with a stone at 2. Up to Black 6 Black's group has no weakness and White's shape is not good (the ▲ is '*hane* at the head of two White stones'). It seems that White invites disaster.

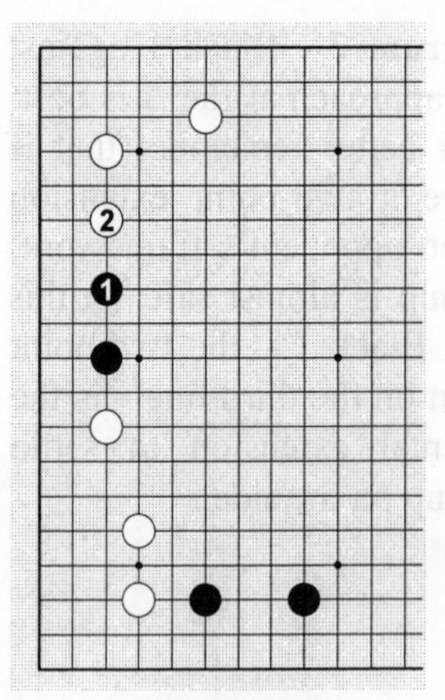

Diagram 4

Diagram 4 - Black's one-point extension is not good. After White 2, Black's group is still under threat. White's group is strong in the corner, and White is attacking. Black has not got enough space to settle the group on the edge. After this Black's group must escape towards the center. It is not a good idea to have a floating group in the opening.

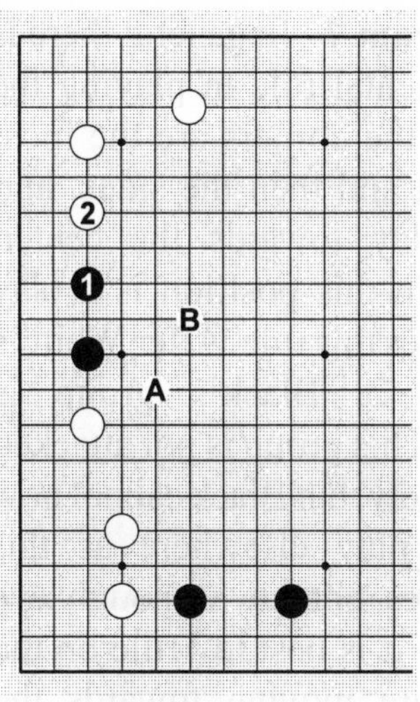

Diagram 5

Diagram 5 - If Black ignores White 2, Black can live, but White has the initiative to create influence or territory while attacking Black's group (with **A** or **B**). Novices often make weak groups thinking that if they live they have succeeded. They should learn to take the effect of White's walls or territory into account too.

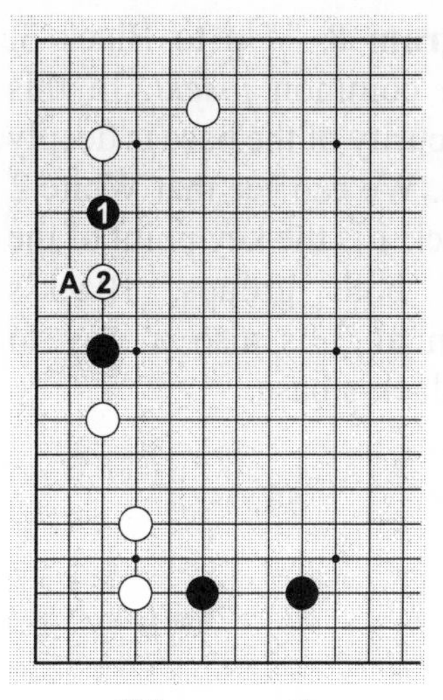

Diagram 6

Diagram 6 - In this situation Black's three-point extension at 1 is possible. Comparing with the two-point extension, it has a problem when White invades at 2. After that Black's group seems to be divided into two. Black can perhaps connect by playing at **A**. But Black will have to pay something for connecting, so the two-point extension is the safest way.

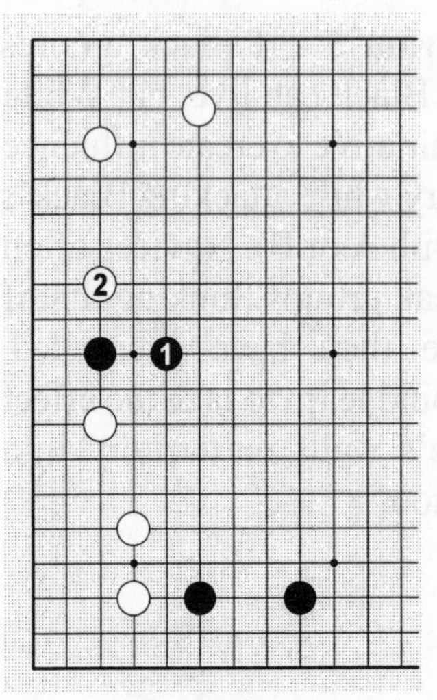

Diagram 7

Diagram 7 - In general there is a fundamental rule in playing the opening: the corners are the most important and then the sides, and finally play towards the center. Black 1 in this position is a play that ignores this rule. After White's approach 2, Black's group is floating. This group is not attacked immediately, but Black cannot now properly play elsewhere as this group does not have enough eye space. So it is best to settle on the side before moving towards the center.

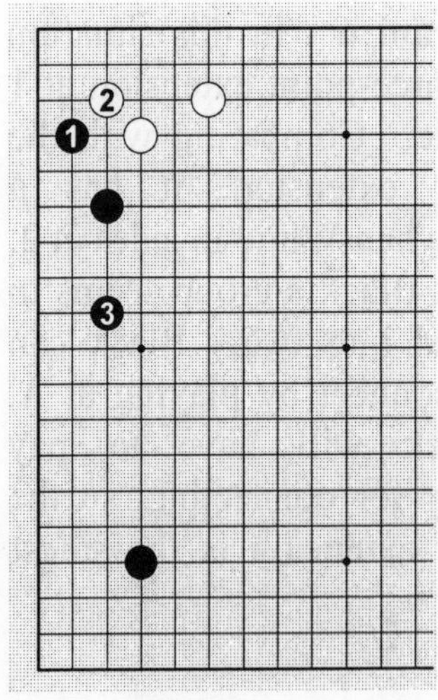

Diagram 8

Diagram 8 - Up to Black 3, this is a common *joseki*. In this *joseki* security of the base is deeply involved. We can see that White 2 after Black 1 is the key point of the base of both groups. Black's extension at 3 is also a way to secure Black's base.

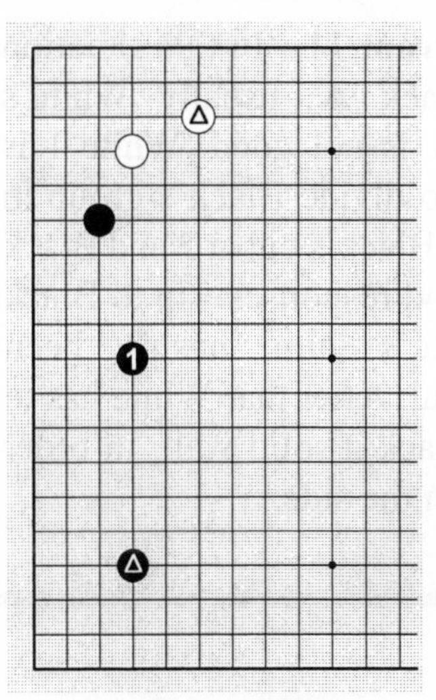

Diagram 9

Diagram 9 - Considering the interval between 1 and ▲, you can extend back to Black 1. Black 1 as a reply to White Δ is an extension that is new for us. A two-point extension on the third line may seem normal here. But the idea is that the wider your extension the more territory you may get. Often Black 1 is more efficient.

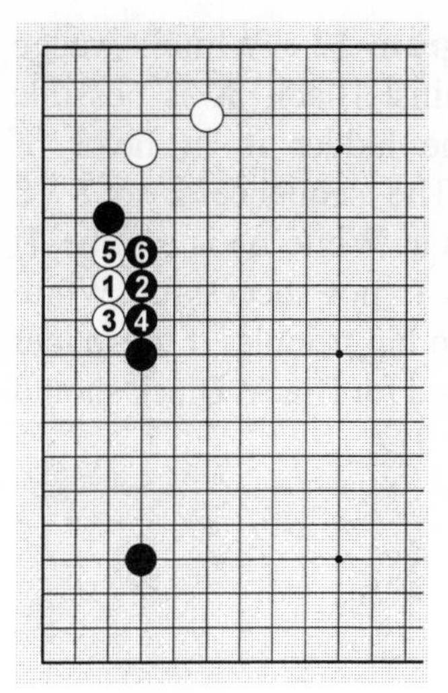

Diagram 10

Diagram 10 - There is a weakness at 1. But up to Black 6, Black will now be able to connect together. White takes some territory, but Black has strong influence towards the center. This result is not bad for Black. So White should choose the timing of the invasion with care.

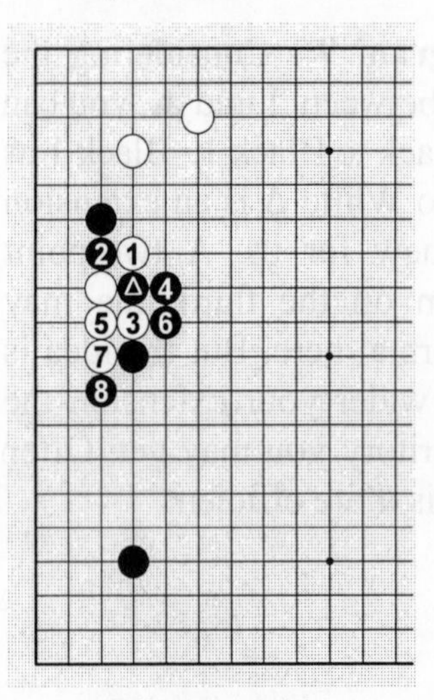

Diagram 11

Diagram 11 - In this situation after Black ▲, usually White's play at 1 is not good. White 1 is aiming to divide Black's group in two, but Black's cut at 2 and Black 8 are good responses. Up to Black 8 White's aim hasn't been successful. After that White has to allow Black a solid wall, in order to live on the side.

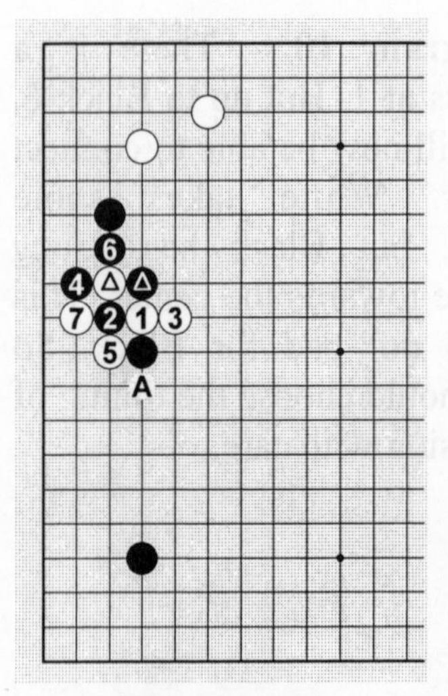

Diagram 12

Diagram 12 - White's wedge at 1 against Black ▲ is possible when the ladder is in favor of White. The sequence 2 to 8 (8 connects at White Δ) is routine. If White **A** is not successful, White will be in big trouble. If the ladder is not good for Black, Black should play 2 at 3.

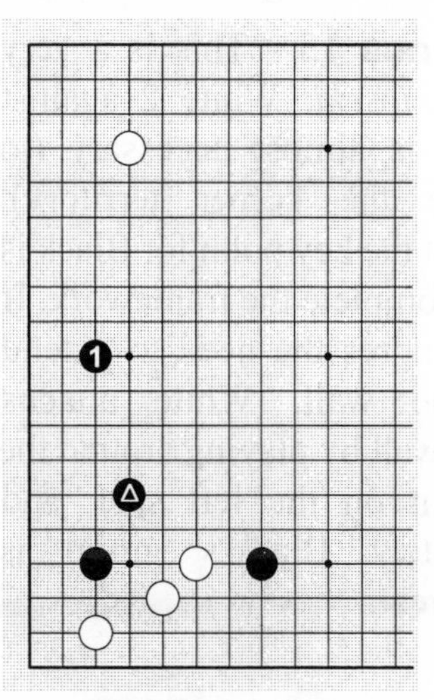

Diagram 13

Diagram 13 - Black 1 here is another three-point extension. When you play the three-point extension of Black 1 from Black ▲, you should consider the balance between the third and fourth lines. The balance of this extension will allow you to connect even if White invades. So it is often played in real games.

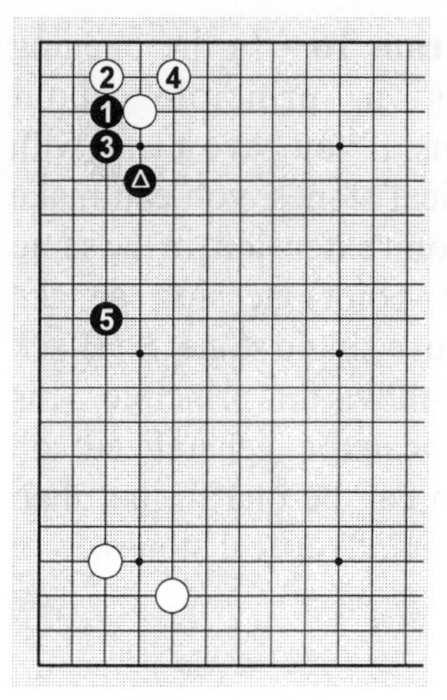

Diagram 14

Diagram 14 - This is a further common *joseki*. Black 1 and 3 are often played to strengthen the group before extending to 5. Up to Black 5 the *joseki* is complete. It is usual to play the three-point extension from the fourth line stone (▲ in this position).

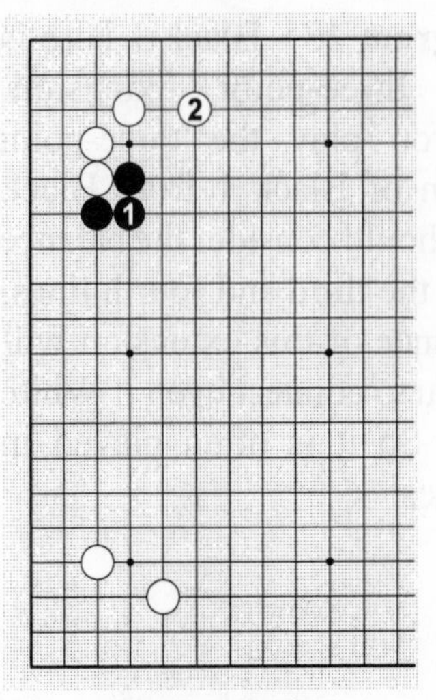

Diagram 15

Diagram 15 - This is a very common *joseki*. White 2 against Black 1 is almost necessary (to complete the corner territory). After that the key point for Black is how to complete the framework. If Black ignores the need to extend from the wall, White attacks Black's wall by playing around the star point on the left side; and immediately Black's group is under threat.

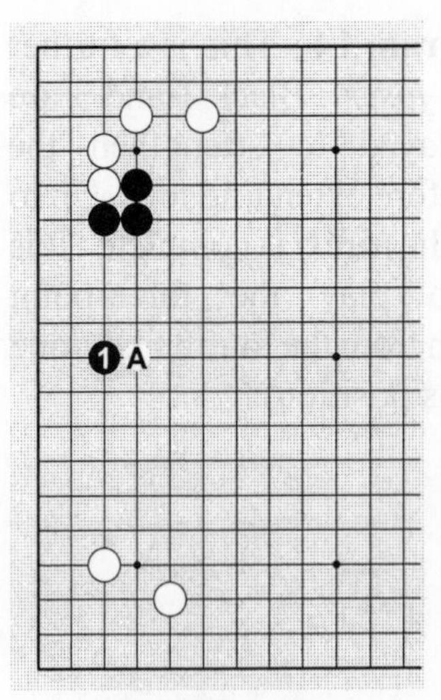

Diagram 16

Diagram 16 - In the opening there is a principle about extensions. If you have a wall with two vertical stones, you can make a three-point extension; in the same way a two-point extension can take place from a single stone. So Black 1 (or **A**) follows this principle. This principle can be generalized: an extension can be one further than the number of vertical stones.

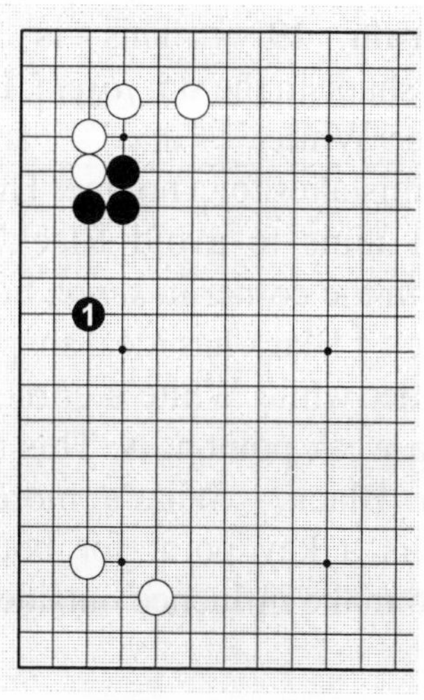

Diagram 17

Diagram 17 - Black 1 is an inefficient extension because the shape of Black's group is over-concentrated. In comparison with **Diagram 16,** this is only one line different, but it is very important. Go pursues efficiency of the stones. This position is not good for Black.

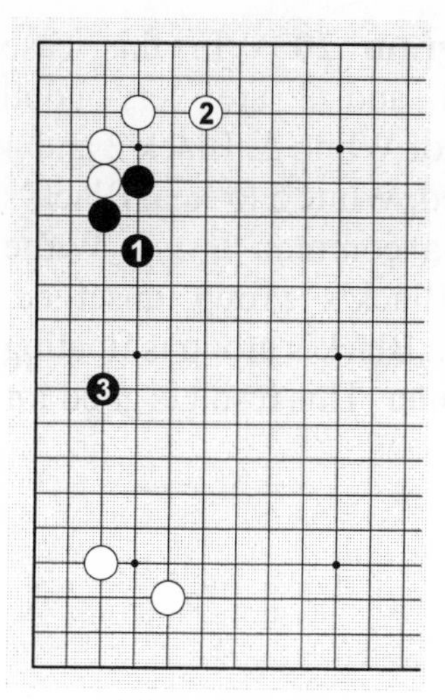

Diagram 18

Diagram 18 - Black's tiger link at 1 is also possible. If White answers at 2, Black's extension at 3 is the best. This is also a common *joseki*, and it restricts White's extension from the lower corner. Comparing with **Diagram 16,** this *joseki* is more efficient. So this type of *joseki* is often played in actual games.

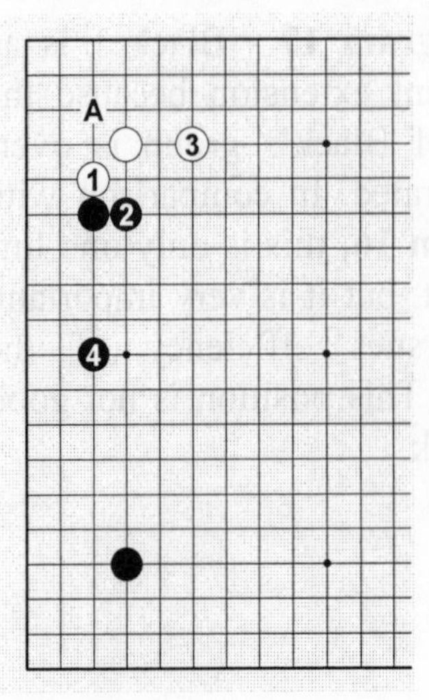

Diagram 19

Diagram 19 - This is a common shape in the star *joseki*. In this case White 1 and 3 are frequent mistakes for a novice. The play at 1 aims to avoid Black's invasion in the corner in *sente*, but up to Black 4 Black has ideal shape on the side, while White's corner still has a weak point at **A**. This is good for Black. What's more, Black 2 is a key point for both players to make influence outside.

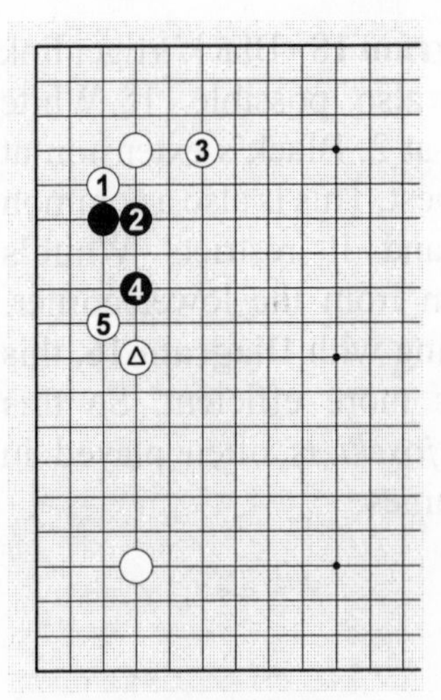

Diagram 20

Diagram 20 - In this case White 1 and 3 are very good because of White Δ. Black 2 and 4 are forced. White 5 to steal Black's base is a common *tesuji*; White makes Black's group unsettled. After that Black's group is floating in the center. This result is good for White.

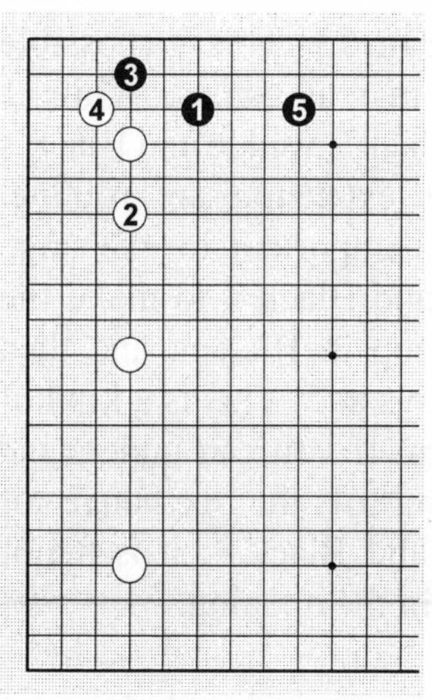

Diagram 21

Diagram 21 - When you approach, you should do so from the unoccupied side. Black's approach at 1 is the correct direction. Up to Black 5 this is a common star *joseki.* In **Diagram 20** Black ignored this rule. So it was inevitable that Black fell behind.

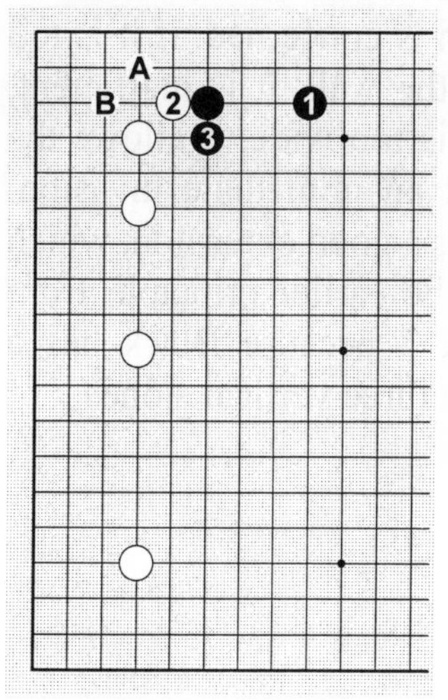

Diagram 22

Diagram 22 - In this situation Black's immediate extension at 1, without the exchange of Black **A** and White **B**, is usually not good. Now White 2 against Black 1 is good. Black 3 is forced and Black's shape is not efficient. So before you extend at 1, you should exchange Black **A** for White **B**.

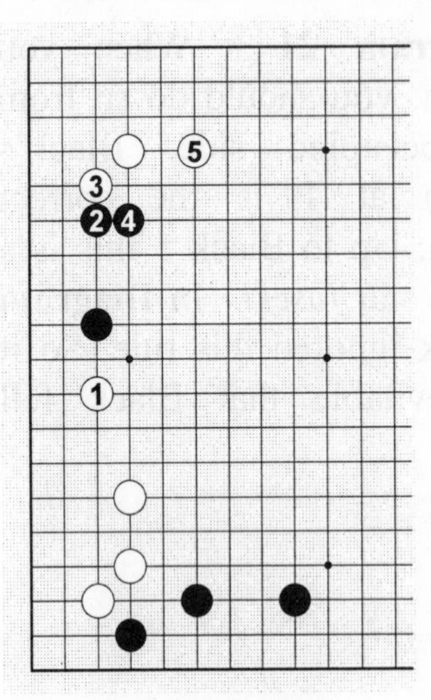

Diagram 23

Diagram 23 - This is a possible situation in real games. White 1 against Black's wedge and Black's two-point extension are routine. Now it is important to exchange White 3 and Black 4 to make the Black group inefficient, and then White plays at 5. This is a kind of set pattern. If you can understand the timing of the exchange of White 3 and Black 4, it is major progress in the opening.

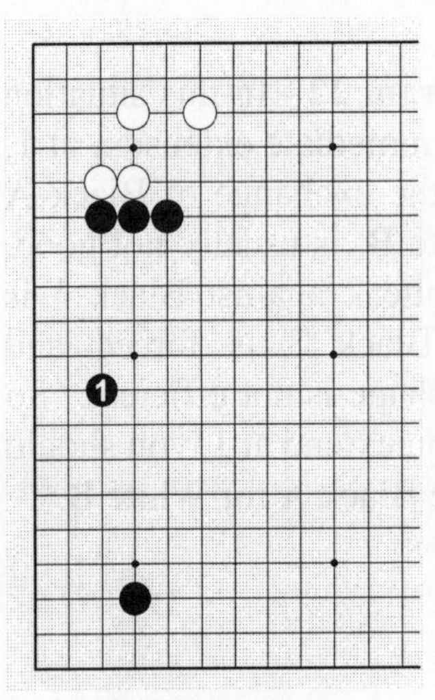

Diagram 24

Diagram 24 - As far as an extension is concerned, if it is too close to the wall, it is inefficient, and if it is too wide, it allows the opponent an immediate invasion. Black 1 is a good extension, which follows the earlier principle from **Diagram 7** because Black has a wall with three vertical stones.

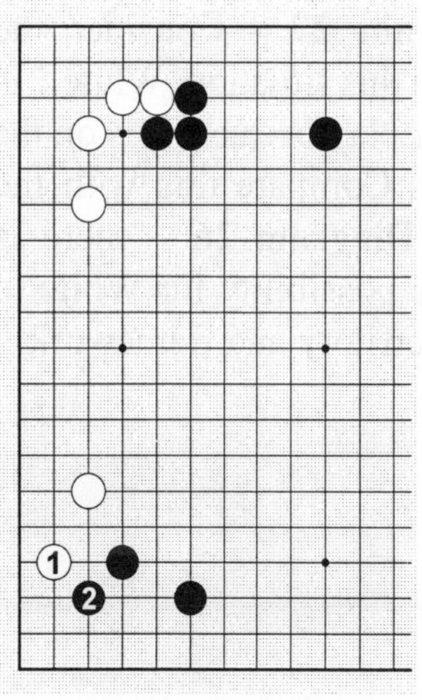

Diagram 25

Diagram 25 - Another important concern in the extension is the balance of the position. In this position, after the exchange of White 1 and Black 2, how should White extend? It may seem to be easy. You should however consider the balance of the position. Normally we talk of the third line as lower and the fourth line as higher. In the opening the balance of higher and lower positions is vital.

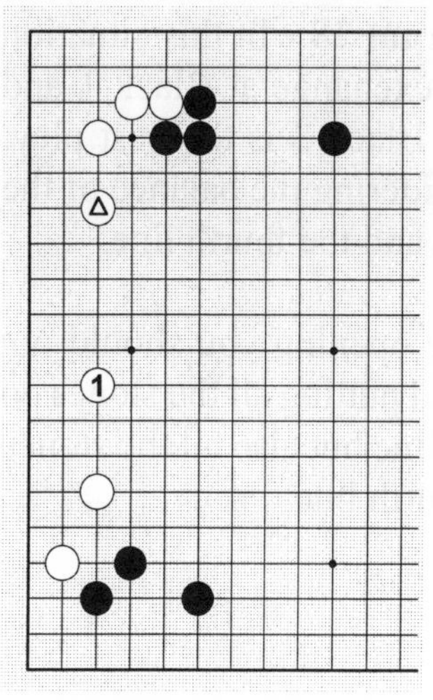

Diagram 26

Diagram 26 - White 1 is the common play, which follows the principle from **Diagram 2.** But looking at the situation carefully, all White's stones are low including Δ. It is not a good idea to put all your stones on the third line in the opening because you can't ever expect a large territory. If one side is on the third line, it is better to occupy the fourth line on the other side.

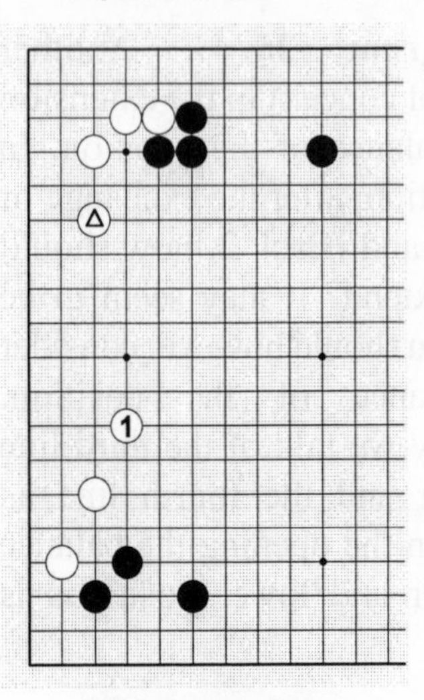

Diagram 27

Diagram 27 - Consider the balance in this situation, White 1 is the proper play because Δ is on the third line. Compare this with the previous **Diagram 26** – there is now more possibility for White to develop territory and framework.

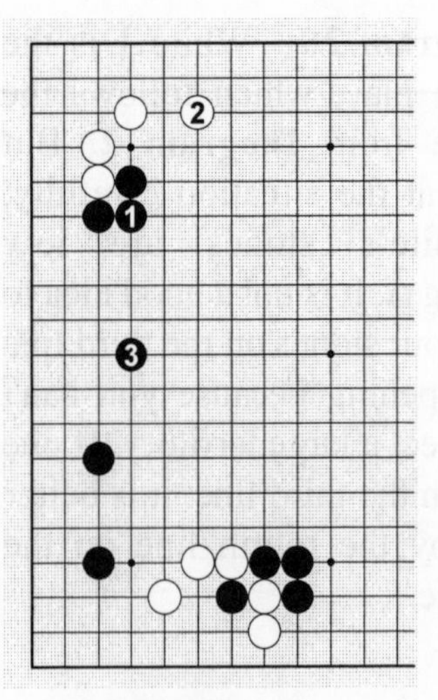

Diagram 28

Diagram 28 - In this situation after the exchange at Black 1 and White 2, Black 3 is the best play, also considering the balance of the third line and the fourth line.

In the opening you should not only avoid putting all the stones on the third line but also all the stones on the fourth line.

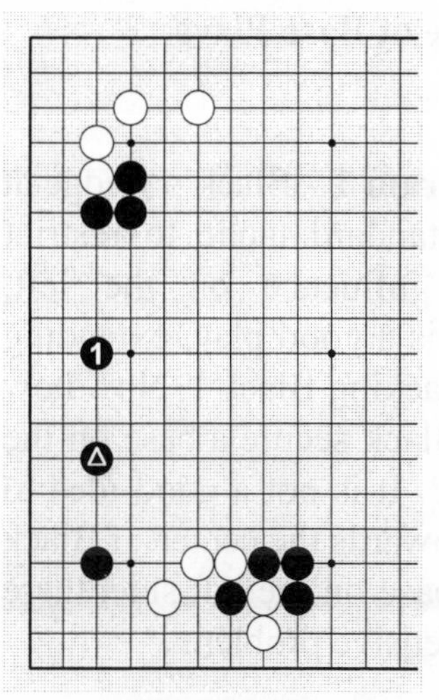

Diagram 29

Diagram 29 - Black's extension at 1 is a maneuver that doesn't consider the balance of the position. Now on the left side Black can't expect a large-scale territory as the stones are all low including ▲. Compared with the previous **Diagram 28**, this is not good for Black. One small mistake can change the result of the game.

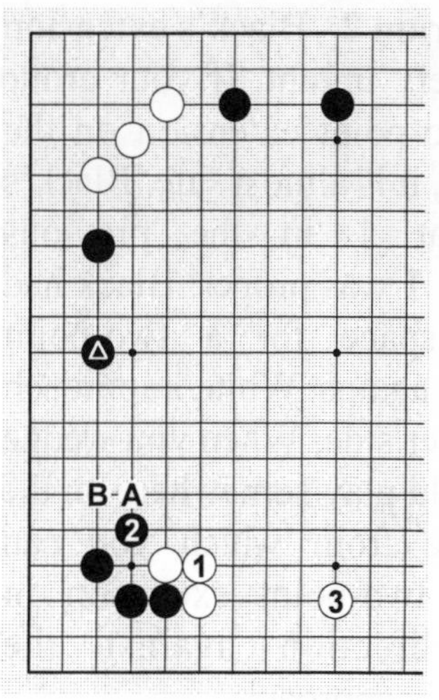

Diagram 30

Diagram 30 - In this situation Black 2 (or **A**) is the best play which takes into account the balance of the third and fourth lines with Black ▲. Black **B** may be a common play but in this case it is not good because Black's upper group with ▲ is very low.

Chapter 4: The Importance of Base Plays

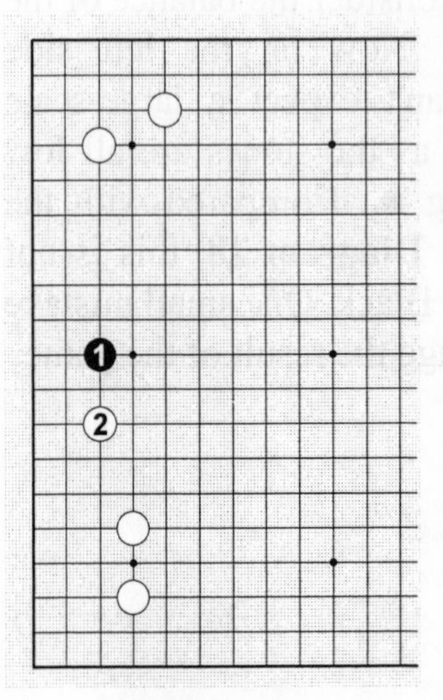

Diagram 1

Diagram 1 - Black's wedge at 1 is a standard tactic to restrict White's influence on the left. White 2 is a good play, extending while attacking Black 1. Now how should Black secure a base on the left side? It is not a good idea to escape towards the center. If Black has the base on the left side, there is no defensive problem.

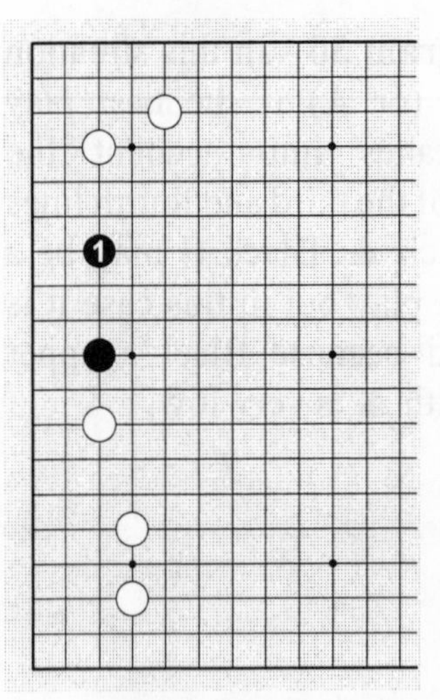

Diagram 2

Diagram 2 - Black's extension at 1 is very urgent. If your group has a two-point extension on the third line, it is almost safe. Black's wedge at 1 in the previous **Diagram 1** was proper: Black had enough space for a two-point extension against White's approach from either side. When you wedge you should play somewhere on the third line from which you can make a two-point extension in either direction against the opponent's approach.

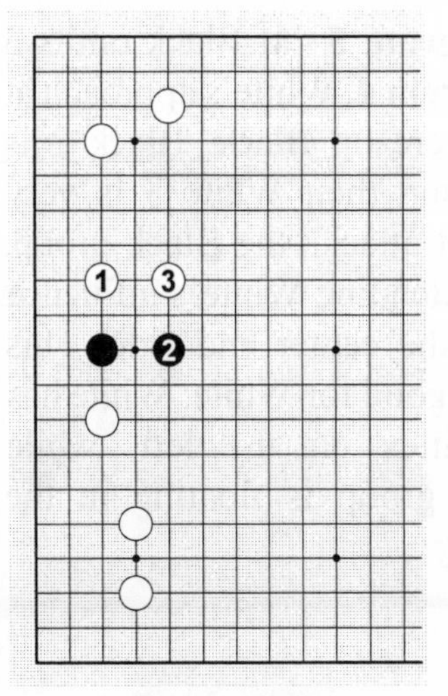

Diagram 3

Diagram 3 - If Black ignores White's approach, White 1 and 3 are very severe on Black. Up to White 3, White has built frameworks on both sides, while Black's group is still unsettled. In general if you have a weak group, the opponent makes a framework or territory while attacking it. Jumping out without a base should be avoided.

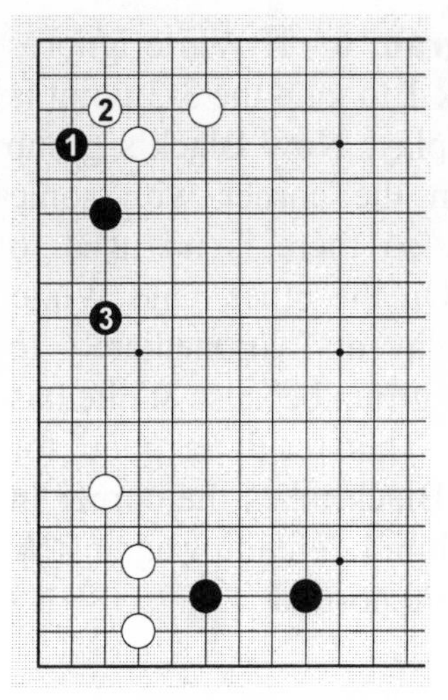

Diagram 4

Diagram 4 - Up to Black 3 this is a common star *joseki,* once more. Looking at every play carefully, you can see that each play involves the base. White 2 against Black 1 is the key point to keep the corner and secure the base of White's group. Black 3 is also important to secure Black's group.

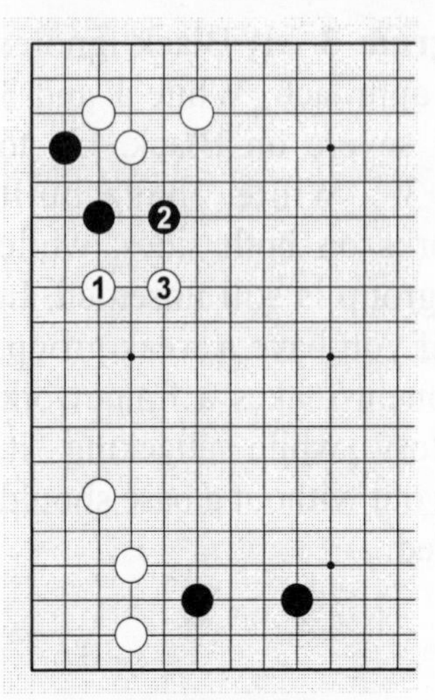

Diagram 5

Diagram 5 - If Black omits 3 in **Diagram 4**, White's approach at 1 is severe on Black. Black 2 is forced and then White 3 is very good. It attacks the Black group, while extending White's influence toward the center and side. This result is good for White: White has possibilities on the left, while Black's group is floating in the center.

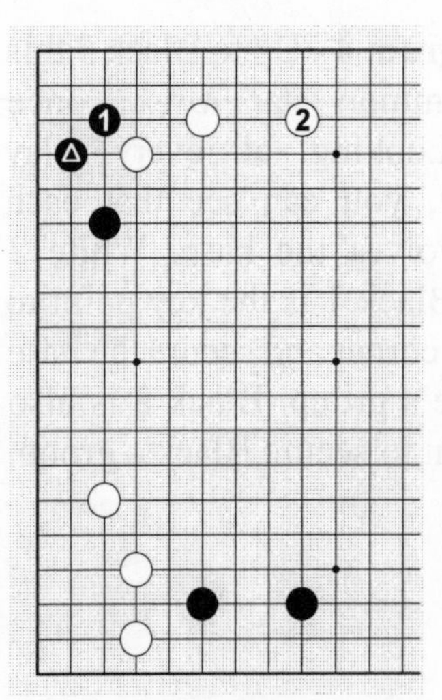

Diagram 6

Diagram 6 - If White ignores ▲, Black 1 to take the 3-3 point is the key play. Now Black's group settles in the corner with some territory, so there is no need to extend. On the other hand White should play at 2 immediately to settle the group because White has no base. This result is good for Black – Black takes the corner in *sente*. White 1 defending against ▲ is therefore normal.

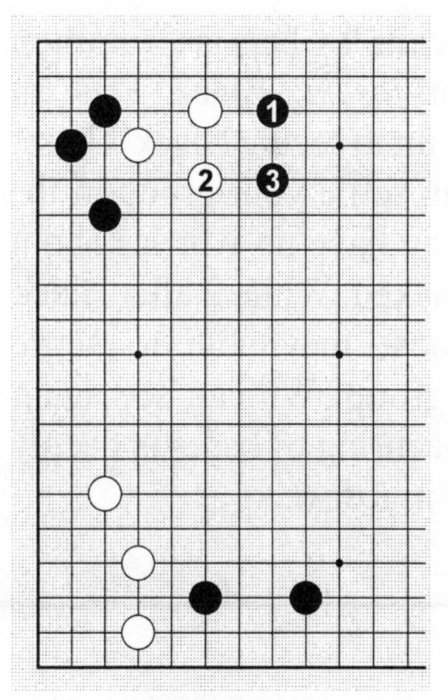

Diagram 7

Diagram 7 - Ignoring Black 1 in **Diagram 6** is very bad. Black's approach at 1 is a good idea, which attacks White's group. White 2 is forced. Up to Black 3 White's group is still under threat. It is not advisable to have a group floating without a base.

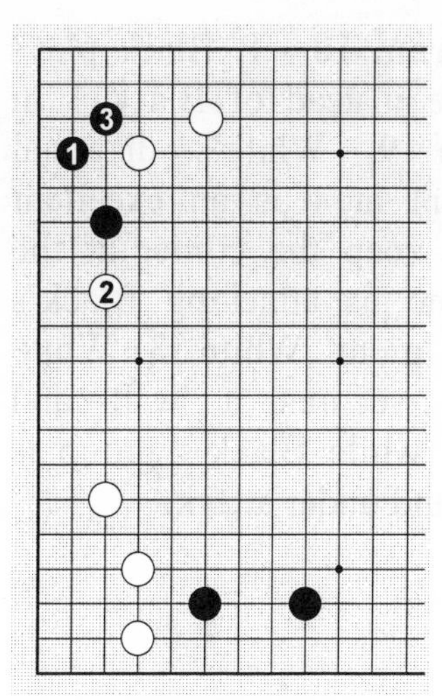

Diagram 8

Diagram 8 - White's approach at 2 against Black 1 aims to stop Black's extension on the side. But if Black takes the 3-3 point at 3, Black's group is settled in the corner. If Black jumped out towards the center, White would play at 3 instead of Black and Black's group would be floating. Black 3 is therefore urgent for both players.

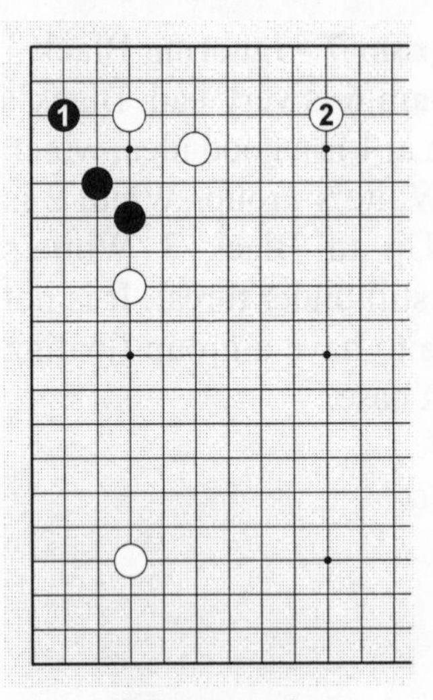

Diagram 9

Diagram 9 - This is a common 3-4 point *joseki*: Black 1 is an urgent point to secure Black's base. If you can settle your group in the corner, you have no worries about being attacked. White 2 after Black 1 is almost inevitable to settle White's group. We can see again that the securing of bases is deeply involved in *joseki*.

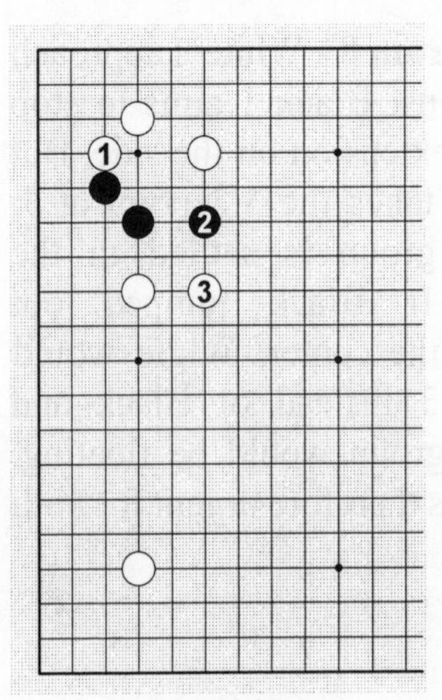

Diagram 10

Diagram 10 - If Black plays elsewhere instead of Black 1 in **Diagram 9**, White's diagonal attachment at 1 is an excellent tactic to keep the corner at the same time as attacking Black's group. Up to White 3 White naturally secures a wall and territory, while Black's group is floating and under attack.

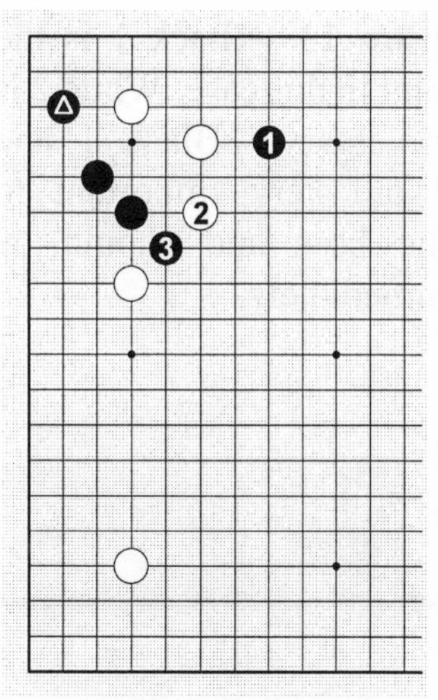

Diagram 11

Diagram 11 - Black ▲ should be played immediately because it involves the security of the base. It is not a good idea for White to ignore Black ▲. Next Black 1 is a good tactic to steal White's base. White 2 is forced and then Black 3 is a key point to attack White in two directions. Now Black can hope to control the whole board.

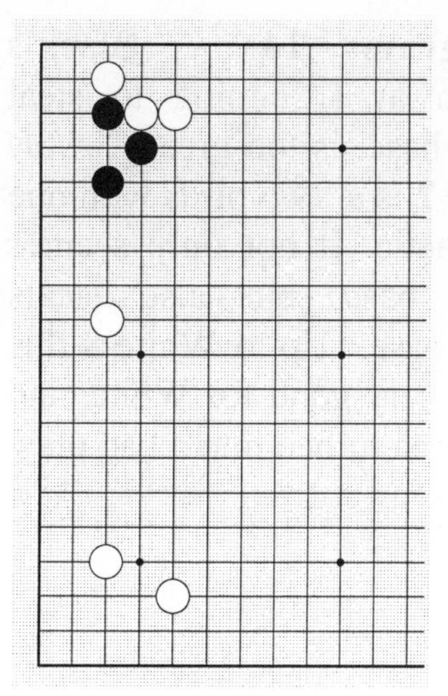

Diagram 12

Diagram 12 - The shape in the top left corner is common in actual games. What is the next play for Black? If you understand the importance of the base, it won't be difficult to solve this one.

Urgent points have priority over big points. If you have a weak group you can't expect a good result, even if you take a big point.

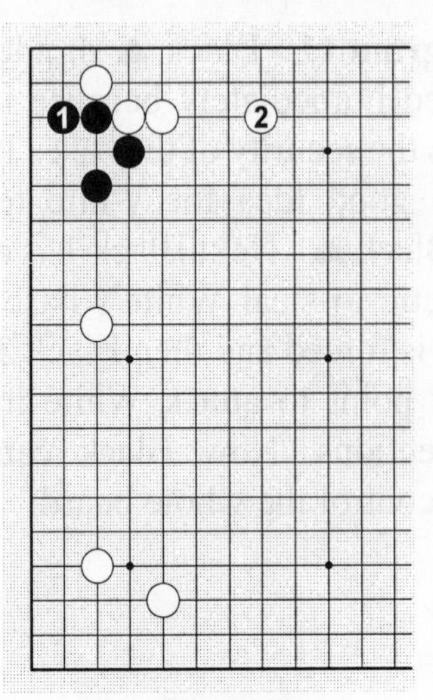

Diagram 13

Diagram 13 - Black 1 is the urgent point in this case. White 2 is almost necessary. Black 1 and White 2 are very important to secure the base and should be played immediately.

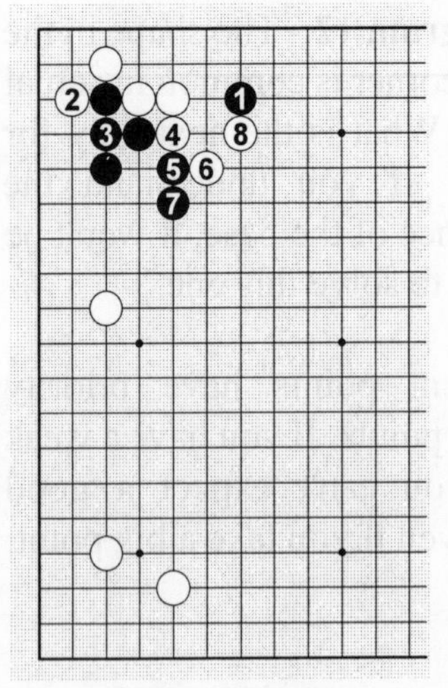

Diagram 14

Diagram 14 - Black's approach at 1, aiming to steal White's base, is too greedy. *Atari* at White 2 is a 'two birds with one stone' tactic. It not only secures White's base, but also steals Black's base. Up to White 8 this result is very good for White, and Black 1 has turned into a bad play.

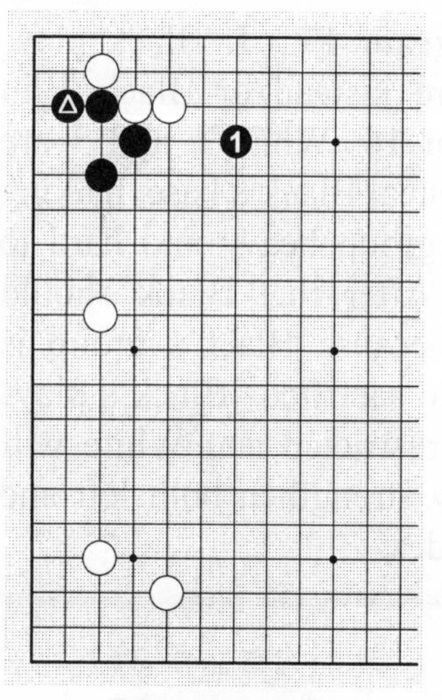

Diagram 15

Diagram 15 - It is essential not to make a floating group in the opening. If White ignores Black ▲, Black 1 is painful for White. White's group can't be killed, but White will have to pay something to live.

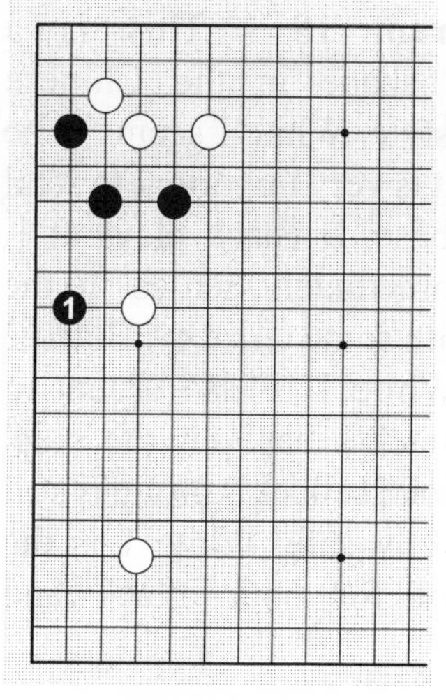

Diagram 16

Diagram 16 - Black 1 is the key point to secure Black's group even though it is on the second line. It is often played in real games. If your group has no base, even though it contains many stones, you will be behind.

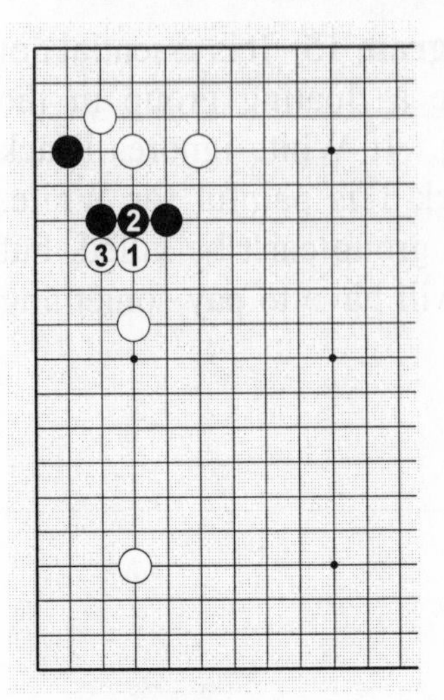

Diagram 17

Diagram 17 - If Black plays elsewhere instead of Black 1 in **Diagram 16**, White 1 and 3 are good to steal Black's base, making Black's group heavy and hard to defend. After that Black should escape because Black's group is too big to sacrifice. Black's plays will be restricted and White will naturally strengthen both left and upper sides.

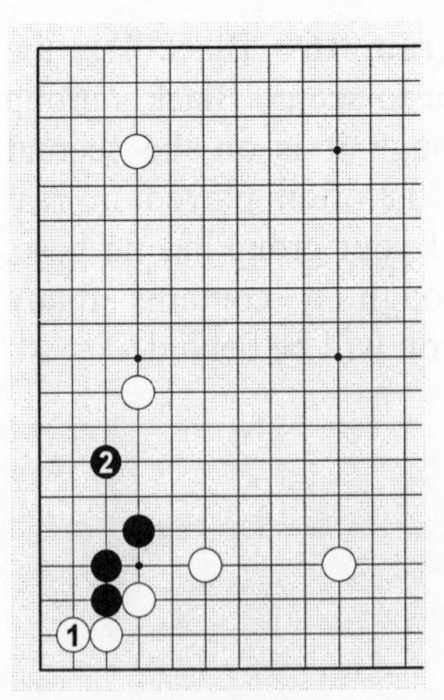

Diagram 18

Diagram 18 - This is a common shape in the Chinese opening style. White 1 seems to be small, but is very important to steal Black's base. If Black plays at 1, Black immediately settles in the corner with some territory. Black 2 against White 1 is also urgent to secure Black's base on the side. After Black 2, Black's group is still not perfectly safe. White 1 is the key point for both attack and defense.

Chapter 5: Making Stones Work Harder

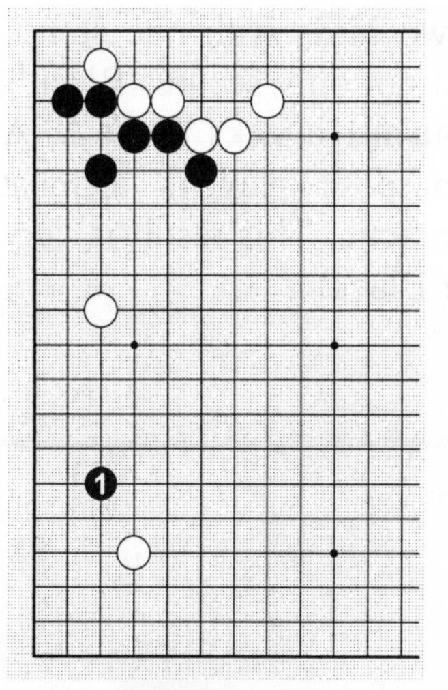

Diagram 1

Diagram 1 - Black has just played at 1. There is a broad choice now for White. What is the most efficient play? If you cannot think in terms of the overall position, you cannot find the answer. You should consider the influence of the Black group in the top corner and the single White stone on the left side before playing.

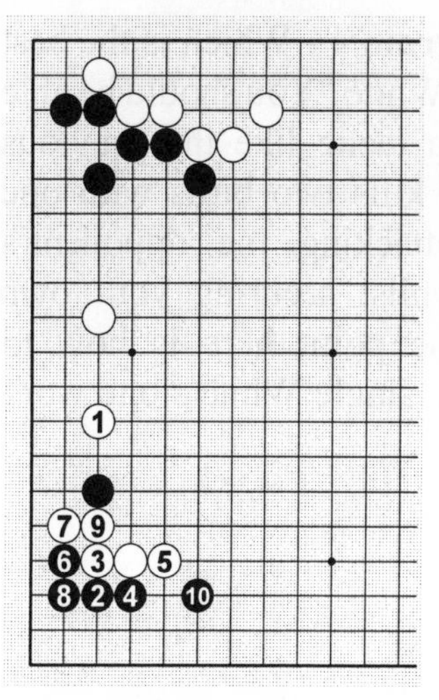

Diagram 2

Diagram 2 - White's two-point extension at 1 is correct and the most efficient maneuver in this case. It steals Black's base, attacking the single stone. Black 2 is usual, invading at the 3-3 point instead of jumping out. Up to Black 10 this is an ordinary pattern. Now White has a good framework on the left, while Black has settled in the corner with some territory. Also Black's wall in the top corner is neutralized.

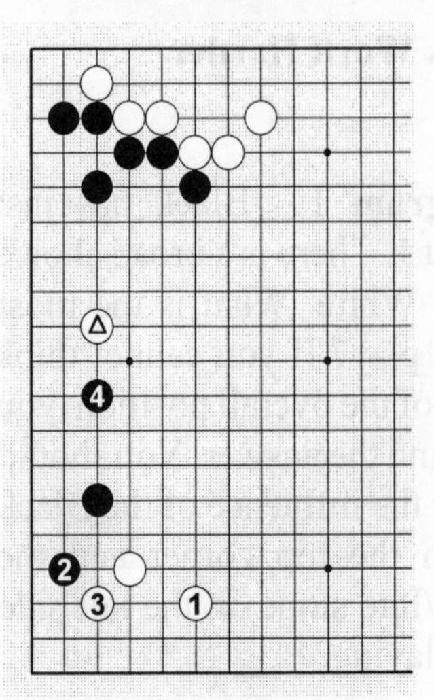

Diagram 3

Diagram 3 - White 1 is a flawed play. After the exchange of Black 2 and White 3, Black 4 is a good "two birds with one stone" tactic. It not only secures Black's group, but also attacks White Δ. A double-purpose play is a most efficient tactic. This result is very good for Black.

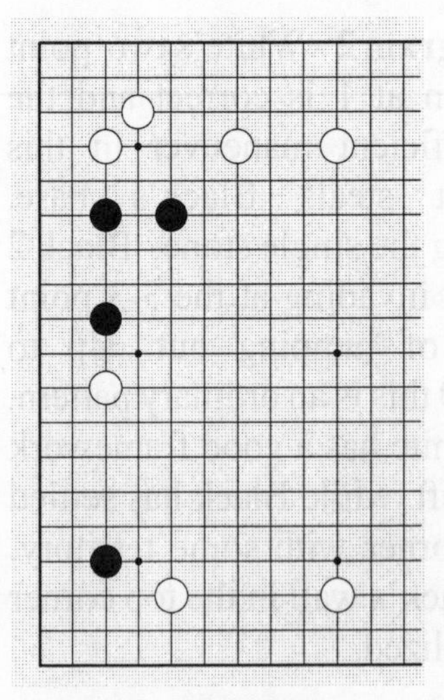

Diagram 4

Diagram 4 - Which is the best play for White? You should be able to find a tactic like the previous one that kills two birds with one stone, attacking the opponent's group whilst securing your own base. The point here is how to make the single White stone work harder.

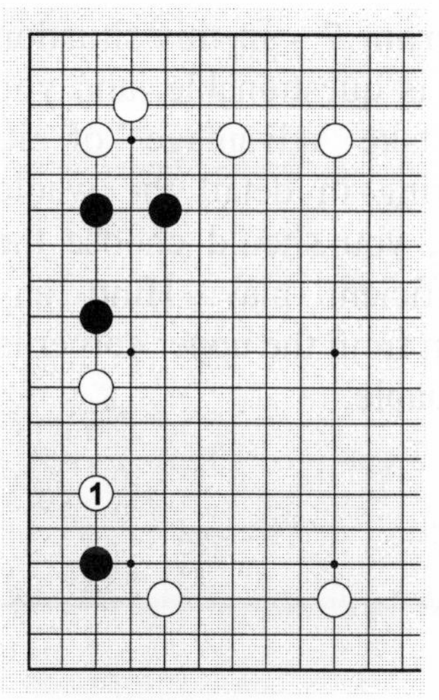

Diagram 5

Diagram 5 - White 1 is an excellent play to secure a base and attack Black's stone. After White 1, Black ought to settle the lower left corner stone. White will strengthen the lower side as a natural result.

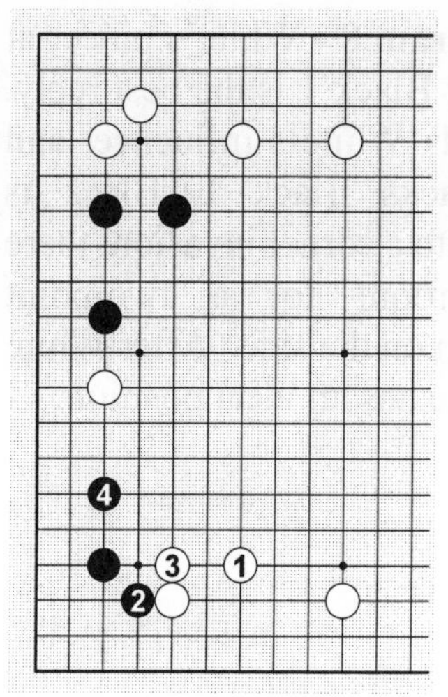

Diagram 6

Diagram 6 - White 1 is a half-baked play, which aims to settle the lower side directly. Black 2 is usually not so good, but in this case it is not bad because White 1 is close to the two-stone wall. Then Black plays at 4. Now White's stone on the left side finds it hard to make a base.

When you decide on the next play, you should consider all aspects of the situation carefully. An inadequate play could be disastrous.

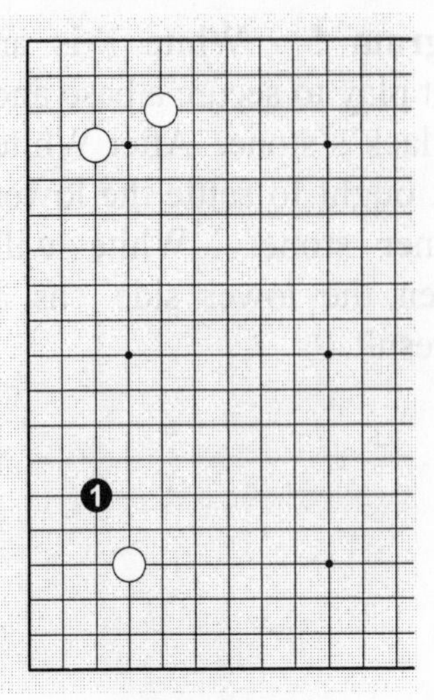

Diagram 7

Diagram 7 - In this situation Black 1 is questionable, and you should take advantage of it. Considering in detail the whole situation, you should choose the most efficient play. Hint: any extension from the upper corner is very valuable.

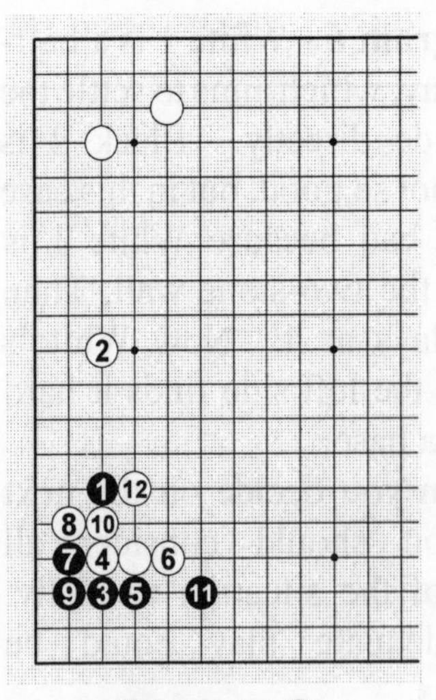

Diagram 8

Diagram 8 - White's pincer at 2 against Black 1 is the best reply. It extends White's influence, and also attacks Black 1. Black is forced into a corner invasion: there is no room for a two-point extension on the side. After White 12, White has an ideal position.

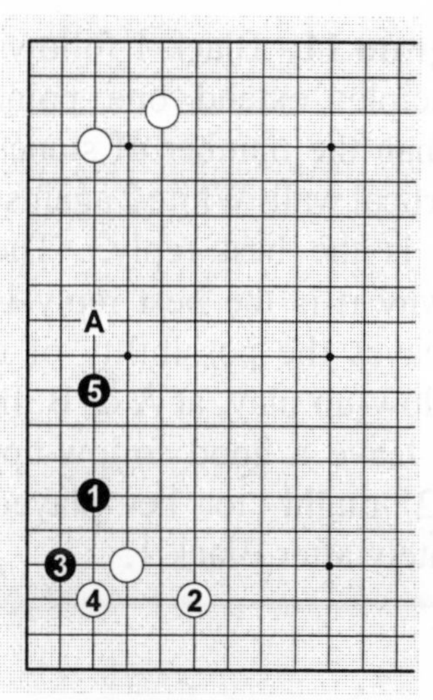

Diagram 9

Diagram 9 - White 2 in this case does not take full advantage of the situation. Up to Black 5 this is a standard pattern, but then Black's group is settled. White's overall position is neutralized: White **A** is no longer a threat to Black's group. Comparing with the **Diagram 8**, the result here is clearly in favor of Black.

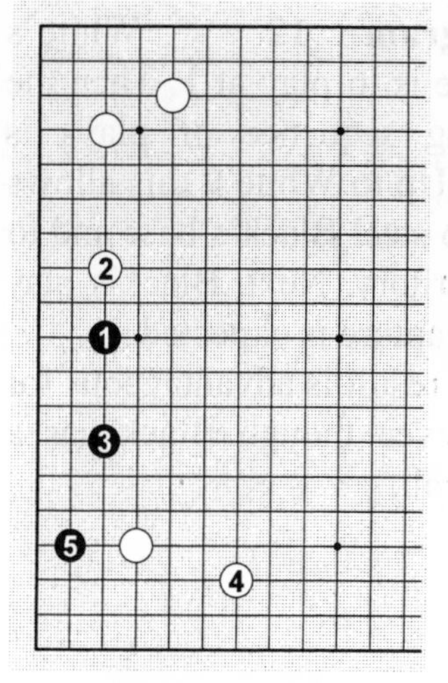

Diagram 10

Diagram 10 - Black's wedge at 1 is the most common idea, when faced with the initial position of the White stones. Up to Black 5 this is the standard play.

Black 1 aims to limit White's possible extension from the enclosure, and leaves the possibility for Black to extend too. After Black 1, White 2 is not a first-rate extension, but is still a good play.

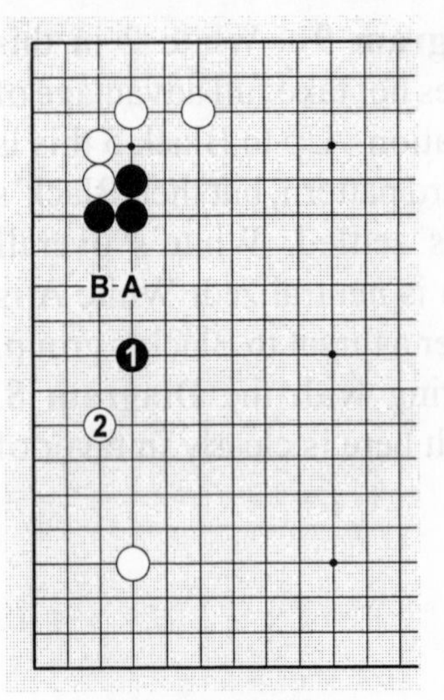

Diagram 11

Diagram 11 - Black 1 follows the principle: extend one point further than the number of stones in the vertical wall. White 2 against Black 1 is the best reply. The reason why it is the best reply is that it leaves the possibility of a good follow-up play, at **A** or **B**. In order to leave a good follow-up, White 2 ought to be played immediately after Black 1.

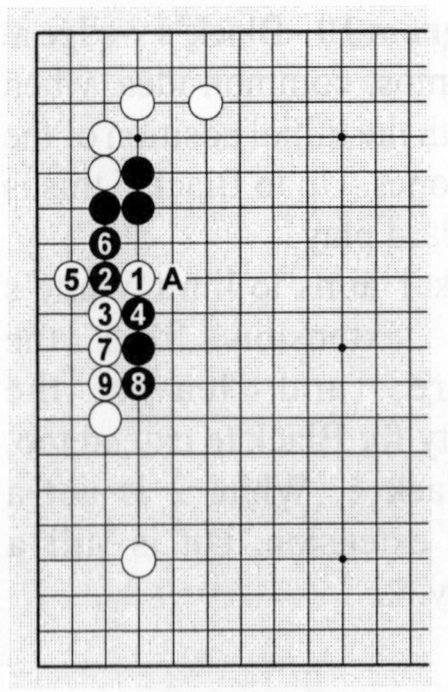

Diagram 12

Diagram 12 - White's objective is to play at 1. Then the following sequence of plays is routine. Up to White 9 this allows White to steal Black's base and to form territory. Next, Black's play at **A** to capture is expected.

This result is advantageous for White, even though Black has a strong wall.

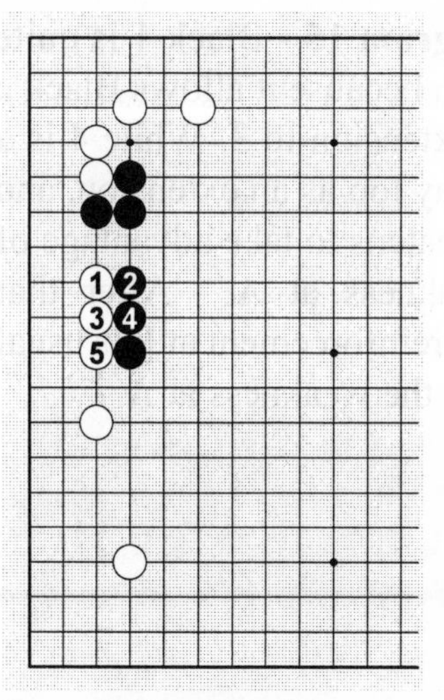

Diagram 13

Diagram 13 - White 1 is also possible. Black 2 against White 1 is the common response. Up to White 5 is straightforward. Now White's territory is not small, but Black has strong influence in the center. The degree of success of this invasion depends on timing.

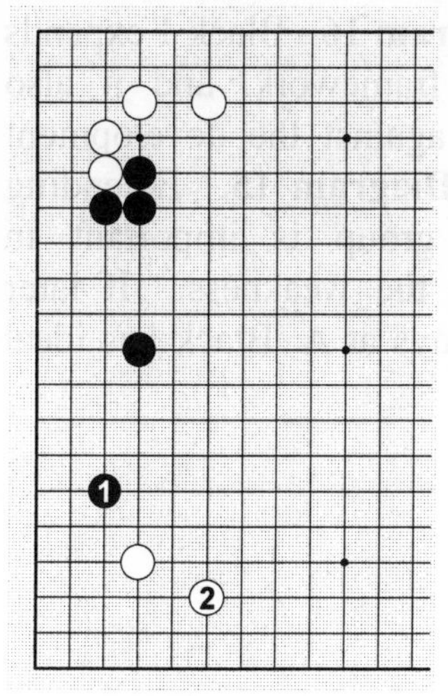

Diagram 14

Diagram 14 - Black 1 prevents the invasion seen in **Diagram 13.** After White 2, Black's group is quite strong. There is a large difference between the positions in **Diagrams 11 and 14**. White 2 in **Diagram 11** must be played immediately if you want to prevent the situation in **Diagram 14** of a strengthened Black group.

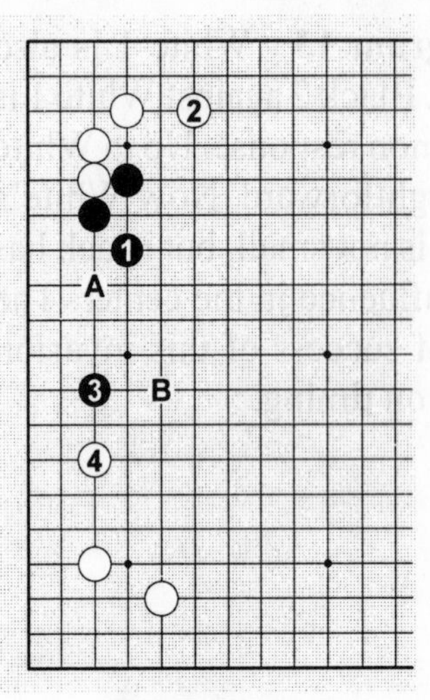

Diagram 15

Diagram 15 - Black 1 is quite common because it allows Black a broad extension to 3. White 4 is a good play too as an extension, and also threatens to take advantage of the weakness at **A**. After that Black's reinforcement at **B** is usual to cover the weakness at **A**.

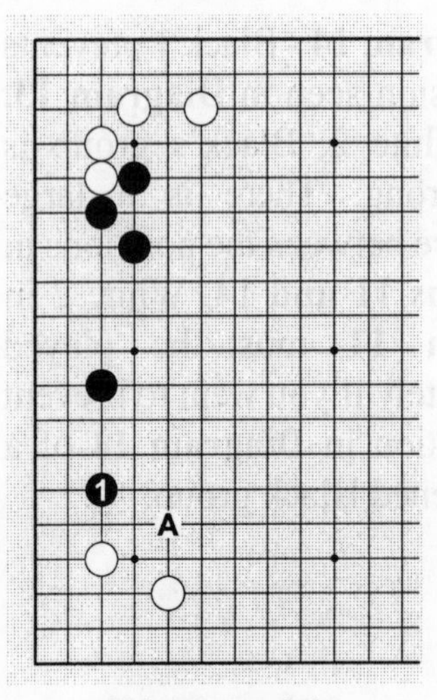

Diagram 16

Diagram 16 - Black 1 expands Black's framework, and it also defends against the development seen in **Diagram 15.** Extending Black's group is important in covering the weakness. If later Black plays at **A**, Black has ideal shape.

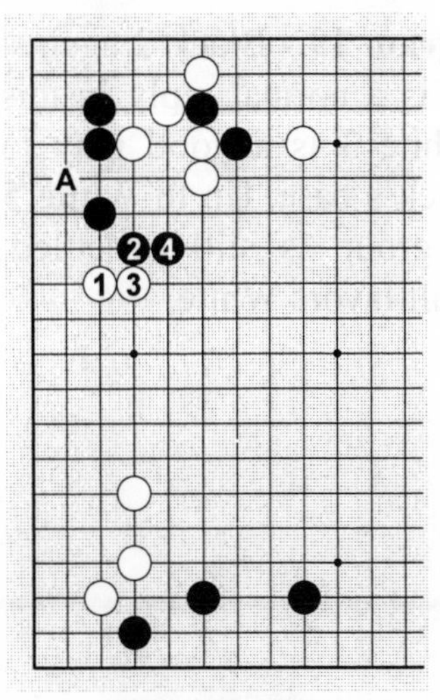

Diagram 17

Diagram 17 - White's approach at 1 is very efficient. It extends White's influence and also aims to take advantage of the weakness at **A**. Black 2 is a good play, to protect that weak point. Up to Black 4 is a sequence that is frequent in practice.

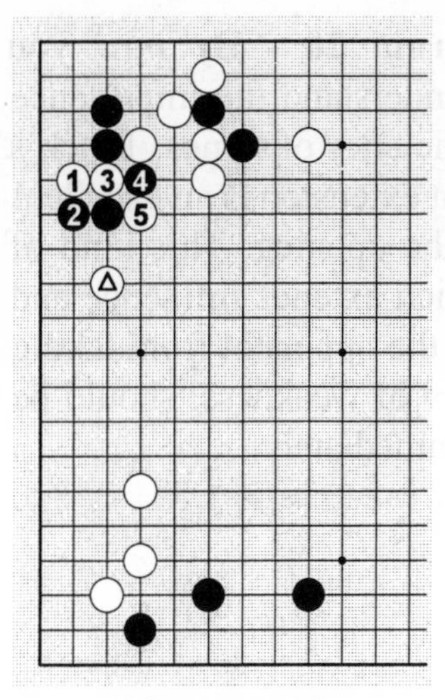

Diagram 18

Diagram 18 - If Black ignores White Δ, White immediately plays at 1. Up to White 5 this is disastrous for Black. Black 2 in **Diagram 17** is therefore the correct reply.

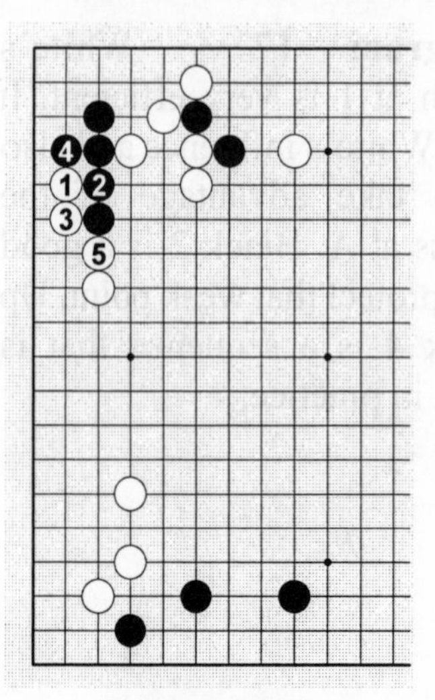

Diagram 19

Diagram 19 - Black 2 against White 1 is a normal reply in this case. White 3 is a good play to steal Black's base. Up to White 5 Black's group is still unsettled. This result favors White.

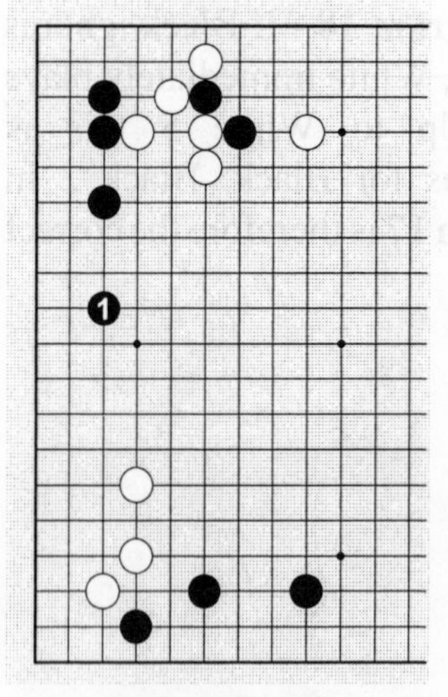

Diagram 20

Diagram 20 - By now you should understand the importance of the efficiency of stones. Black's two-point extension is an excellent play in the opening. This kind of play, which extends influence and prevents the opponent from taking advantage of weakness, should be played immediately.

SECTION 2

EXAMPLES ON THE FUNDAMENTALS

Problem 1 - What are Frameworks Worth?

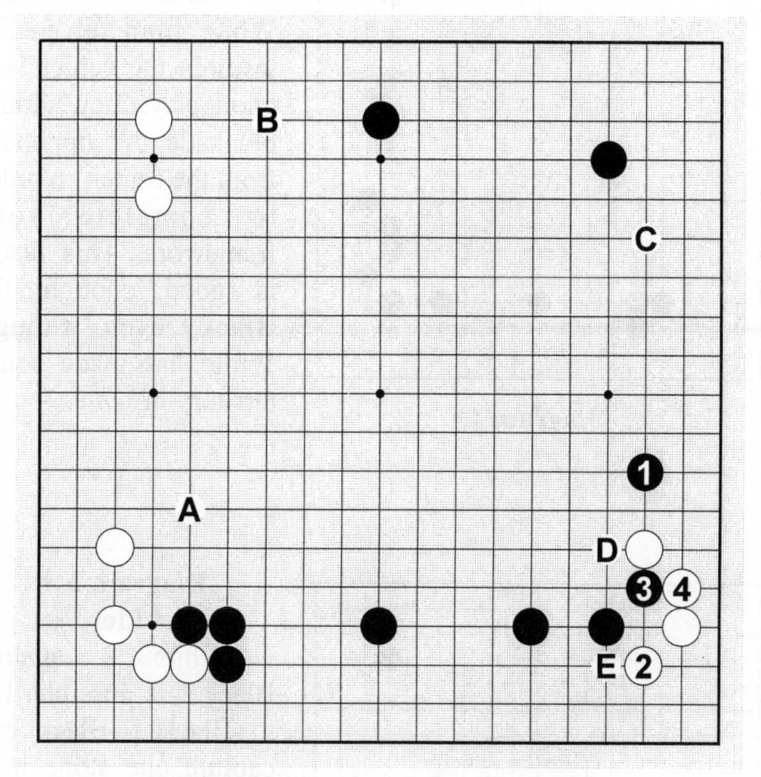

Problem Diagram – Black to play

In the bottom right corner there is a star *joseki* in process. After White 4, Black should decide whether to play elsewhere or continue to maneuver in this area to complete the *joseki*. If you understand the value of a framework, you can solve this problem easily; choose the correct answer from **A** to **E**.

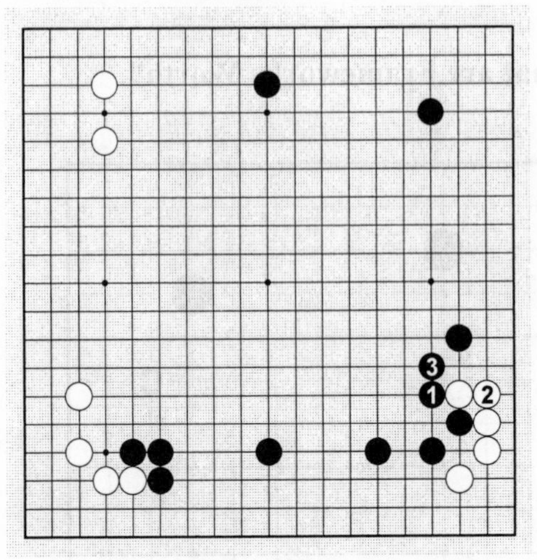

Diagram 1

Diagram 1
Correct Answer

Black 1 to stop White from advancing towards the center is a good play. You should blockade the opponent from the center, in order to complete your framework. This result is good enough for Black even though White has made some territory in *sente*.

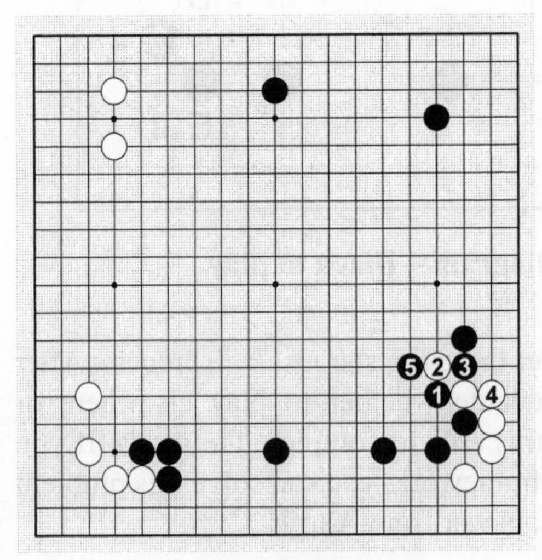

Diagram 2

Diagram 2
Ladder

White 2 against Black 1 is possible. Up to Black 5 Black can capture one stone in a ladder. Comparing with the answer in **Diagram 1,** Black's framework is much stronger, but now White can make use of a later ladder-breaker.

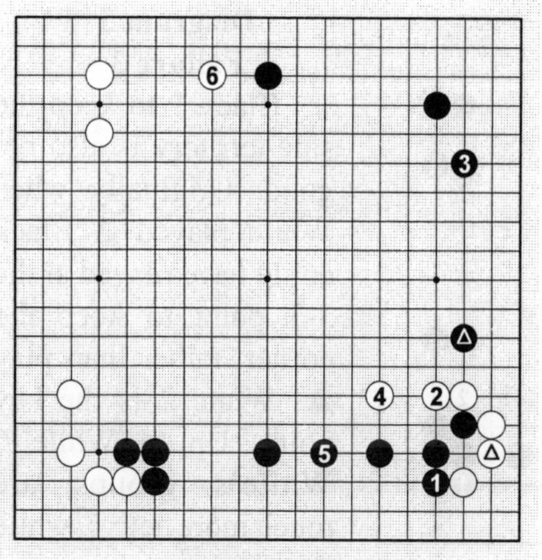

Diagram 3

Diagram 3
Failure 1

Black 1 to emphasize territory is not good in this case. White 2, poking a head into the center, is an excellent play. Now the exchange of ▲ and Δ turns out to be bad for Black, and Black can't expect a large-scale framework on the lower side.

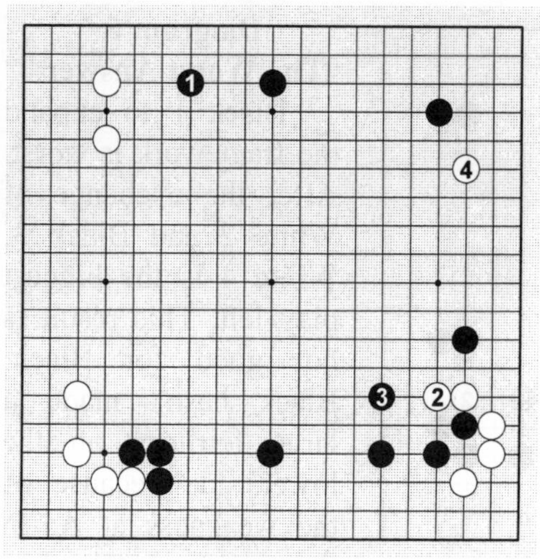

Diagram 4

Diagram 4
Failure 2

Usually we think Black's extension at 1 is a good play, which prevents White from expanding. But in this case White 2 is the key point. If Black stops White from advancing towards center, White 4 is a good approach. This result is an unsuccessful opening for Black.

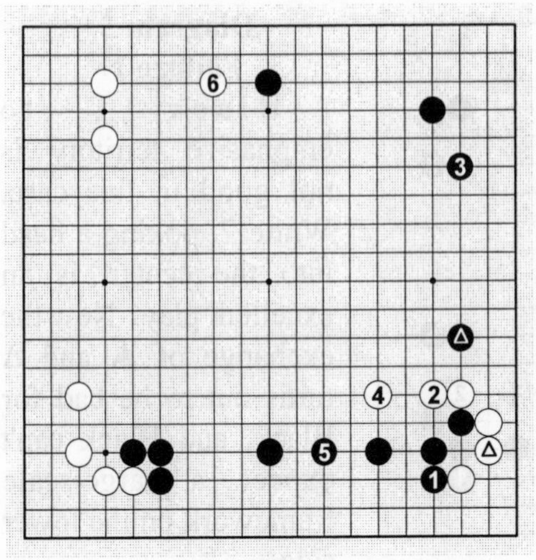

Diagram 5

Diagram 5
Failure 3

Black 1 to keep the side territory is also not good. Originally when White played Δ Black could have played at the 3-3 point to keep the corner, rather than play ▲. White 2 is the key point. Up to White 6 White's groups are much more active, while Black's groups are withered and lifeless.

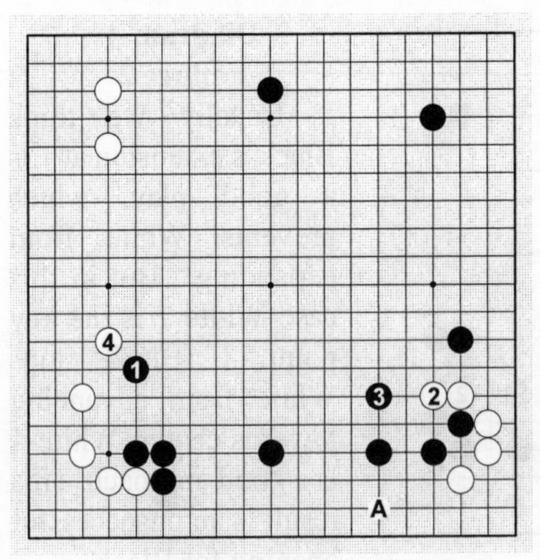

Diagram 6

Diagram 6
The Worst Answer

Black 1 to expand the framework is worst. After the exchange of White 2 and Black 3, White 4 is the biggest play left. This result is not good for Black: Black hasn't made a large territory on the lower side because of the weakness at **A**. In this case Black's consistent focal-point style is not successful.

Problem 2 - Is Playing Away Good?

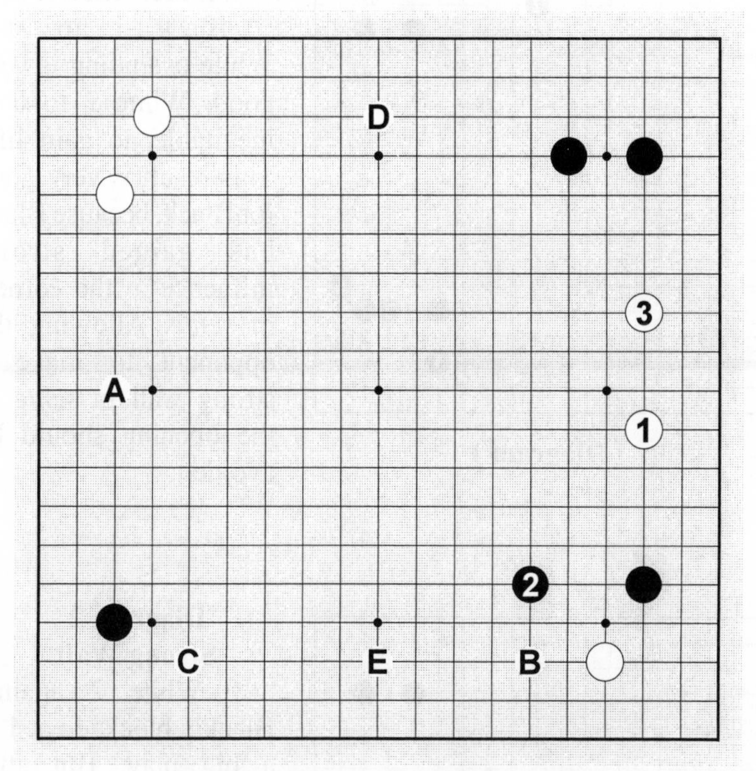

Problem Diagram – Black to Play

White 3, after the exchange of White 1 and Black 2, aims not to allow Black to extend from the top right corner. It is based on the reading that Black can't capture White's corner stone, even if Black plays there first. The security of the base is deeply involved in this problem; choose the correct answer from **A to E**.

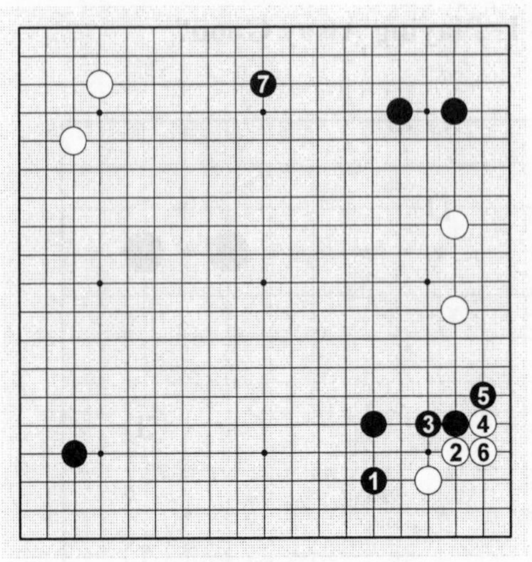

Diagram 1

Diagram 1
Correct Answer

Black 1 to stop White extending is very good. White 2 to 6 is inevitable, to gain life. This result is very good for Black, because Black has gained strong influence in the corner, in *sente*. Allowing the opponent to make a strong wall in *sente* in the opening should be avoided.

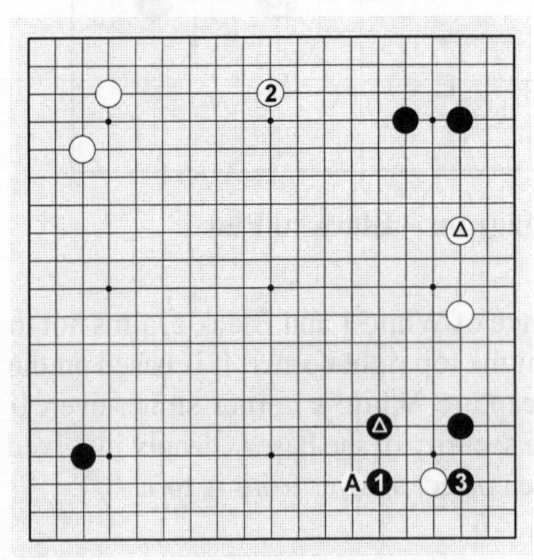

Diagram 2

Diagram 2
Strong Wall

White 2 against Black's blockade at 1 is a big play. But after Black 3, Black has a nice territory and strong wall. Furthermore there is almost no *aji* (potential) left in the corner. Originally White should have answered at **A** instead of playing Δ, when Black played ▲.

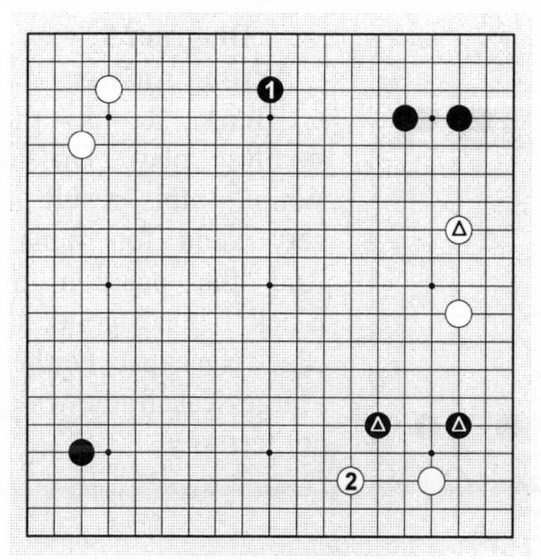

Diagram 3

Diagram 3
Missing
The Opportunity

Black 1 is a big play to extend the influence from the top right corner, and also restrict White's influence. But after White 2, Black's ▲ are very weak. Now Δ turns into a good play.

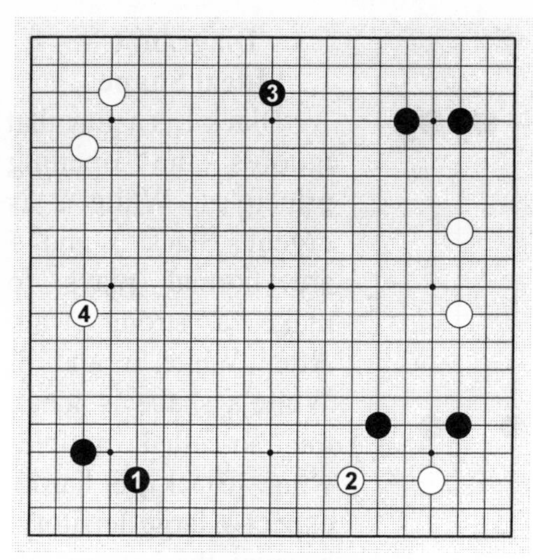

Diagram 4

Diagram 4
Just a Large Play

Black's corner enclosure is very big. But after White 2, Black has missed the opportunity to take the lead. After that, Black 3 and White 4 are almost *miai* (equivalent points). This result is good for White.

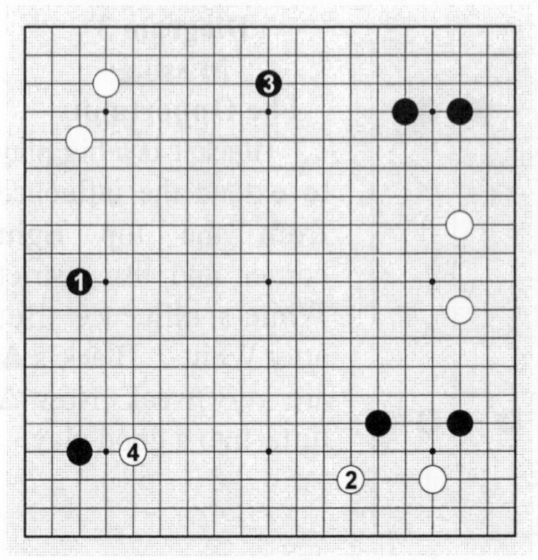

Diagram 5

Diagram 5
Wrong Answer

Black 1 is the smallest play. Up to White 4 this result is very good for White. And the position of Black 1 is not good, so Black can expect neither a large-scale framework, nor territory.

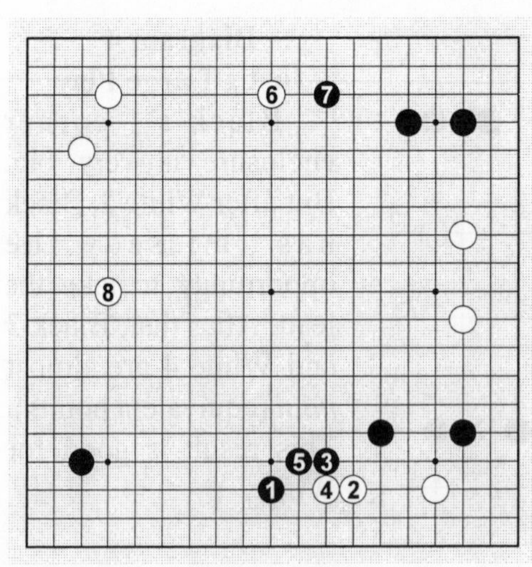

Diagram 6

Diagram 6
Ideal Shape

Black 1 is a play that ignores the opening principles. White 2 is urgent. Black 3 and 5 are normal plays to make a strong wall. After White 6 and 8, White's shape is ideal, the so-called double-wing. Black can hardly expect a large territory, because the bottom left corner is not yet enclosed. So this result is not good for Black.

Problem 3 Choice at a Crossroads

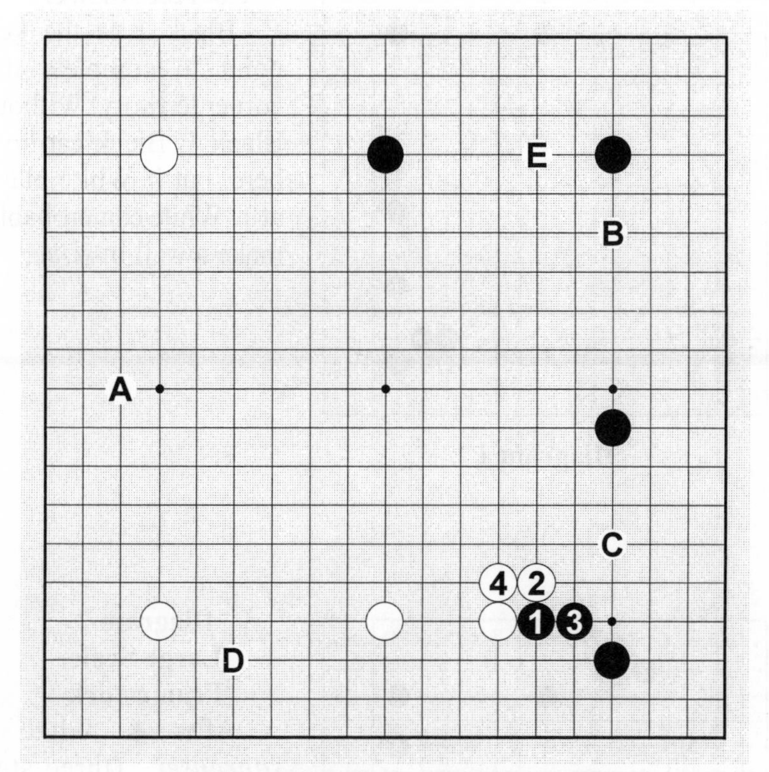

Problem Diagram – Black to play

Black's attachment at 1 aims to strengthen the group in the corner. Up to White 4 it seems to be successful, but allowing White to make a strong wall is inevitable. Now you should decide whether to reinforce the corner, or play elsewhere. Choose the correct play from **A** to **E**.

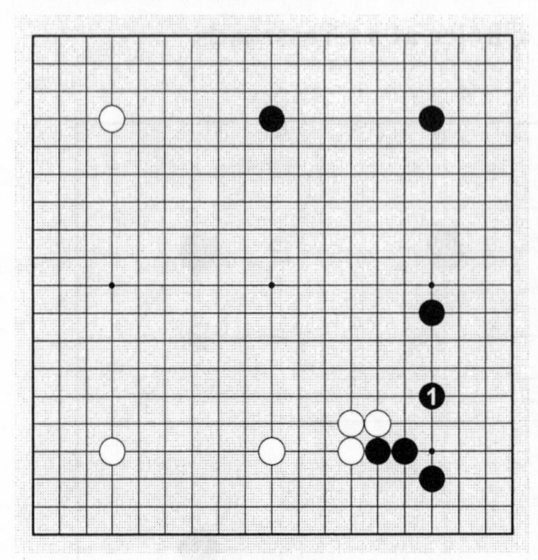

Diagram 1

Diagram 1
Correct Answer

Black 1 is the key point to complete the corner territory. Without Black 1, Black can live here, but if White plays at 1, White can probably make a wall in *sente*.

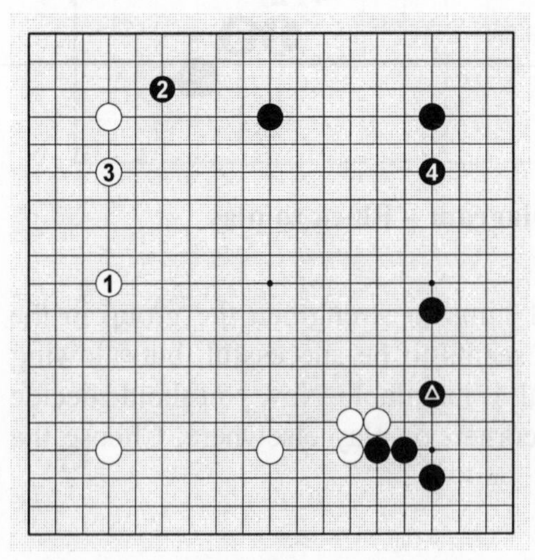

Diagram 2

Diagram 2
Large Scale Framework

After ▲, White 1 *sanrensei* (three-star formation) is usual. Then we can expect the sequence 2 to 4. Both players try to construct large-scale frameworks, but Black's territory on the right is good enough to retain the advantage of playing first.

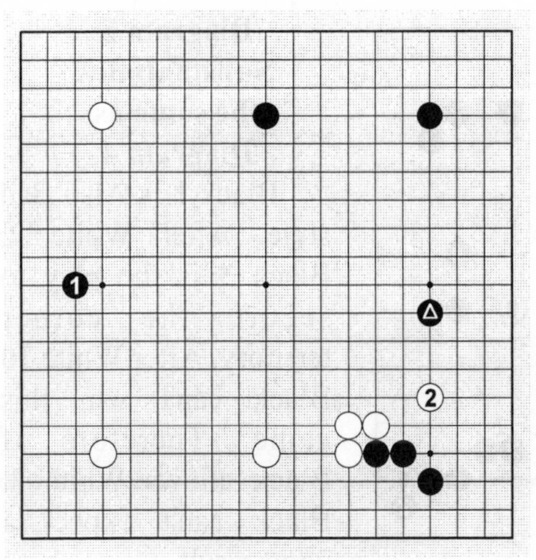

Diagram 3

Diagram 3
Separation

Black's wedge at 1 aims to prevent White from having a *sanrensei*. But after White 2, Black ▲ is very weak, as it is isolated from the corner group.

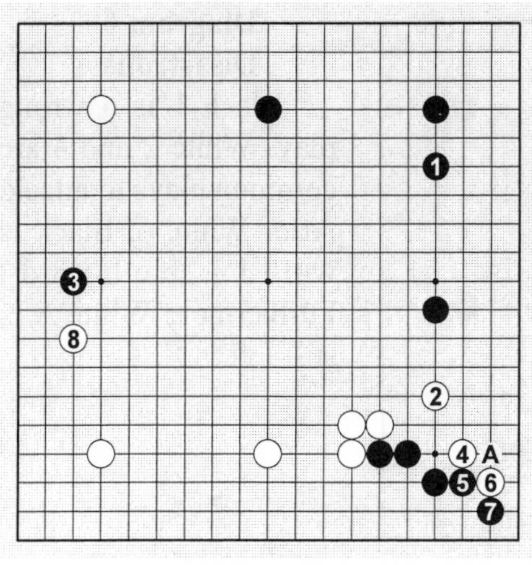

Diagram 4

Diagram 4
Too Early

Black's corner enclosure at 1 is not good. After White 2, Black's framework in the top right corner is shrinking away. Black ignores White again by playing at 3. Then after the exchange of White 4 to Black 7, White plays at 8. Black's corner group has to live with just two eyes if White connects at **A**. This result is not good for Black.

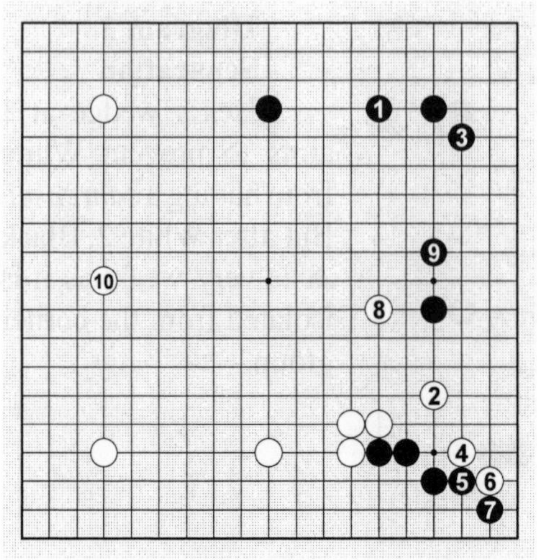

Diagram 5

Diagram 5
Substantially the same as Diagram 4

Black 1 Is Also Bad style. After White 2, Black 3 is the play to secure the corner territory. After White 10 Black can't win this game. Therefore if Black allows White 2, Black can't expect a good result.

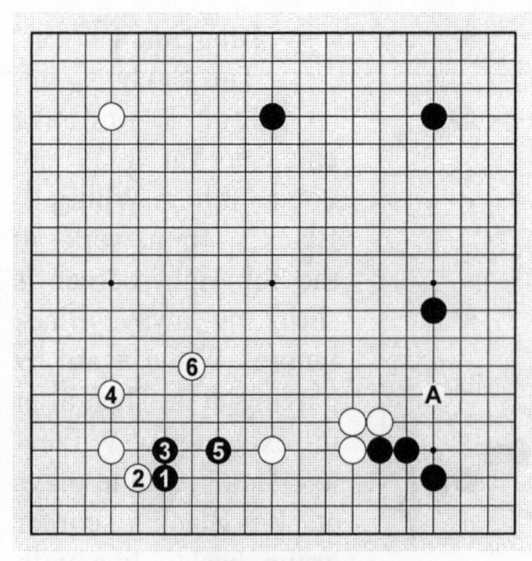

Diagram 6

Diagram 6
Disastrous

Black 1 is a wrong play. White 2 and 4 are common plays to attack. After White 6, Black is well behind. Furthermore White **A** is still left.

Problem 4 A Necessary Reinforcement

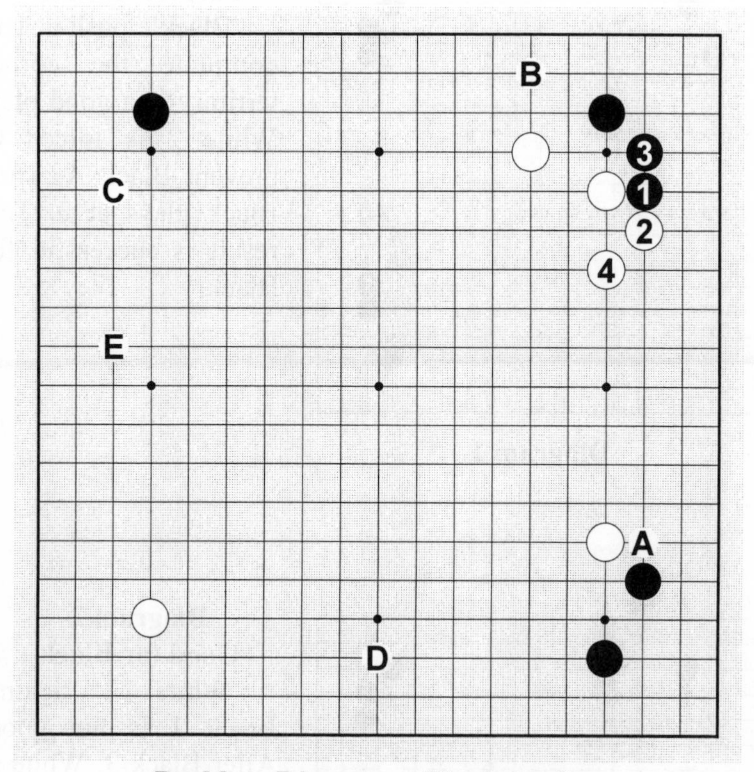

Problem Diagram – Black to play

In the top right corner there is a 4-5 point *joseki* in process. Up to White 4 Black takes territory, while White completes the wall. Black should decide whether to continue to play in the corner or play elsewhere. Choose the correct one from **A** to **E**.

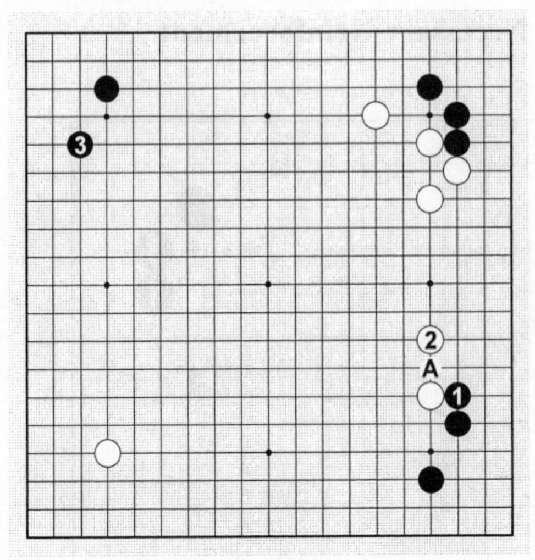

Diagram 1

Diagram 1
Correct Answer

Black's push at 1 to complete the corner territory is a good play. White 2 is forced to prevent Black **A**. Then Black plays at 3. This result is successful for Black.

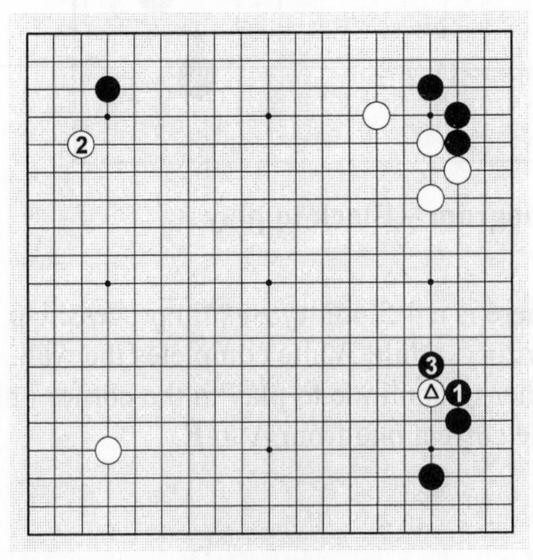

Diagram 2

Diagram 2
Good for Black

White 2 against Black 1 is not good. After Black 3, White Δ is almost useless and White's shape in the top right corner has shrunk because of Black 3. This result is not good for White.

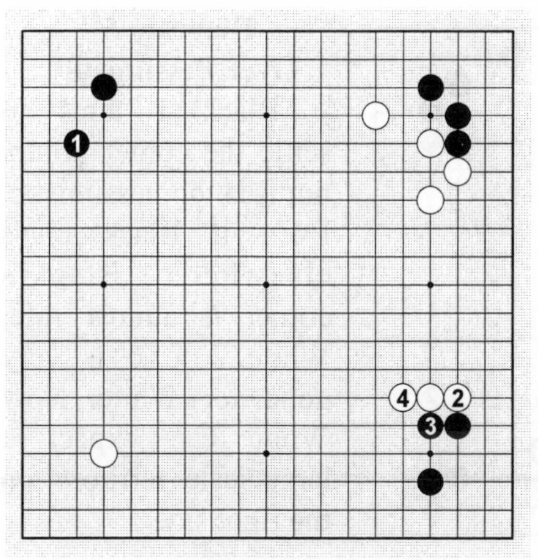

Diagram 3

Diagram 3
Ideal Shape

Black 1 is a big play. But after White 2 and 4, White has ideal shape on the right side. White 4 against Black 3 is the key point. If White allows Black to play at 4, White's group becomes weak, while Black's group is strengthened.

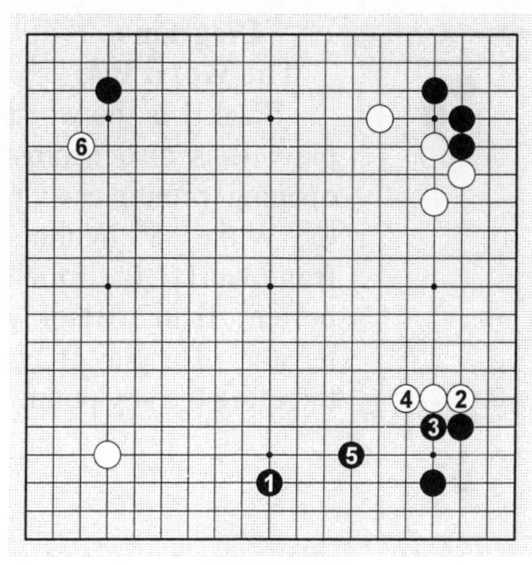

Diagram 4

Diagram 4
Bias Towards the Lower Side

Black 1 is a play that takes too much account of the lower side. After White 2 and 4, Black 5 is usual. Up to White 6 this result is good for White, because White has an ideal shape on the right, while Black's shape is biased towards the lower side.

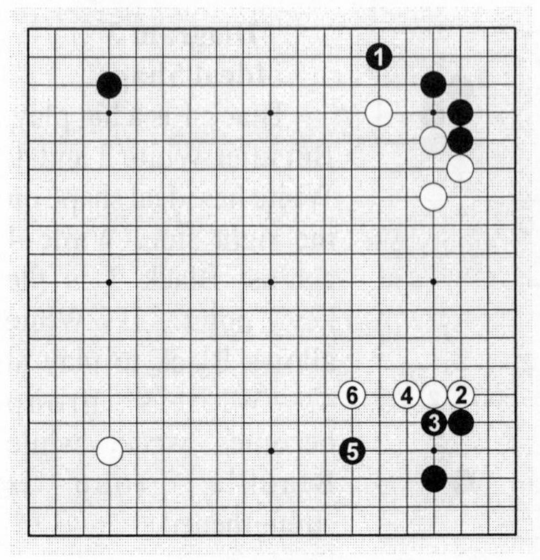

Diagram 5

Diagram 5
Over Pessimistic

Black 1 aims to settle the corner group, but it is too pessimistic. Even if Black plays elsewhere, Black's corner is almost safe. White 2 to 6 is very good for White. Now White can expect a large-scale territory on the right side.

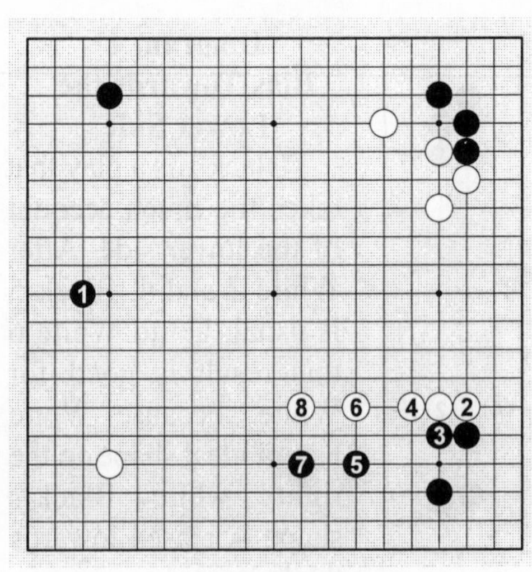

Diagram 6

Diagram 6
The Worst Play

Black 1 is the worst play. It is also against opening principles. Up to White 8 White's framework is much better than Black's territory. The play at 2 is therefore the key point.

Problem 5 A Framework Completed

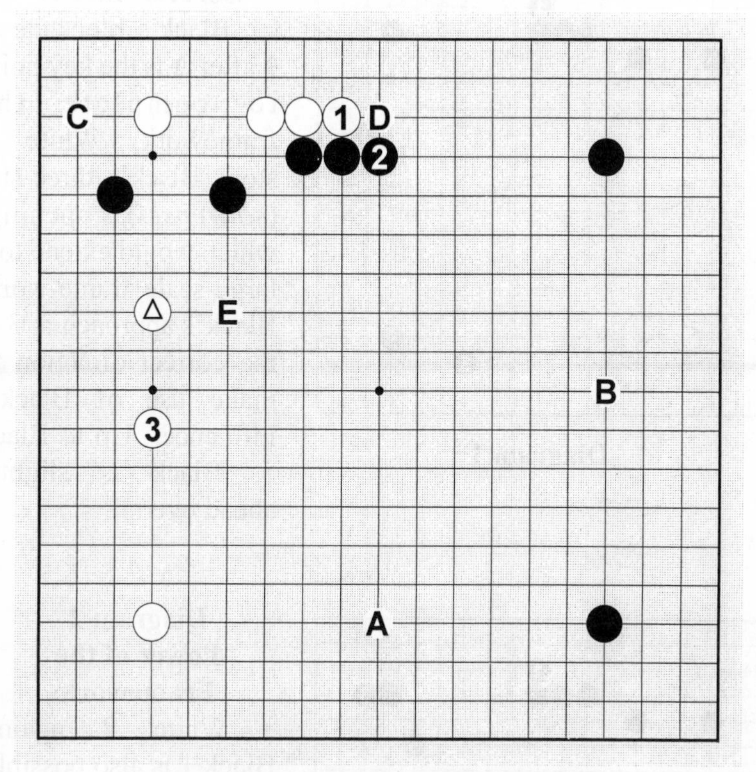

Problem Diagram – Black to play

White has just played at 3 after the exchange of White 1 and Black 2. White 3 aims to settle White Δ. Now what is the best play to complete Black's framework? Choose from **A** to **E**.

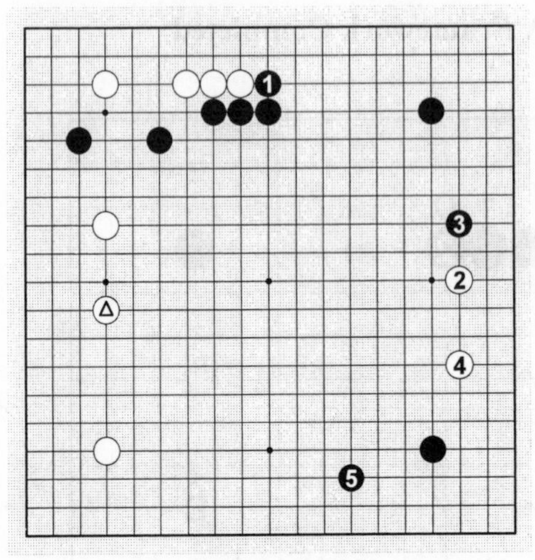

Diagram 1

Diagram 1
Correct Answer

Black's blockade at 1 after Δ is the key point to complete the framework. White 2 stops Black's three-star (*sanrensei*) opening, which would extend to a large-scale frame-work. Black's approach at 3 is the correct direction to make use of Black's influence. Up to Black 5, Black is slightly ahead overall.

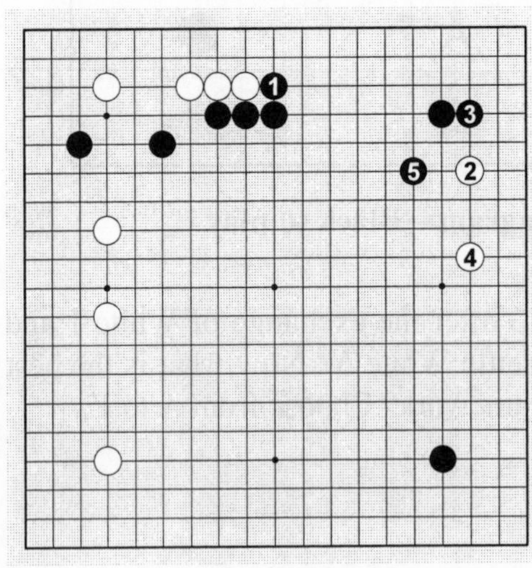

Diagram 2

Diagram 2
Power of the Framework

White 2 against Black 1 is also possible. In this case Black 3 to keep the corner is a good play, because the framework hardly works if Black next allows White's invasion in the corner. After Black's knight's play at 5 against White's extension at 4, Black has a large-scale territory.

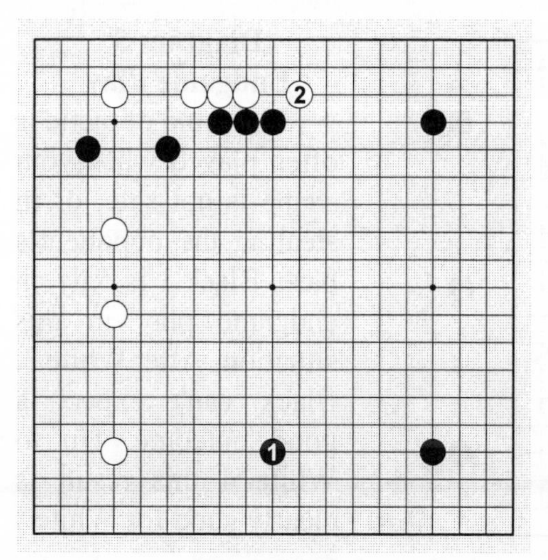

Diagram 3

Diagram 3
Worthless Wall

Black 1 is a big play. But after White 2, Black's wall doesn't work very well. Completing the framework comes before a big play.

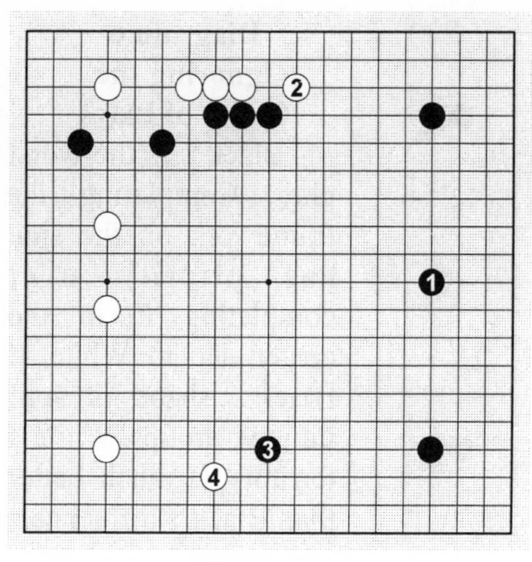

Diagram 4

Diagram 4
***Sanrensei* Formation**

Black 1 is a play to build up the framework. But after White 2, Black's framework is incomplete. After White 4 White's territory is better than Black's influence.

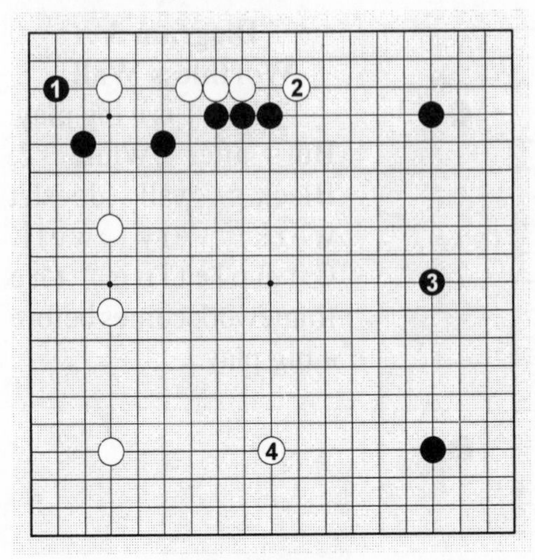

Diagram 5

Diagram 5
Endgame Play

This kind of tactic is often played when your shape is not safe, or in stealing the opponent's base. Black 1 is only an endgame play in this situation. After White 2, Black can't expect a good outcome. Up to White 4 this result is clearly good for White.

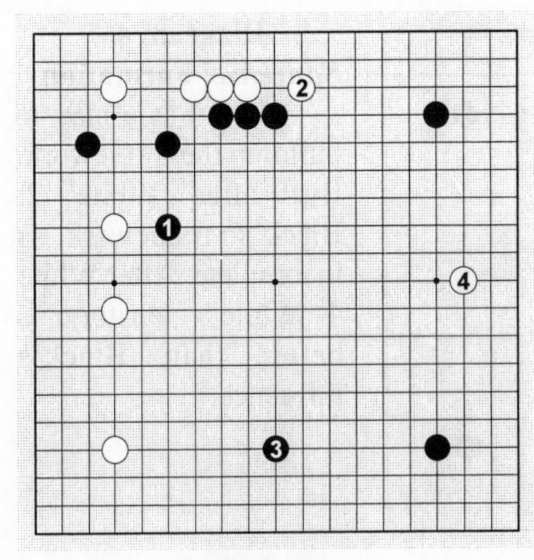

Diagram 6

Diagram 6
Ignoring the Order of Plays

Black 1 is the worst play. Completing the framework on the side has priority over completing it in the center. Up to White 4, Black's shape is split into two groups. White's territory is much better than Black's influence.

Problem 6 Punishing the Loose Play

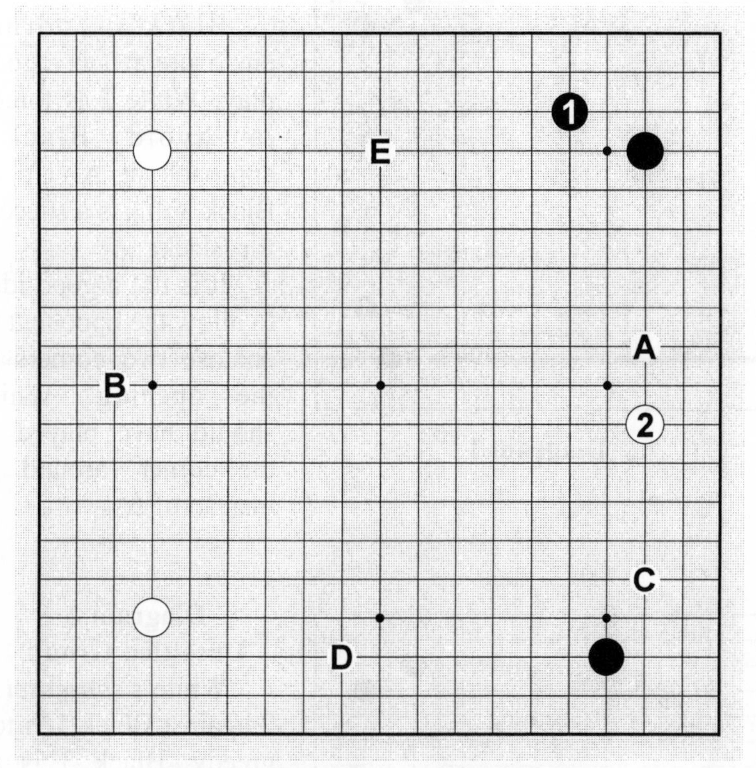

Problem Diagram – Black to play

White has just played at 2 after Black's enclosure at 1. White 2 is against the rule in the opening: play the corners, then the sides, and finally the center. Going against this rule is usually not good. After six plays, there is only one correct reply for Black, which is rare so early in the game. Choose the correct answer from **A** to **E**.

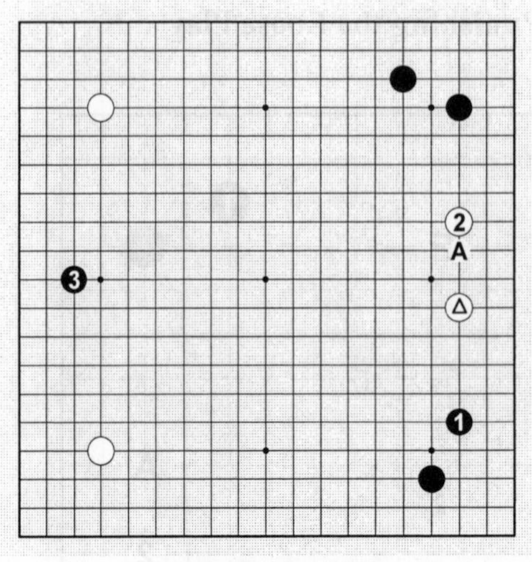

Diagram 1

Diagram 1
Correct Answer

Black's corner enclosure at 1 is a good play. White 2 is forced to avoid Black's approach at **A**. Up to Black 3 this is a success for Black.

It is not a good idea to allow the opponent to enclose two corners in the opening. White should have played in the corner (around 1) instead of Δ.

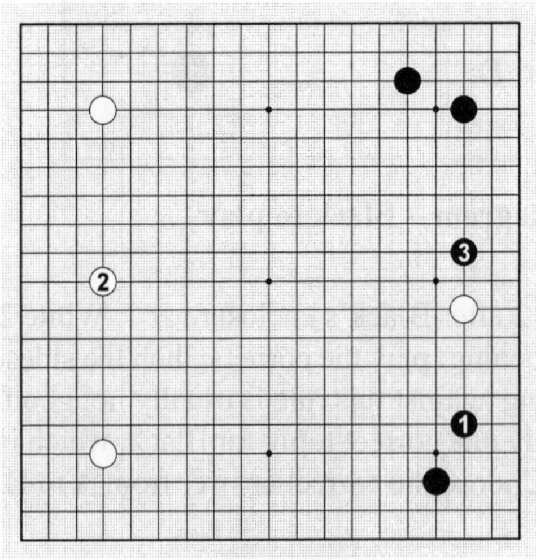

Diagram 2

Diagram 2
Unsettled Group

White's *sanrensei* at 2 against Black 1 is too greedy. Black 3 is an excellent 'two birds with one stone' tactic, to expand the influence and attack White on the right side. This is clearly good for Black.

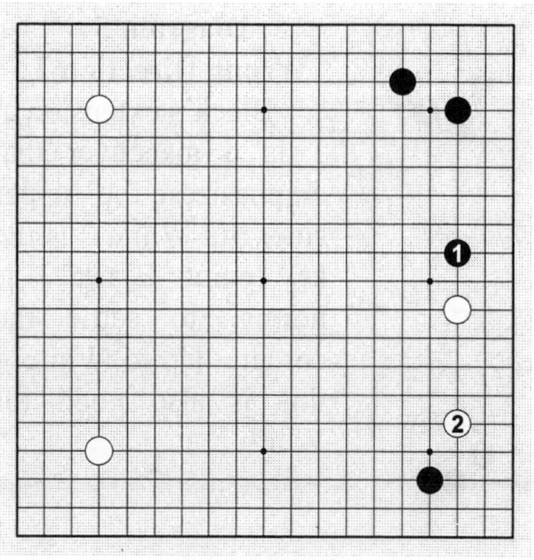

Diagram 3

Diagram 3
Failing to Punish

Black 1 is a good play for expansion. But in this case White 2 is very good to settle White's group on the right side, at the same time preventing Black's corner enclosure. After White 2, Black has failed to take advantage of White's bad play.

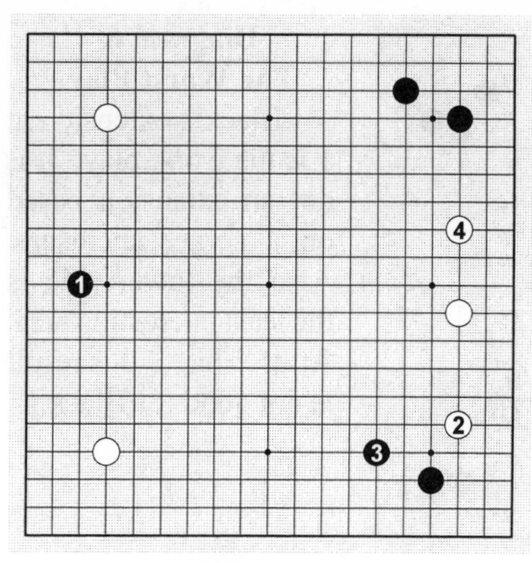

Diagram 4

Diagram 4
Wrong Direction 1

Black 1 prevents White's three-star formation (*sanrensei*). But it is too early. White 2 and 4, to take the right side, are good plays; in this case the right side is more interesting than the left side. Up to White 4 this result is good for White.

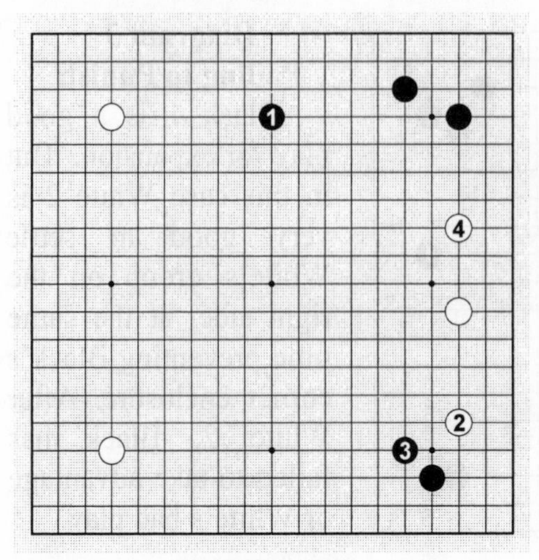

Diagram 4

Diagram 5
Wrong Direction 2

Black's extension at 1 is a maneuver that emphasizes the upper side. But White 2 is the key point. Black 3 is normal to settle the corner. Up to White 4 this is also good for White.

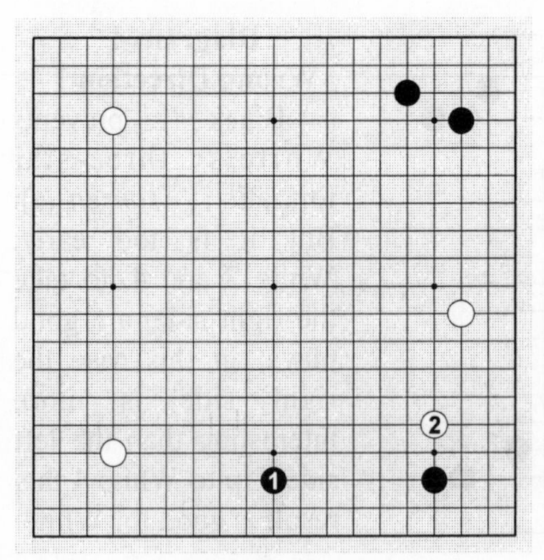

Diagram 6

Diagram 6
The Worst Play

Black's extension at 1 is the worst play. It is not an extension based on a corner enclosure. Also the lower side is the least interesting area. After White 2 this result is not good for Black.

Problem 7 The Corners are Big

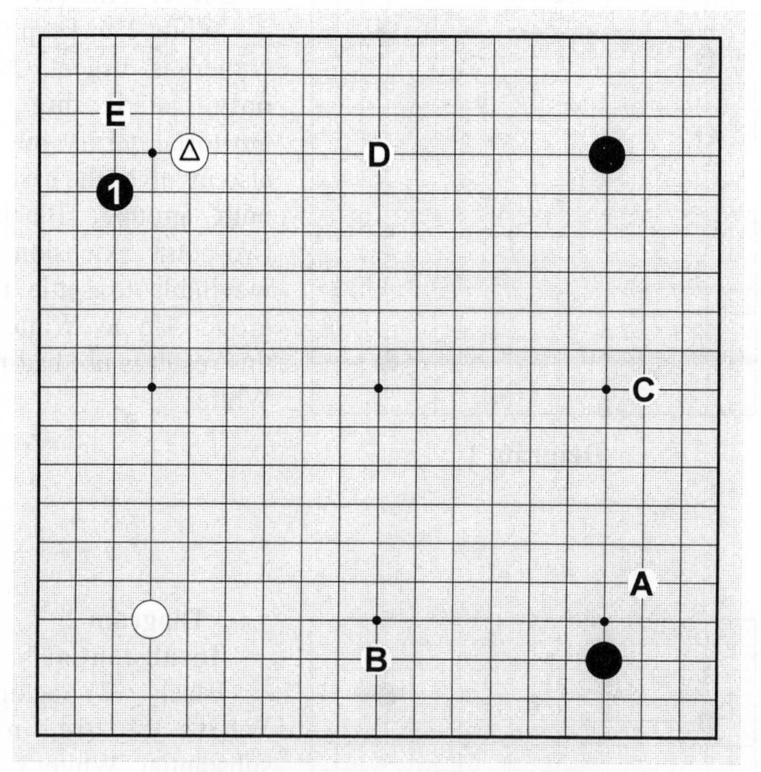

Problem Diagram - White to Play

Black's approach at 1 against White Δ at the 5-4 point is rather unusual. Playing Black 1 at the 3-3 point or 4-3 point instead is more usual. Now White should decide whether to answer in the corner or play elsewhere. Choose the next play from **A** to **E**.

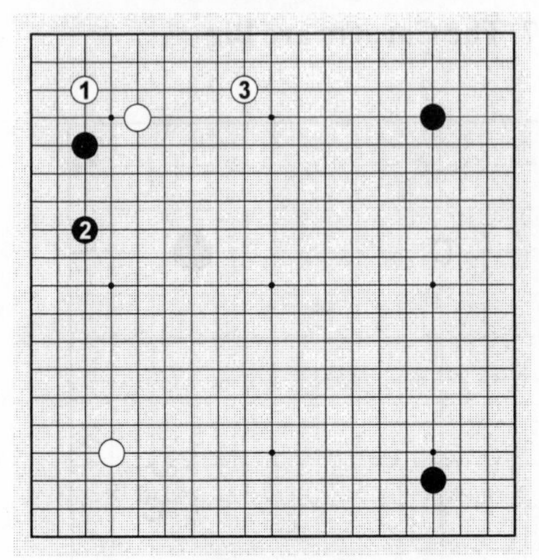

Diagram 1

Diagram 1
Correct Answer

White 1 to keep the corner is urgent. Not only is it big in territorial terms but it also involves the base of both groups. Black's two-point extension is inevitable to settle the group. Up to White 3 this result is not bad for White.

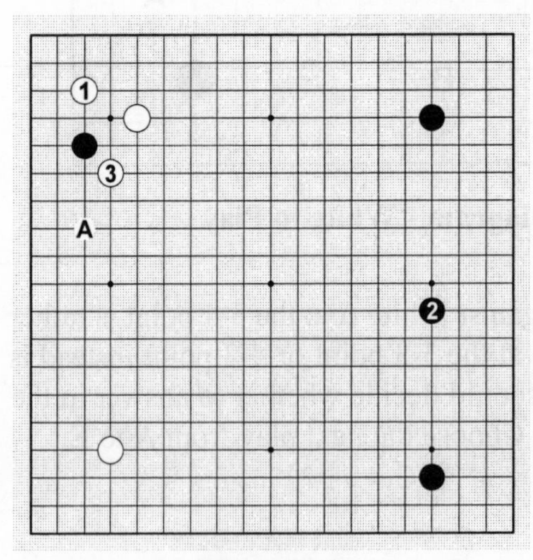

Diagram 2

Diagram 2
Insubstantial

Black 2 against White 1 is not substantial. White 3, to press Black's one stone, is a good play. Now White has quite a good territory in the corner and also has strong influence. Black should have played at **A** instead of 2.

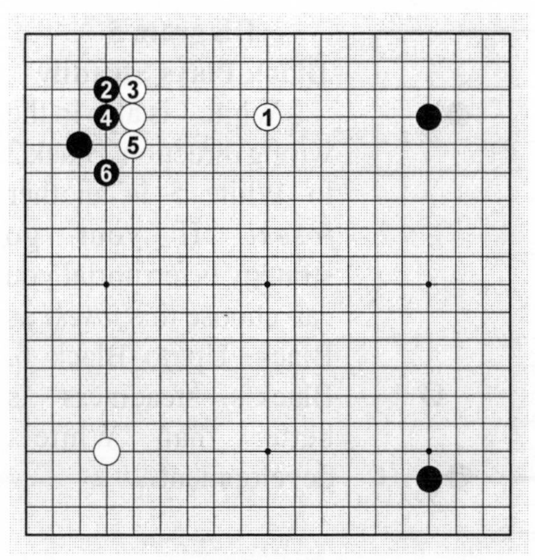

Diagram 3

Diagram 3
Joseki

White 1 takes much account of the upper side. After the sequence 2 to 6, Black has taken the corner, while White has taken the upper side. But this result is not good for White: Black's territory in the corner is better than White's framework on the upper side even though the sequence may seem normal.

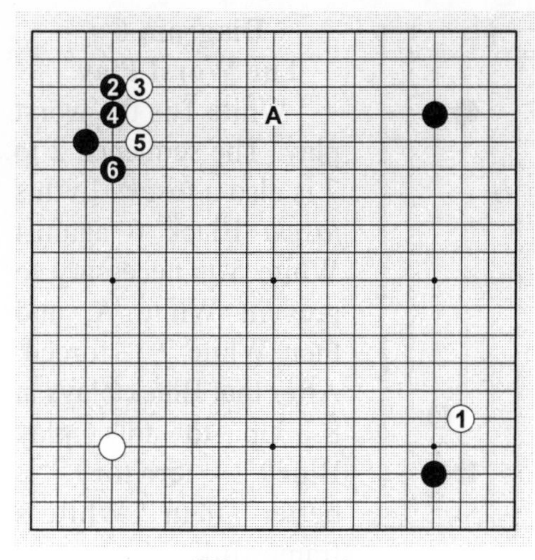

Diagram 4

Diagram 4
Wrong Direction

White 1 is also not good. Black 2 to 6 to take the corner is very good. After Black 6, White should answer on the upper side (around **A**). This **Diagram is** similar to the previous one.

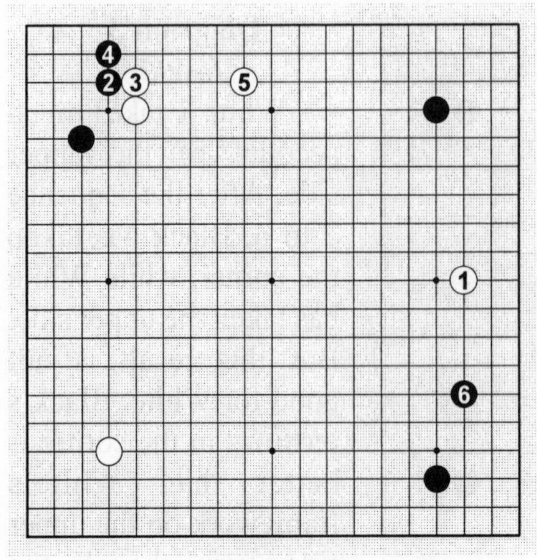

Diagram 5

Diagram 5
Black Plays Steadily

White 1 is also in the wrong direction. Black 2 to White 5 is another *joseki*. If your go strategy is territorial you can choose this *joseki* as Black. Up to Black 6, Black's steadiness is better than White's development.

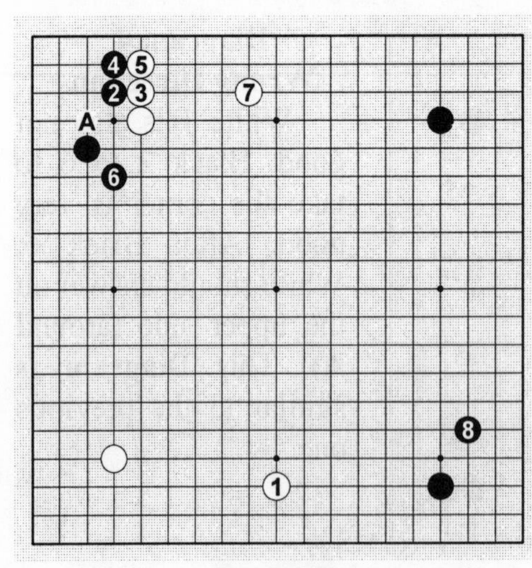

Diagram 6

Diagram 6
The Worst Play

White 1 is the worst play. The sequence 2 to 7 is also a *joseki*. In this *joseki* Black 6 against White 5 is necessary to prevent White **A**, and then White 7 is forced. After that Black plays at 8. Up to this play Black's territory is better than White's framework.

Problem 8 Limiting Outside Influence

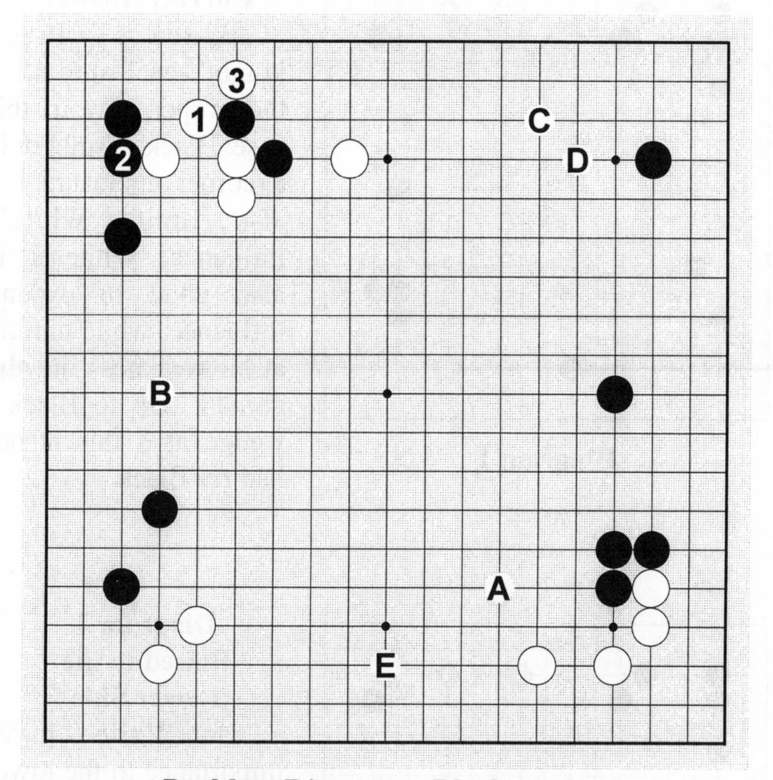

Problem Diagram – Black to play

In the top left corner, a star *joseki* has been completed. In this *joseki* Black takes territory, while allowing White to build strong influence. You should decide whether to limit that influence, or play a big point. Choose the correct answer from **A** to **E**.

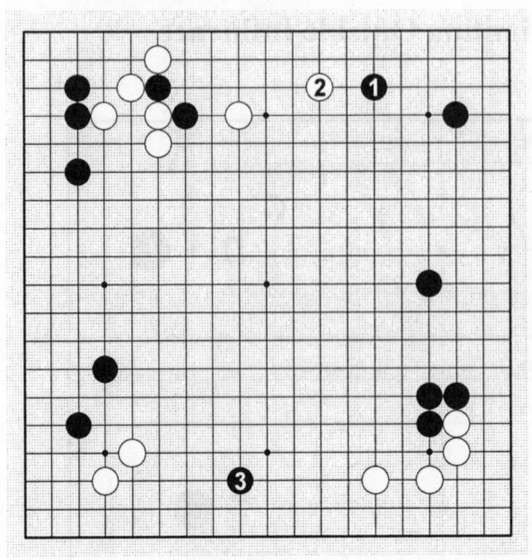

Diagram 1

Diagram 1
Correct Answer

Black's large knight's enclosure at 1 is the proper play in this case. Black 1 is not only a corner enclosure but also limits White's influence. White 2 is also good to expand influence, while aiming at a weakness in the corner. Up to Black's wedge at 3 this is not bad for Black.

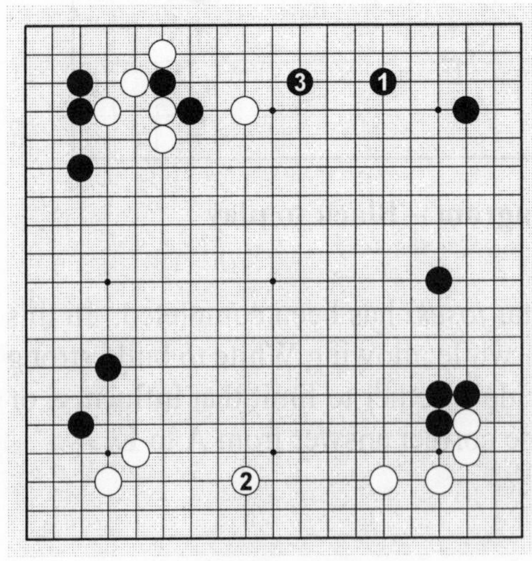

Diagram 2

Diagram 2
Biased to the Lower Side

If White gives importance to the lower side by playing at 2, Black's two-point extension at 2 is very good. On the whole White's shape is concentrated on the lower side, while Black's shape has much more potential for future development.

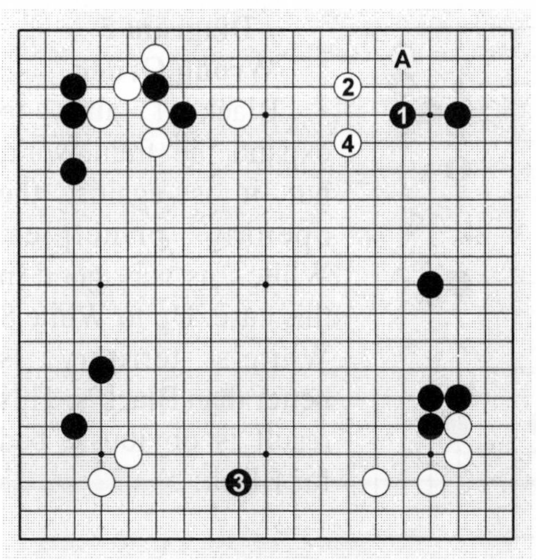

Diagram 3

Diagram 3
Difference

Black 1 is a corner enclosure too, but it is worse here than the large knight's enclosure. White 2 is an excellent play, and then Black 3 and White 4 are routine. Comparing with the correct answer, Black's corner has an obvious weakness at **A**. This result is bad for Black.

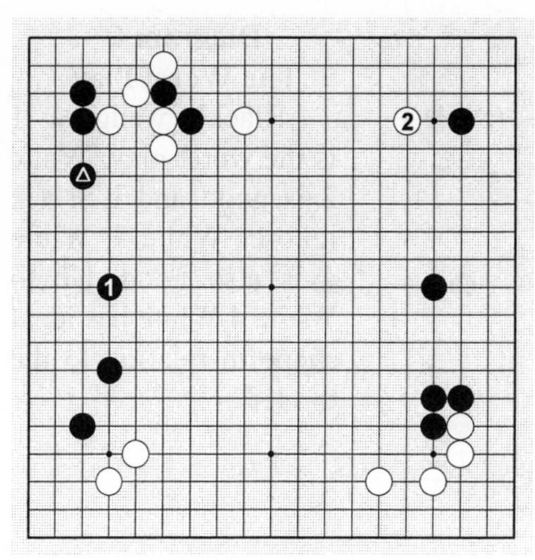

Diagram 4

Diagram 4
Wrong Direction

Black 1 is the big play to keep the territory on the left side, but this area is not interesting, because ▲ is on the third line. White's approach at 2 is an excellent play. After White 2, White can expect a large-scale framework. This result is good for White.

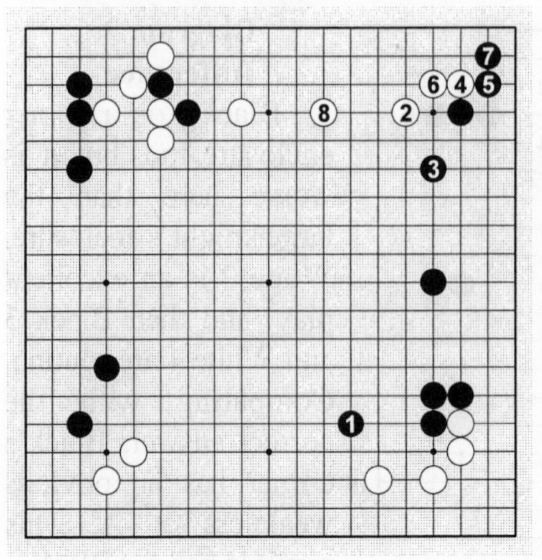

Diagram 5

Diagram 5
Wrong Order

Black 1 aims to expand the framework, but it is against the opening principles. White 2 is very good in this case. Up to White 8 White's territory is better than Black's. This result is obviously bad for Black.

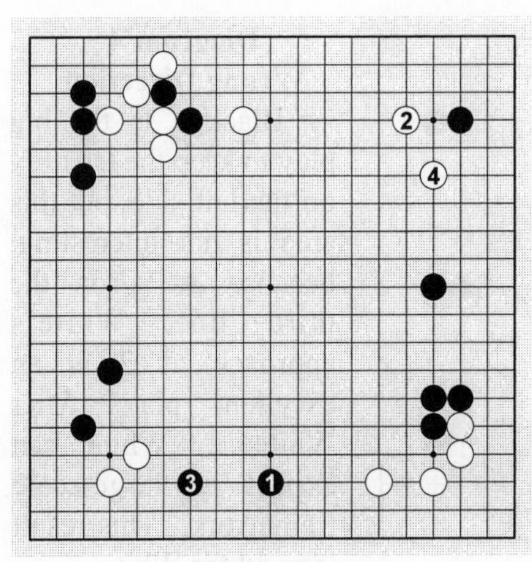

Diagram 6

Diagram 6
The Worst Play

Black's wedge at 1 is the worst play. White 2 is good and if Black ignores White 2, White 4 is also good. Up to White 4 White has ideal shape in relation to the top left.

Problem 9 Judgment of Future Potential

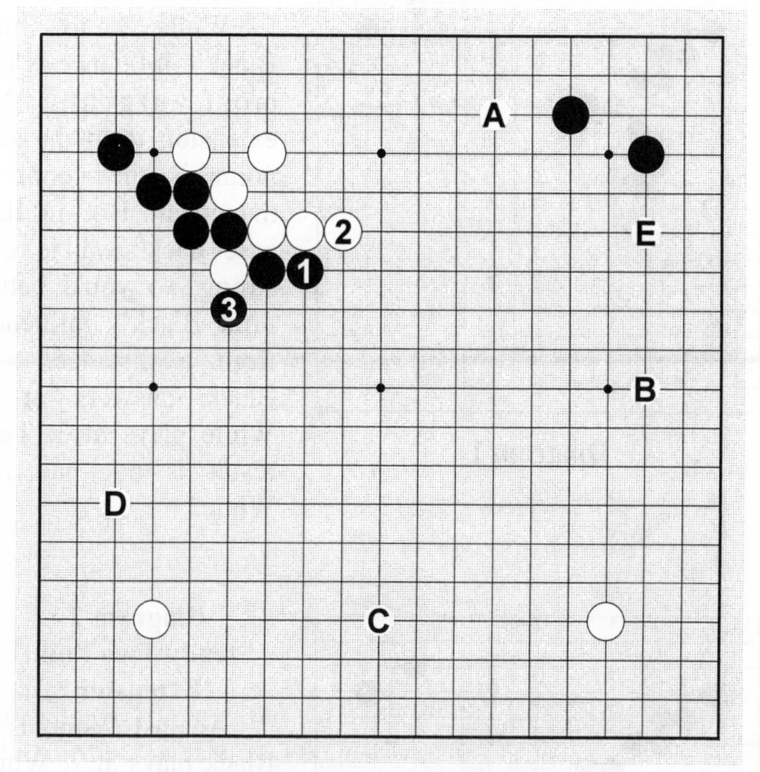

Problem Diagram – White to play

A large-scale *joseki* has just been completed. Up to Black 3 Black has formed a large wall on the left side, while White has a good wall on the upper side. The question is how to improve these walls or limit these influences, and you should also decide whose wall has greatest future potential. Choose the correct answer from **A** to **E**.

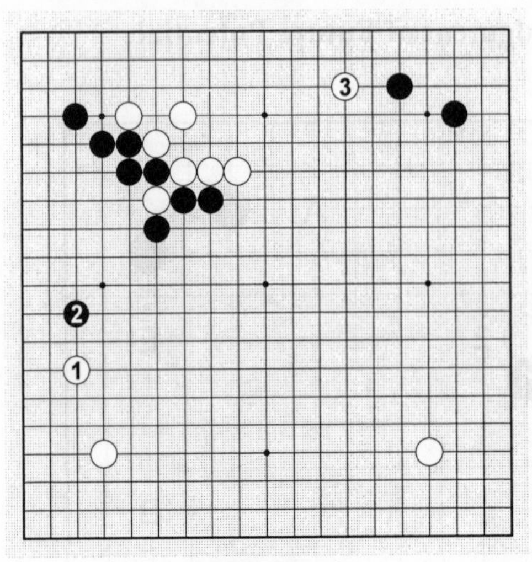

Diagram 1

Diagram 1
Correct Answer

White 1 to limit Black's influence is the most urgent. An extension from the star point is the common maneuver. But in this case Black's wall is very strong, so you'd better limit Black's influence from a distance. If Black answers at 2 White plays at 3. This result is not bad for White.

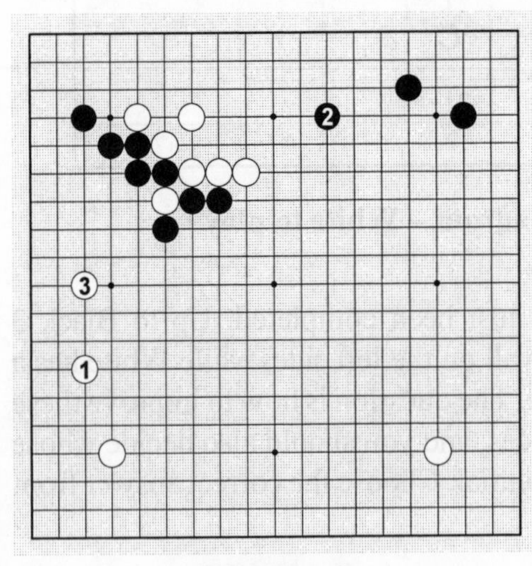

Diagram 2

Diagram 2
Steady Two Point Extension

Against White 1, if Black plays at 2, White 3 next is ordinary. But up to this play Black's influence has almost disappeared.

In general if the opponent has a strong wall, you should make steady plays like White 1 and 3.

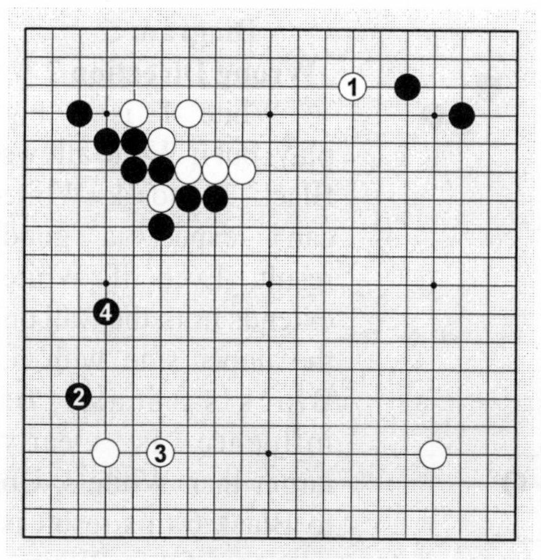

Diagram 3

Diagram 3
Scale of Influence

White 1 makes a good job of expansion on the top side. But you should see that Black's influence over the left side is much stronger than White's influence over the upper side. Up to Black 4 Black's framework is ideal.

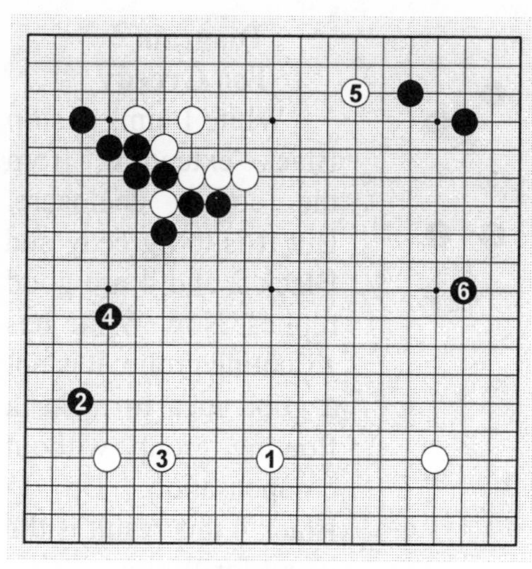

Diagram 4

Diagram 4
Wrong Direction 1

White 1 to complete the *sanrensei* is in the wrong direction. Black's 2 and 4 are good to complete Black's framework, and then White 5 is a normal tactic to extend the influence. However, up to Black 6 Black is clearly ahead.

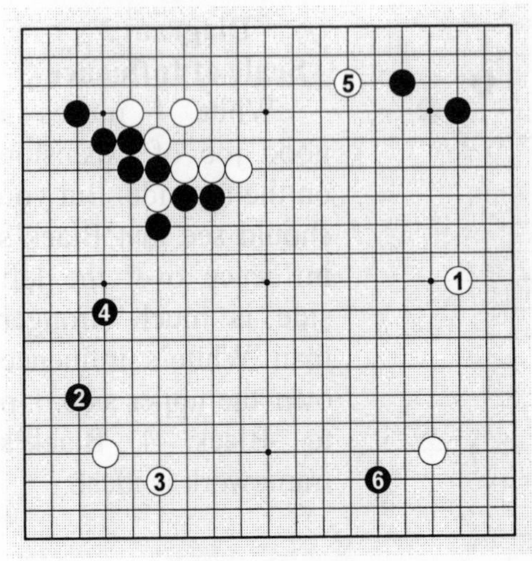

Diagram 5

Diagram 5
Wrong Direction 2

White 1 is a big play, but if White allows Black 2 and 4, White can't expect a good result. Even if White extends from the wall on the upper side with 5, Black's scale of influence is clearly larger than White's. Up to Black 6 this result is unsuccessful for White.

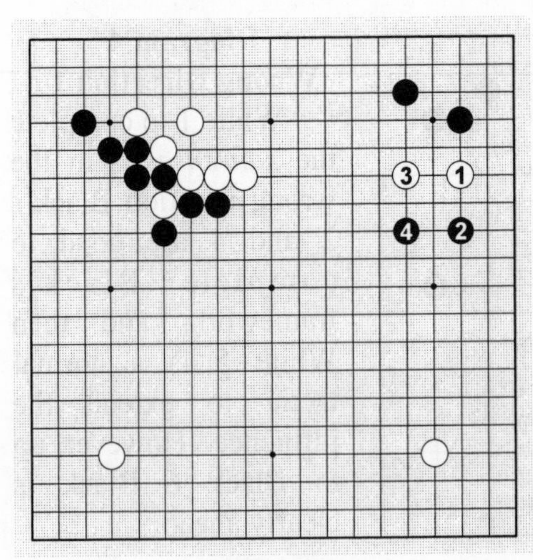

Diagram 6

Diagram 6
Too Greedy

White 1 aims to stop Black extending from the corner enclosure. But it is too greedy and Black 2 and 4 are good replies. Now White has a floating group; it is not a good idea to make a floating group without compensation. Up to Black 4 this result is the worst for White.

Problem 10 Taking Account of Thickness

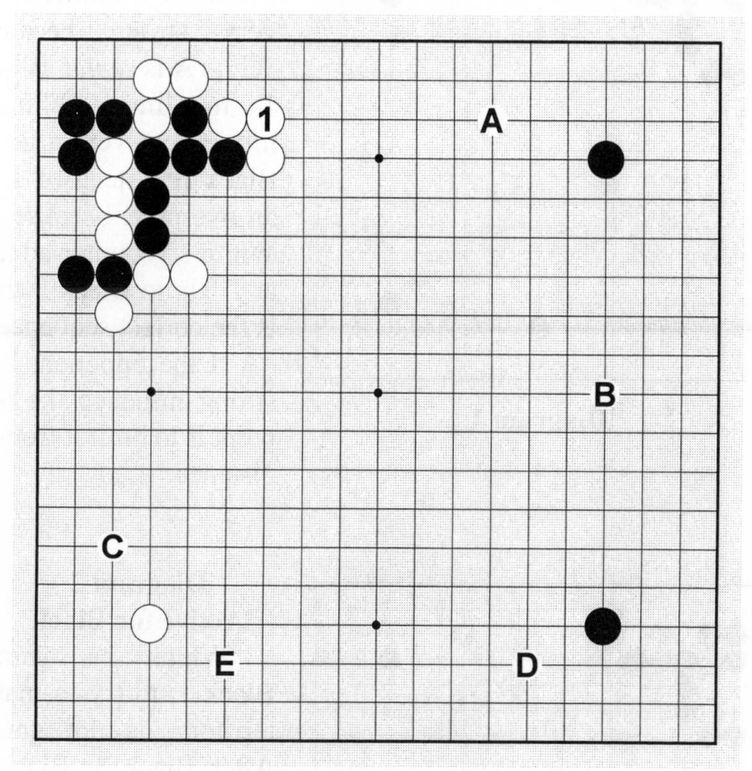

Problem Diagram – Black to play

With White 1 a *joseki* is completed in the top left corner. Black takes territory in the corner, while White has a strong influence outside. The question is how to limit White's influence. Choose the correct answer from **A** to **E**.

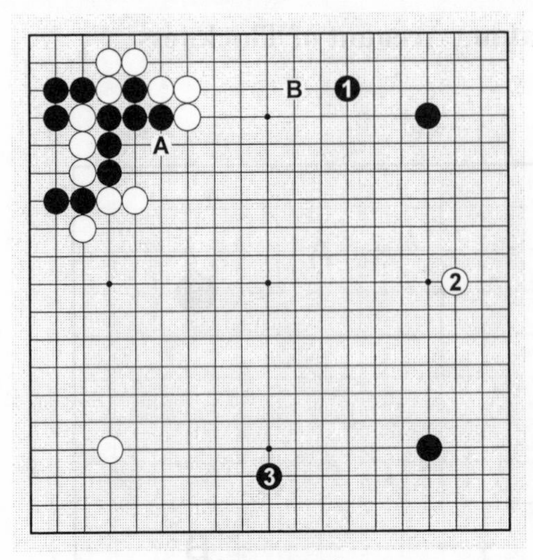

Diagram 1

Diagram 1
Correct Answer

White's influence is very strong because White **A** is *sente*. Black 1 to limit White's influence is very urgent. Black **B** instead of 1 is an overplay, because of White's counter-attack at 1. Up to Black 3 this is the correct sequence.

If the opponent has strong influence, the key point is to limit it from a distance.

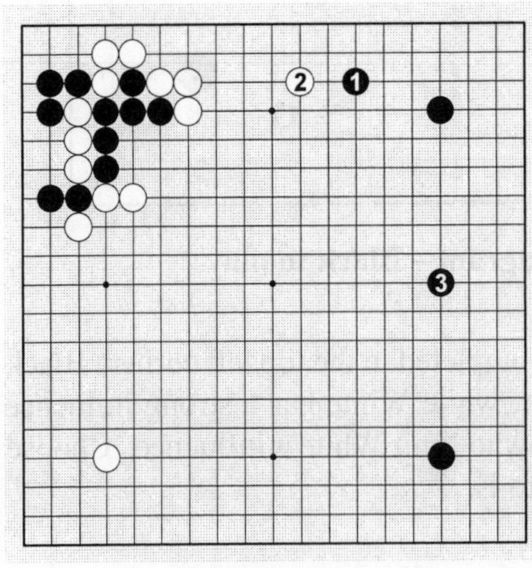

Diagram 2

Diagram 2
Active for Black

White 2 against Black 1, to try to make territory, is not good. After Black 3, Black's shape is more active. This result is good for Black.

In general the ideal way of using influence is to make a large-scale framework, or to attack the opponent's weak group.

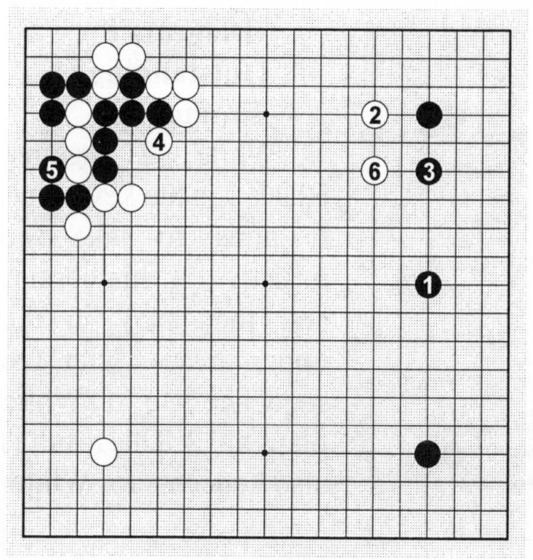

Diagram 3

Diagram 3
Ideal Shape

Black 1 aims to expand influence on the right. But White 2 and 6 to complete the framework, after the exchange of White 4 and Black 5, are very good. After White 6, White has an ideal shape expanding the upper side into the center.

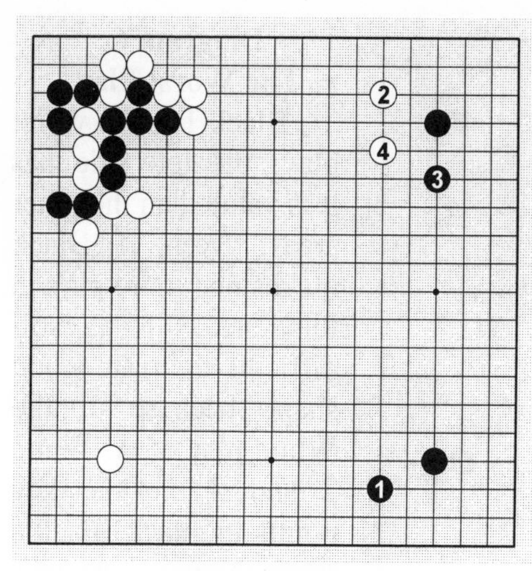

Diagram 4

Diagram 4
Wrong Direction

Black 1 is in the wrong direction. After allowing White 2, Black can't expect a good result. In this situation the focus is the upper area. Up to White 4, White has again completed an ideal framework.

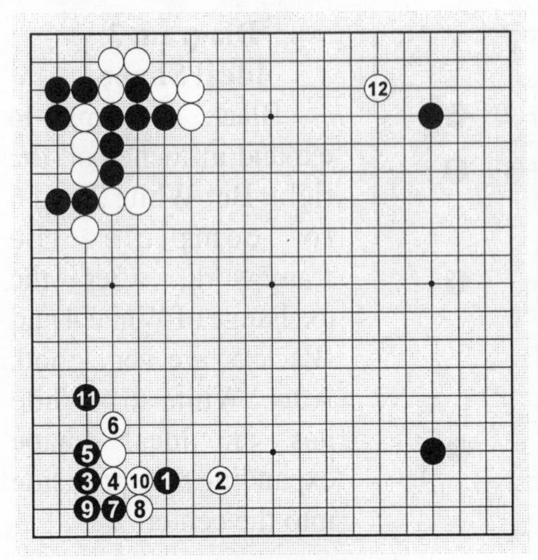

Diagram 5

Diagram 5
Outstanding Framework

White 2 against Black 1 is the key point. It aims to take the initiative in this corner, and then play in the upper area. After the sequence 3 to 11, White plays at 12. This result is also a success for White.

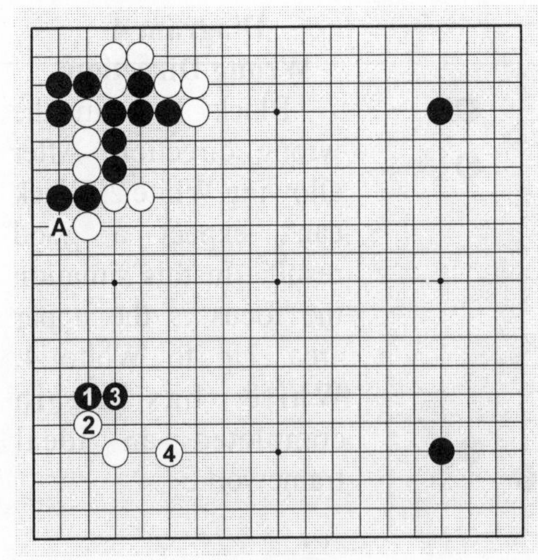

Diagram 6

Diagram 6
The Worst Play

Black 1 is the worst play: the left side has less value than the other areas. Even if Black makes one more play in this area, it is still difficult to make good shape because of the White play at **A**. White 2 and 4 are the key points to attack Black's group. Now Black needs an extension to settle it. Then White can play in the upper area.

Problem 11 A Deceptively Large Place to Play

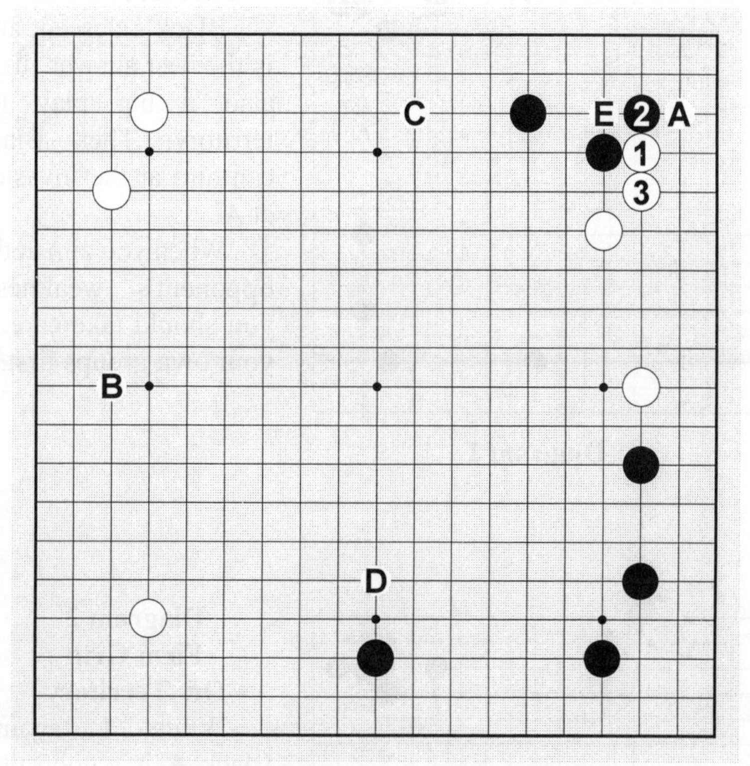

Problem Diagram – Black to Play

White has just settled the group by playing at 1 and 3. Now Black should decide whether to answer or play elsewhere. There is a deceptively large place to play. Choose the correct answer from **A** to **E**.

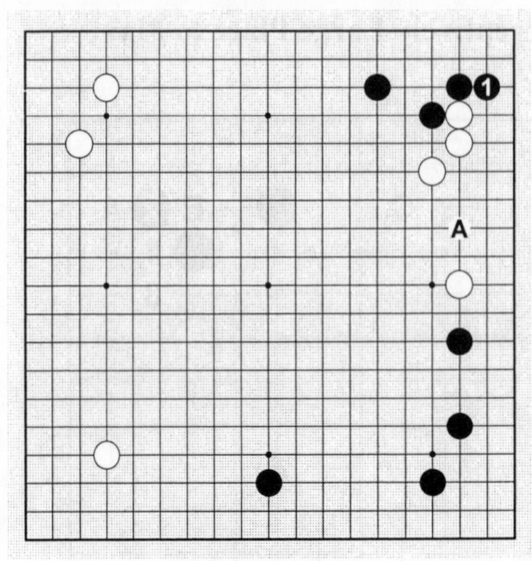

Diagram 1

Diagram 1
Correct Answer

Black's descent at 1 is the best answer. It is also a big play for territory. Then Black can aim at the invasion at **A**.

When you aim at the opponent's weakness, you should take care of your own groups first.

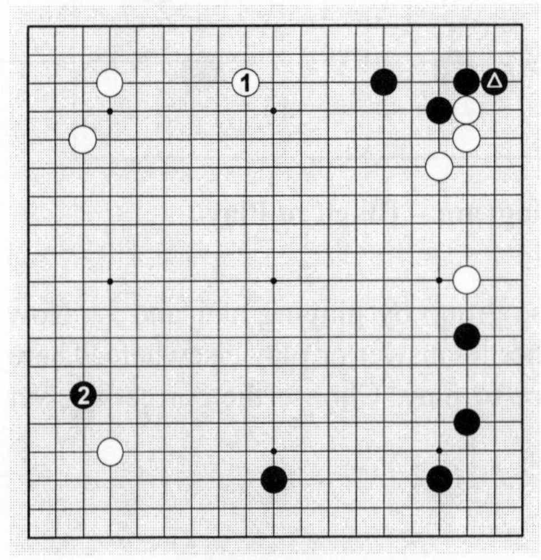

Diagram 2

Diagram 2
Firm Grip
On Territory

White 1 against Black ▲ is a good play to extend the influence from the enclosure. Then Black plays at 2. Up to this point Black's solid territory is better.

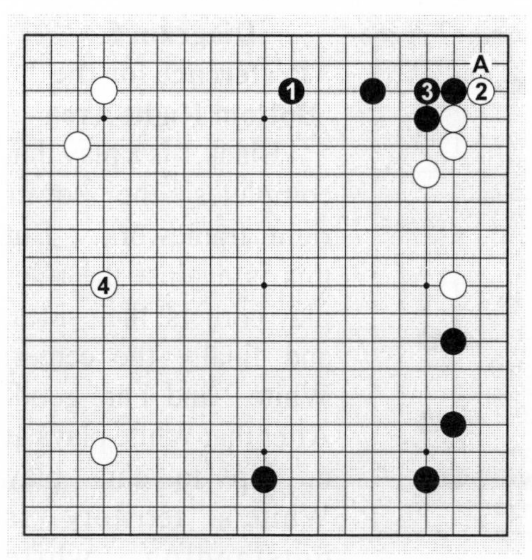

Diagram 3

Diagram 3
Slow

Black's extension at 1 emphasizes the upper side. But White 2 is very good. Black 3 is a normal answer in this case. Then White takes the big point at 4. This result is very positive for White. If White later plays at **A**, Black's territory is not large.

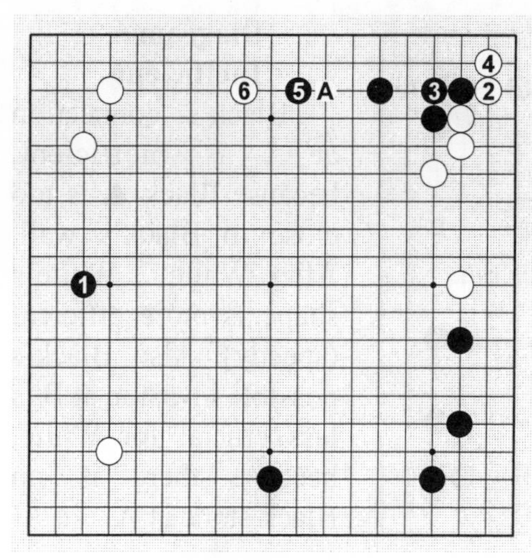

Diagram 4

Diagram 4
Insubstantial

Black's wedge at 1 prevents White from expanding on the left. But if Black allows White 2, the result will be insubstantial for Black. White 4 is a good play, which attacks the base of Black's group, and then Black 5 is forced: if Black allows White **A**, Black's group has no base for life. Up to White 6 this is clearly good for White.

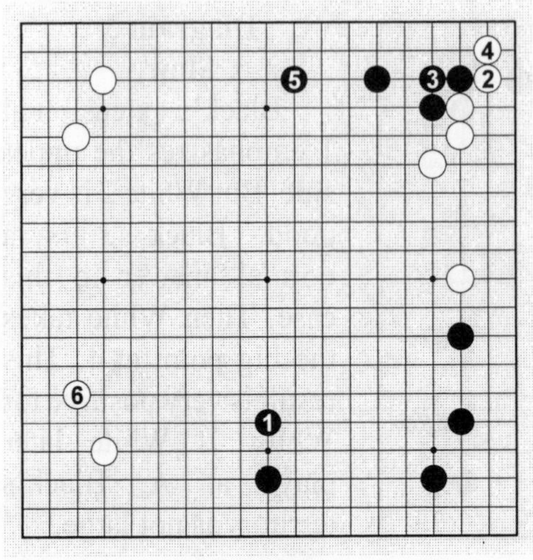

Diagram 5

Diagram 5
Preference for the Bottom Right Area

Black 1 is a play that completes the lower right framework. But this is against the rule: play corners, then sides, and finally the center. White 2 and 4 are good. After that White plays at 6. Up to this play White's territory is outstanding, while Black's shape is biased to the bottom right area.

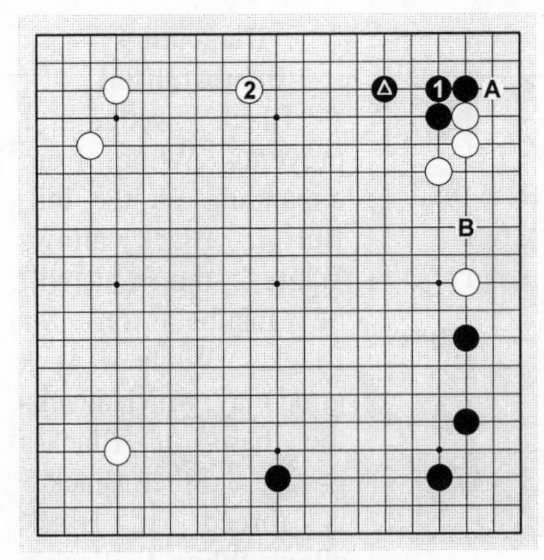

Diagram 6

Diagram 6
Inefficient

Black's connection at 1 is inefficient, because Black ▲ is too close to Black's wall. After White 2 White's shape is more efficient (speedy). Also Black's possible invasion at **B** is less crucial for White, because there is no Black stone at **A**.

Problem 12 The Scale of a Framework

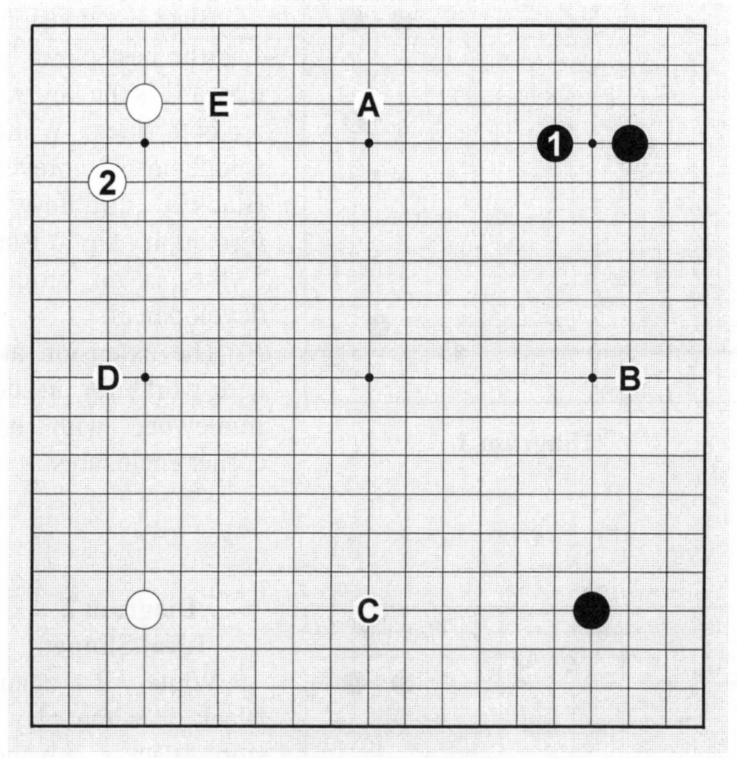

Problem Diagram – Black to Play

Black 1 and White 2 have just been played. Now there are no empty corners. According to the opening principles the next play should be an extension on the side. In a simple territorial game, it is important to understand quite precisely the scale of the frameworks. If you understand the value of a corner enclosure, you will find the answer easily. Choose the correct answer from **A** to **E**.

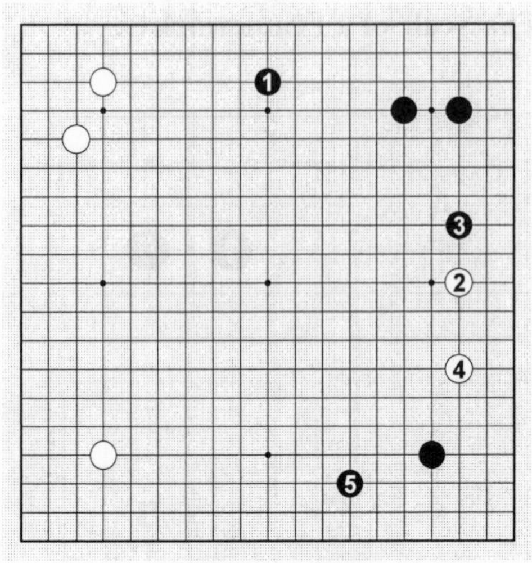

Diagram 1

Diagram 1
Correct Answer

Black's extension at 1 is the best play. The play at 1 is the key point for both sides. White's wedge at 2 prevents Black's double-wing formation. Up to Black 5 this is an ordinary development.

The extension at 1 here works for an ideal framework with both corner enclosures.

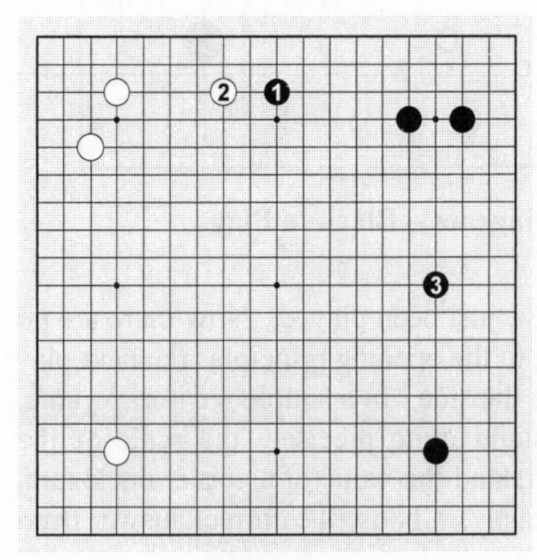

Diagram 2

Diagram 2
Ideal Shape

White 2 against Black 1 is the play to stop Black's advance, but it is not big enough. Black 3 is very good, and the result is clearly bad for White. Black has an ideal shape stretching from the upper to right sides.

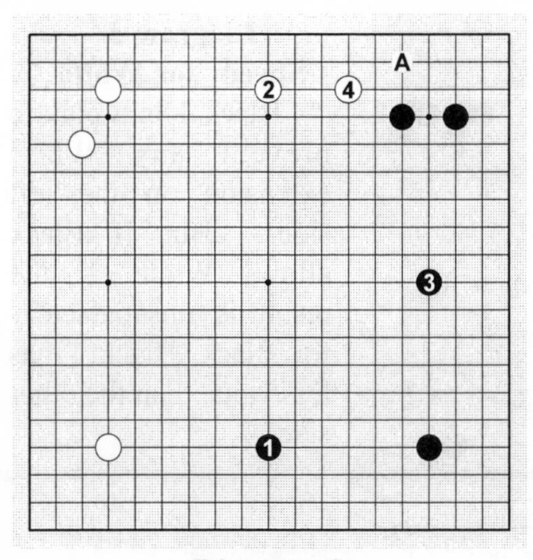

Diagram 3

Diagram 3
The Back Door Is Open

Black's extension at 1 expands the lower side, but the value of 1 is inferior to that of White 2. In general the value of an extension from a corner enclosure is greater than from a star point in the corner. Black 3 is a consistent plan of expansion. However, up to White 4, White is ahead, as Black's upper right corner is open at **A**.

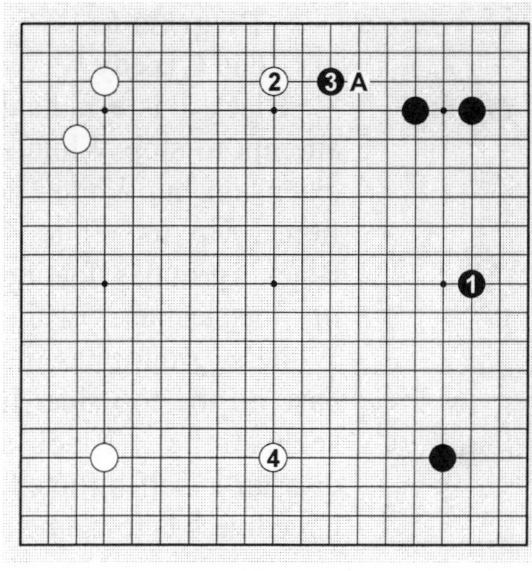

Diagram 4

Diagram 4
Withered Shape

Black 1 is a good play to extend influence, but is inferior to White 2. Black 3 is a big play, to prevent White **A**. Then White extends at 4. Up to this point White is very positive, while Black's shape is somewhat withered.

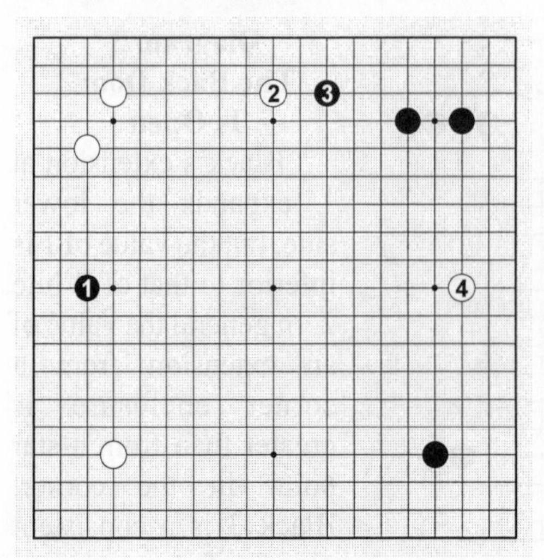

Diagram 5

Diagram 5
Speedy for White

Black 1 is a play to prevent any White extension on the left side. But if Black allows White 2, the result is unsatisfactory for Black. Black 1 has less value than the other sides.

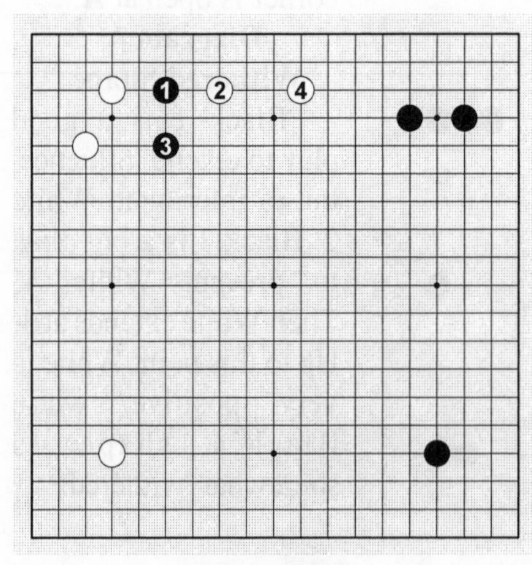

Diagram 6

Diagram 6
Too Greedy

Black 1 is a radical attempt to stop White's extension, but White 2 is fierce. Up to White 4 Black's group is floating in the center, while White's group has its base on the top side. It seems that Black's disaster is self-inflicted. Greediness is to blame.

Problem 13 Speedy Strategy

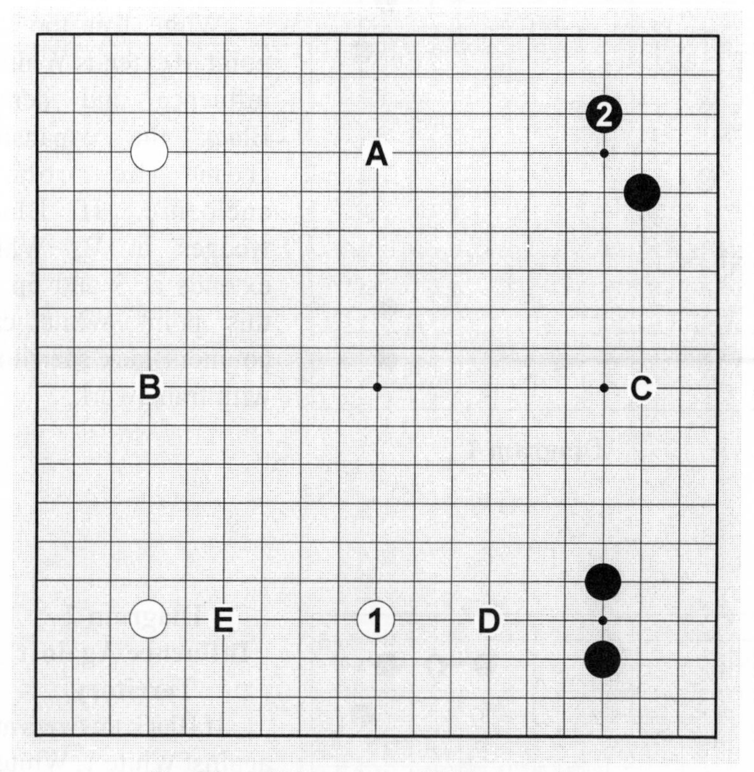

Problem Diagram – White to play

White 1 is a speedy play to prevent Black's extension on the lower side. But usually allowing two corner enclosures is not good. Now Black is ahead in solid territory. White should choose a play that counters Black's solidity, from **A** to **E**.

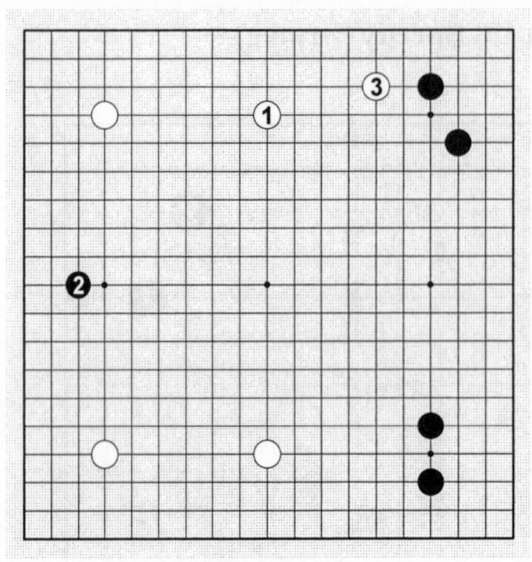

Diagram 1

Diagram 1
Correct Answer

White 1 is the key point. It extends White's influence and denies Black the expansion from the corner enclosure. If Black wedges at 2, White extends at 3 and up to this point White can counter Black's territory with framework.

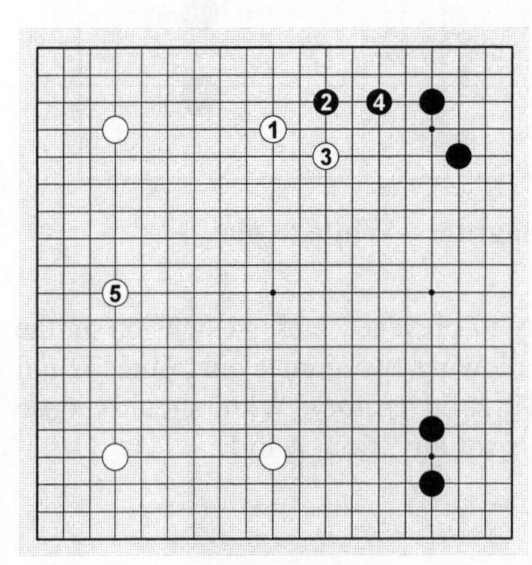

Diagram 2

Diagram 2
Influence Against Territory

If Black answers at 2 against White 1, White's knight's shape at 3 is good. Black 4 is forced. After that White forms a large-scale framework with White 5. White's framework is good enough to compete with Black's territory.

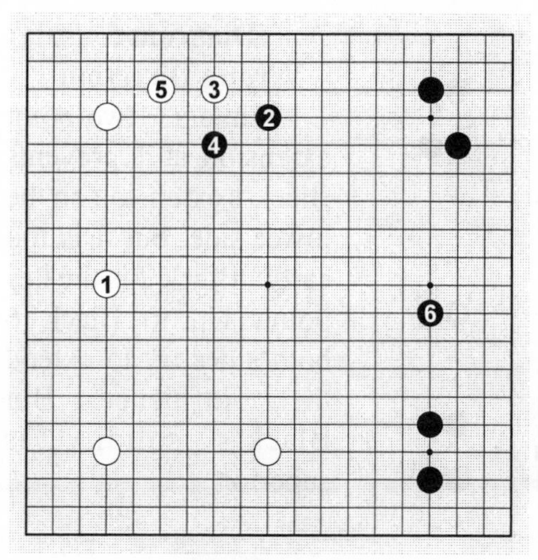

Diagram 3

Diagram 3
Ideal Formation

White 1 is consistent, to form a large framework, but Black 2 and 4 are also good. Up to Black 6, Black's formation is ideal, while White's is both smaller and thinner, since Black's framework is based on the corner enclosures.

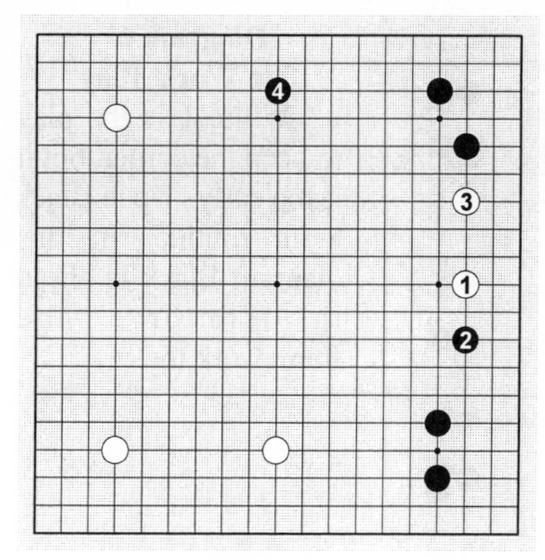

Diagram 4

Diagram 4
Thin for White

White 1 is a big play to prevent Black's extension. But after the exchange of Black 2 and White 3, Black 4 is another good extension. This result is good for Black.

In this case White should try to form a large-scale framework because Black has already made two corner enclosures.

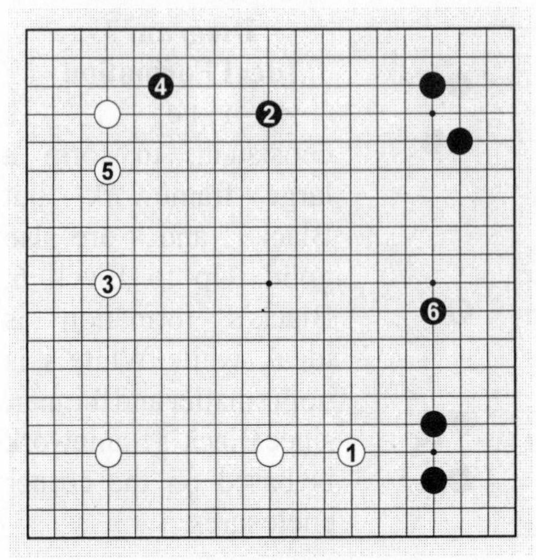

Diagram 5

Diagram 5
Wrong Direction

White's two-point extension at 1 prevents Black's extension on the lower side, but it is too early. Black 2 is the key point. Up to Black 6 both sides try to extend their influence. But Black's solidity is superior.

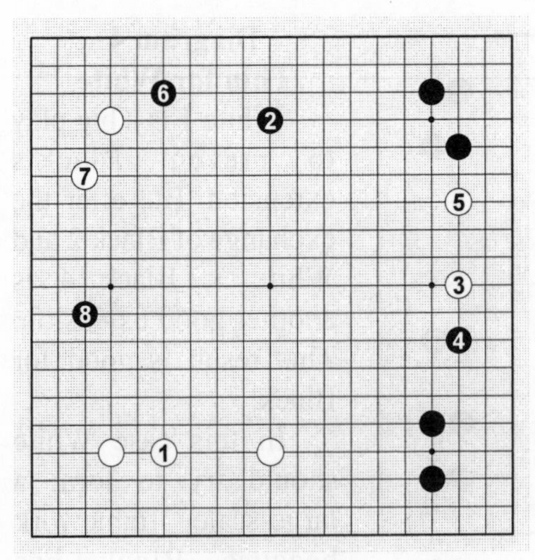

Diagram 6

Diagram 6
The Worst Play

White 1 is the play to keep the corner, but it is too early. Up to Black 8 is routine. In this diagram Black is ahead in territory, and framework too.

Problem 14 Exploiting Your Enclosure

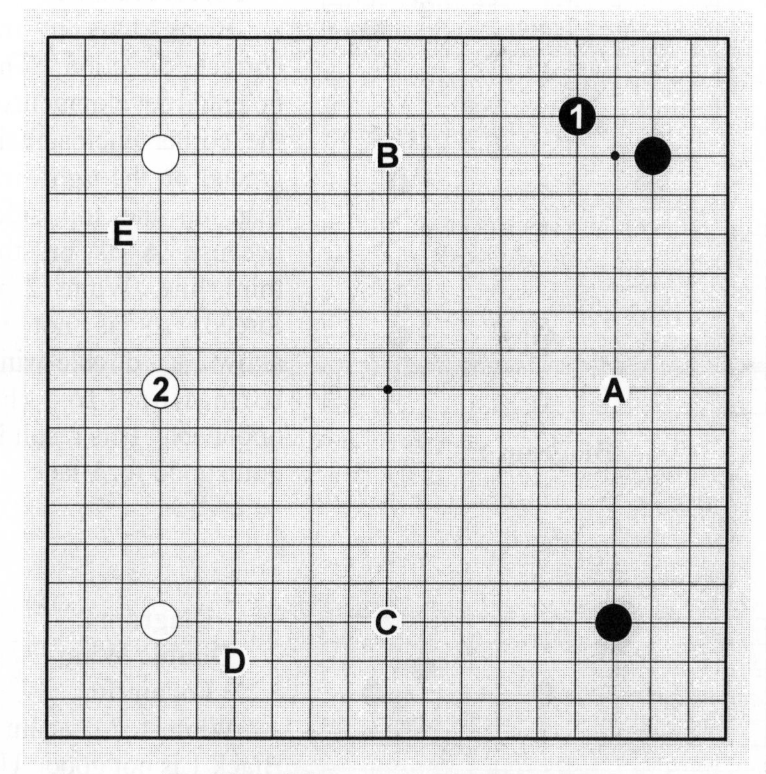

Problem Diagram – Black to play

White has just completed the three-star opening, after Black's corner enclosure. Now Black should decide whether to expand the influence or limit the opponent's influence. Make full use of the corner enclosure. Choose the correct answer from **A** to **E**.

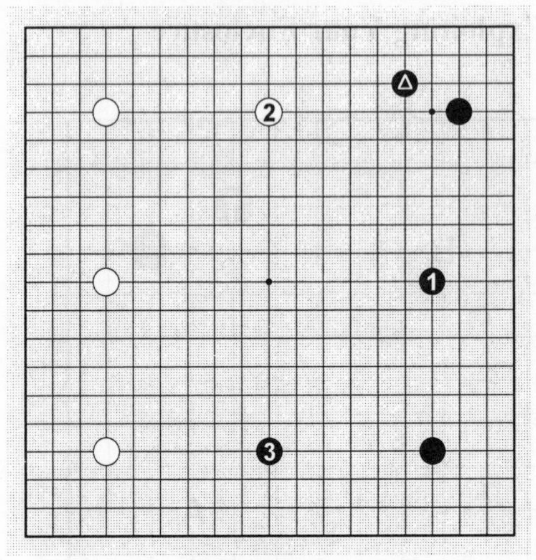

Diagram 1

Diagram 1
Correct Answer

Black 1 is in the correct direction. The potential development of the corner enclosure is greater on the right side than on the top side, because ▲ is on the third line. White 2 is forced, so as not to allow a double-wing formation to the opponent. This result is quite good for Black.

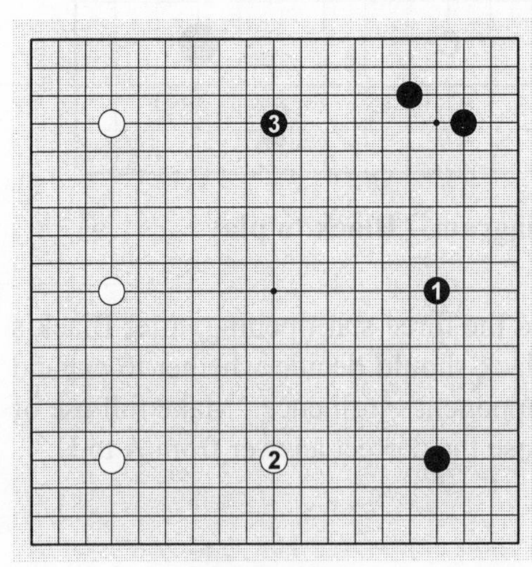

Diagram 2

Diagram 2
Double Wing Formation

White 2 against Black 1 is not good. Up to Black 3, Black has the ideal shape called a double-wing formation.

In the opening it is better not to allow the opponent a double-wing formation.

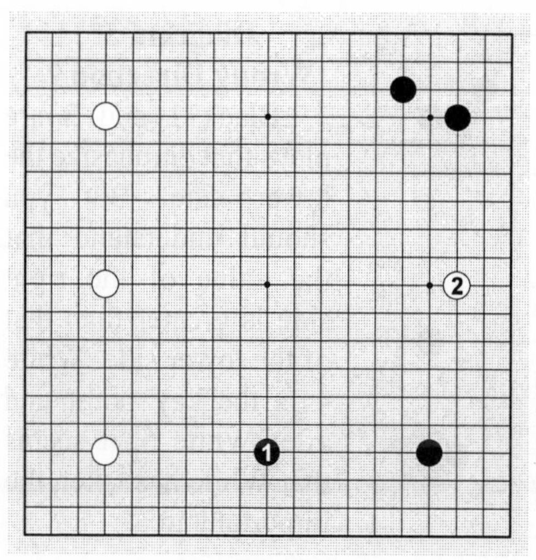

Diagram 3

Diagram 3
Wrong Direction 1

Black 1 is the second-best play, but if White 2 is allowed, Black's shape will be split into two. If your stones are divided into two groups, you can hardly expect a large-scale territory.

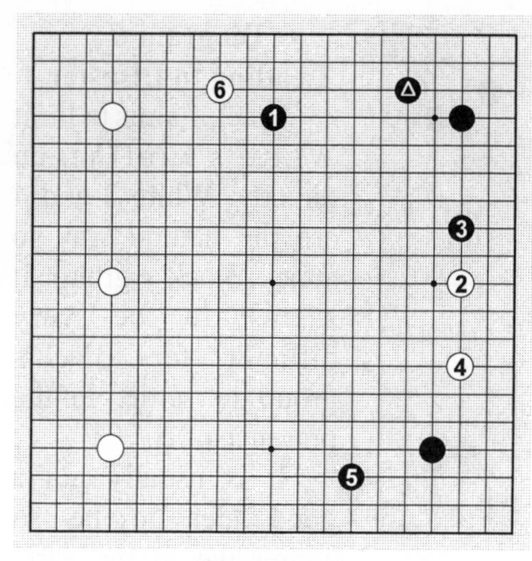

Diagram 4

Diagram 4
Active for White

Black 1 is the point to extend on the top side from the corner enclosure. But it is inferior to White 2, because ▲ is on the third line. White's wedge at 2 is the key point, and up to White 6, White is more active.

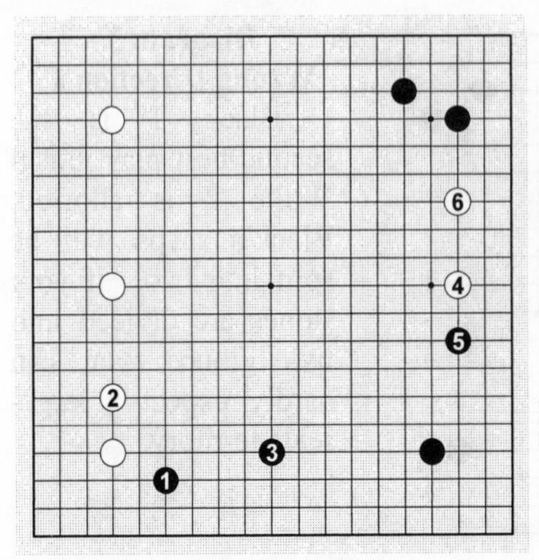

Diagram 5

Diagram 5
Wrong Direction 2

Black 1 and 3 are plays that emphasize the lower side. But you should understand that the value of the right side is greater than that of the lower side. White 4 is the key point and after White 6, it seems that White has taken the important area.

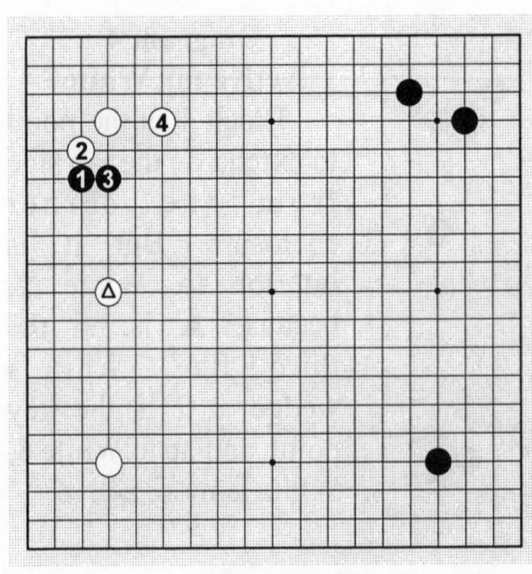

Diagram 6

Diagram 6
Leading to Disaster

Black 1 aims to limit White's influence directly. White 2 and 4 are the natural way to attack Black's group. It seems to be very difficult for Black's group to settle, in the presence of Δ.

It is usually not a good idea to be so aggressive in the early stages of the opening.

Problem 15 Decision on the Direction

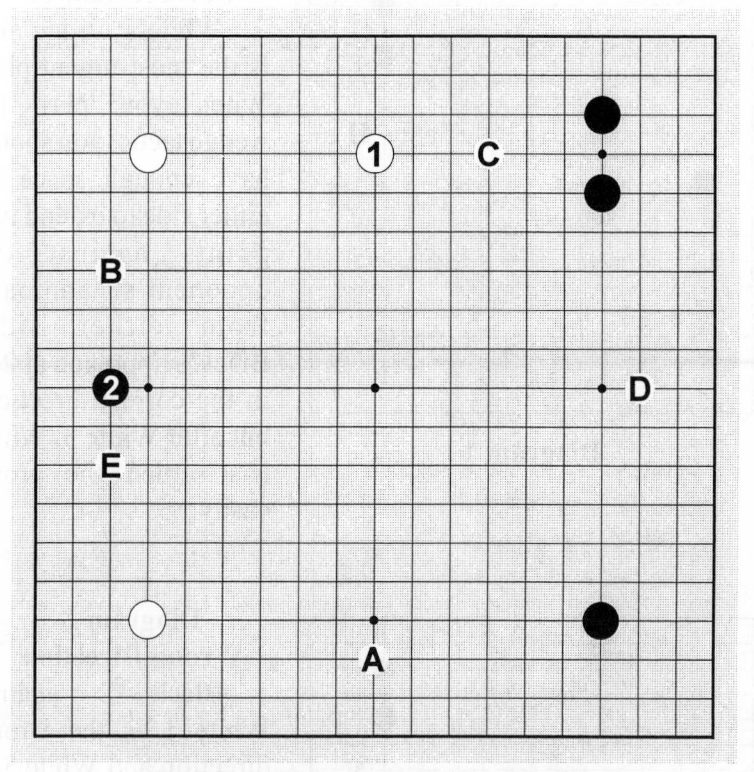

Problem Diagram – White to play

White 1 is a big play and Black's wedge at 2 is also good. Now White should decide whether to expand influence or limit the opponent's influence. Choose the correct answer from **A** to **E**.

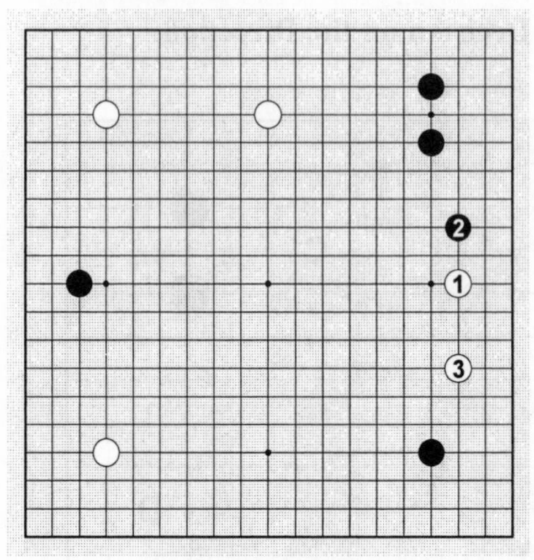

Diagram 1

Diagram 1
Correct Answer

White's wedge at 1 is the most urgent play. When you play the wedge tactic, you should have enough space on either side to extend two points against the opponent's approach from either side. Black's approach at 2 is in the correct direction, but after White 3, White has settled the group easily.

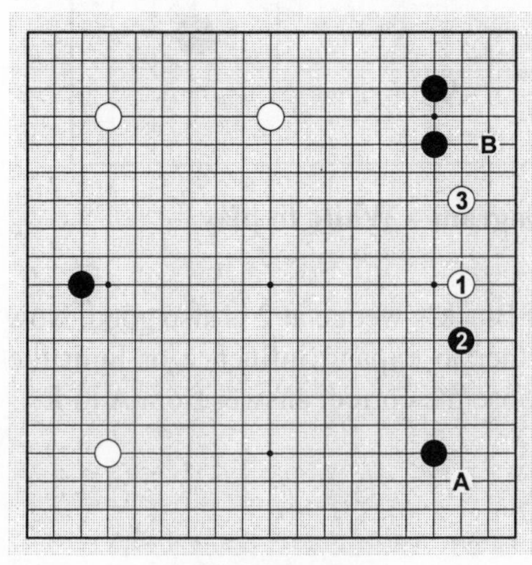

Diagram 2

Diagram 2
Wrong Direction

Black 2 against White 1 is the wrong direction and White 3 is a good extension. Now Black's corner enclosure has a weakness at **B**, and also Black's bottom right corner territory is not perfect because of the weakness at **A**.

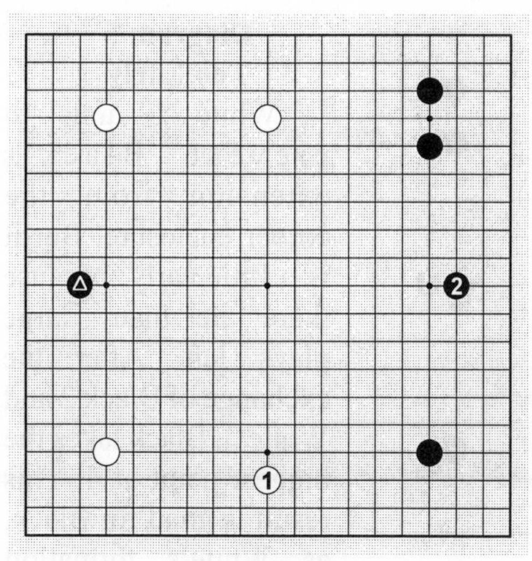

Diagram 3

Diagram 3
Second Best Play

White 1 is the second-best play. However, if White allows Black 2 White is behind. Black has ideal shape on the right, while White's shape is divided into two groups by ▲.

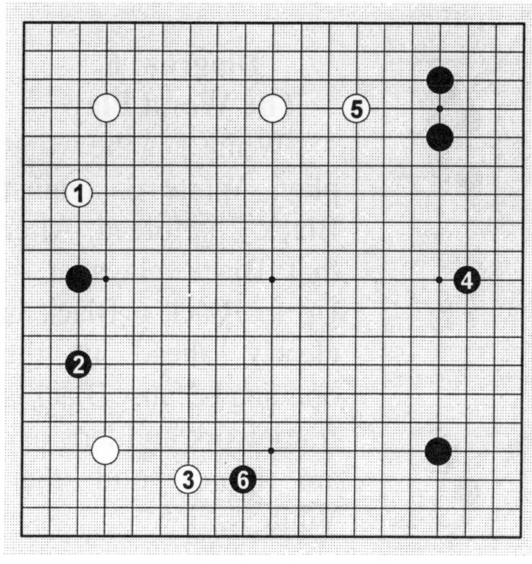

Diagram 4

Diagram 4
White Takes *Gote*
On the Left Side

White's large knight's shape at 1 aims to keep the corner and attack Black's one stone on the left. But when Black plays 2 White's answer at 3 is almost necessary. That means Black takes the biggest play at 4. Up to Black 6 this result is again good for Black.

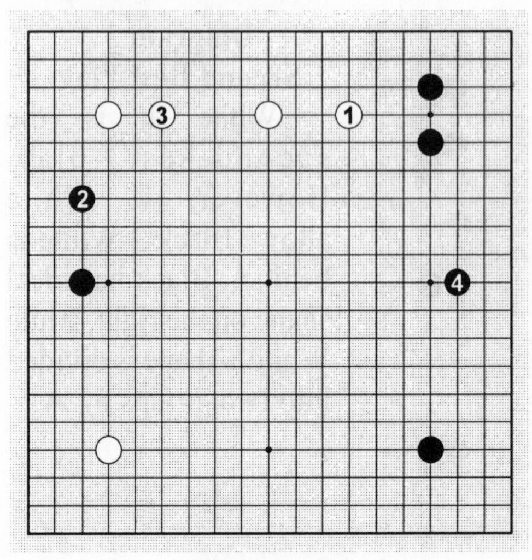

Diagram 5

Diagram 5
Too Early

White 1 aims to prevent Black's extension from the corner enclosure. But it is a little early, because there are many large plays left. After the exchange of Black 2 and White 3, Black takes the biggest point at 4. This result is good for Black, as White's formation favors the upper side, while Black has ideal shape with 4.

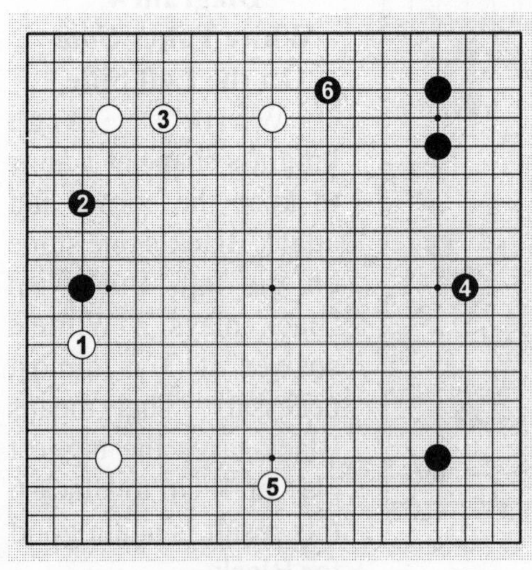

Diagram 6

Diagram 6
The Worst Play

White 1 is the worst play. White 3 against Black 2 is forced. After that Black plays at 4. Up to Black 6 Black is clearly ahead in the opening because Black's framework and territory are more solid than White's.

Problem 16 Double Wing Formation

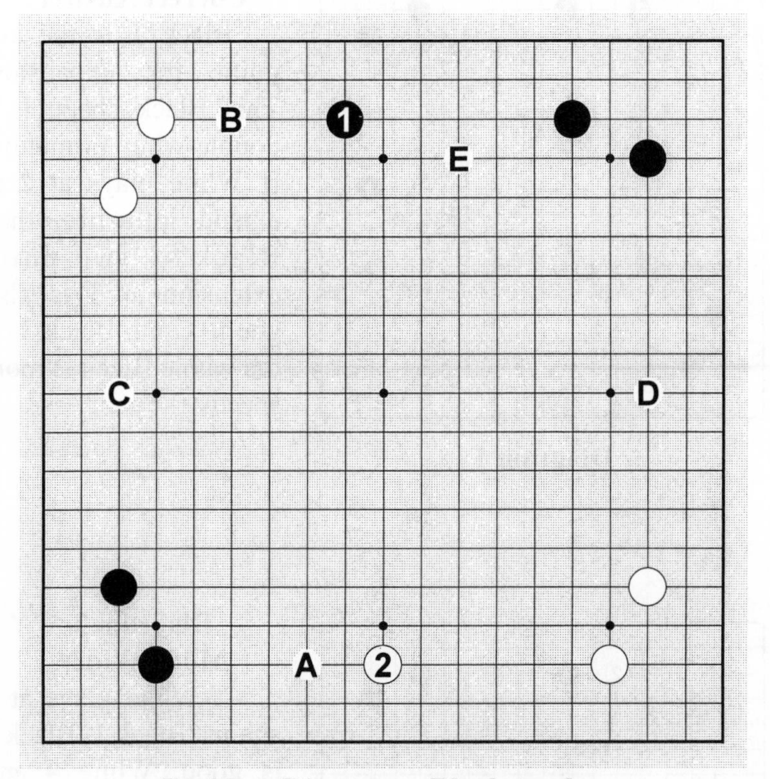

Problem Diagram – Black to play

All four corners have been enclosed, two by each side. In a simple territorial game, taking the wider area could be the correct answer. Remembering that the double-wing formation is an ideal shape in the opening, choose the correct answer from **A** to **E**.

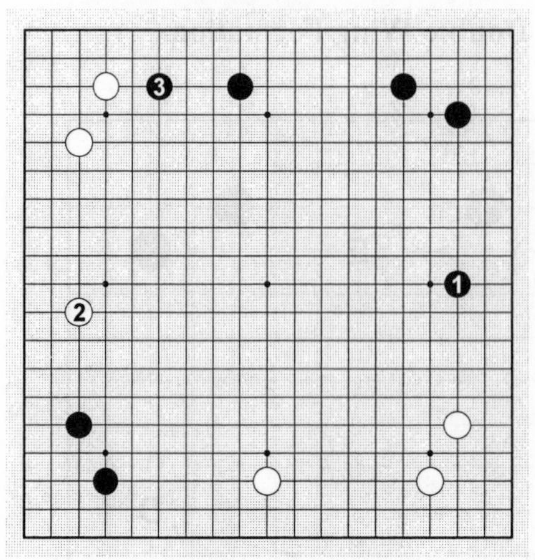

Diagram 1

Diagram 1
Correct Answer

Black 1 is the key point for expansion. This Black shape is a double-wing formation. If White plays at 2 to extend influence, then Black's two-point extension at 3 is also good. Up to Black 3 on the whole Black is more speedy.

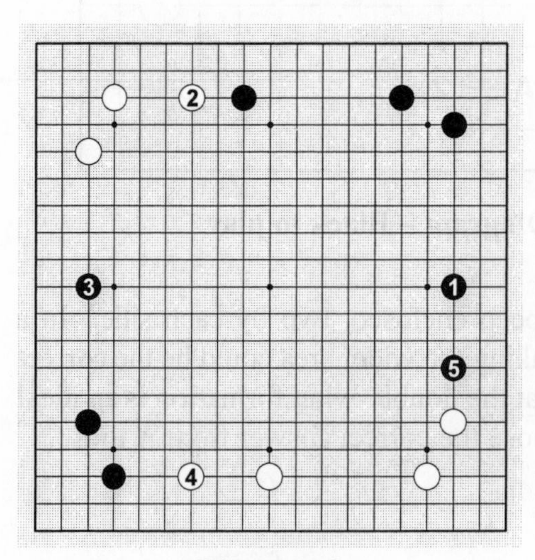

Diagram 2

Diagram 2
Much Wider

If White plays at 2 against Black 1, Black 3 is good. White 4 and Black 5 are then routine; they seem at first glance to be small, but are in fact large plays. Up to Black 5, Black's scale of framework is greater than White's.

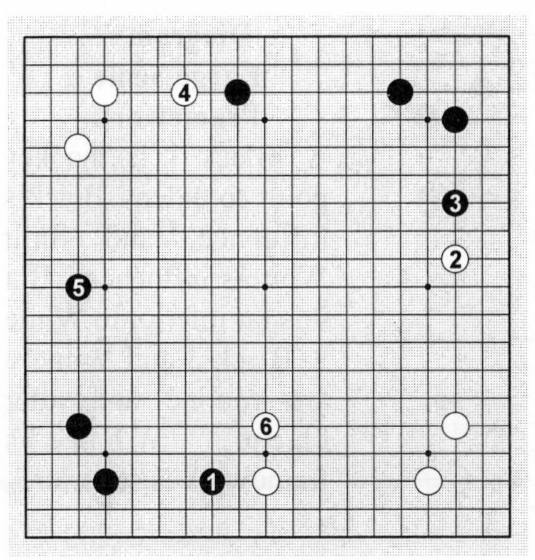

Diagram 3

Diagram 3
Second Best Play

Black 1 prefers the lower side. It is very big, but if Black allows White 2, White has the double-wing formation. Up to White 6, White's framework is better than Black's.

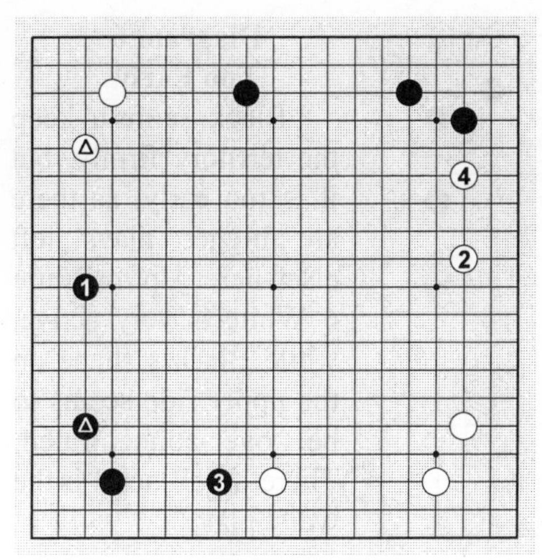

Diagram 4

Diagram 4
Too Low

Black 1 is the point to extend Black's influence from the corner enclosure. However, its value is inferior to that of the right side, because both Black ▲ and White Δ are on the third line. White 2 is the key to extending White's influence. Up to White 4, this is a success for White.

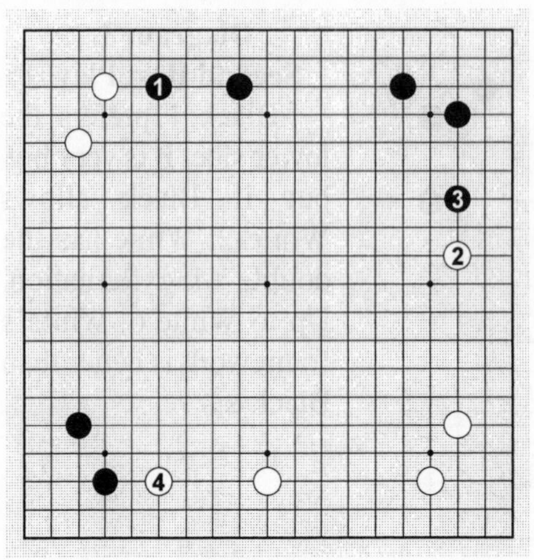

Diagram 5

Diagram 5
Large Scale Framework

Black 1 is the key point to extend Black's influence, and limit White's influence. But it is far inferior to White 2. Black 3 and White 4 are routine and after them, White's framework is superior.

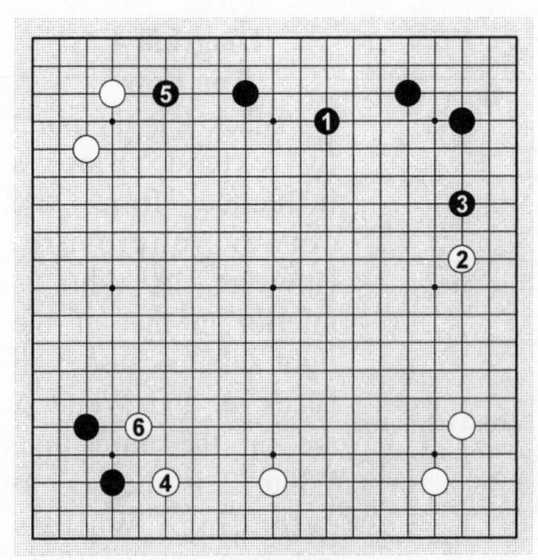

Diagram 6

Diagram 6
Too Early

Black 1 aims to keep the territory firmly, but it is too early, as there are bigger plays left elsewhere. Up to White 6 White is very active, while Black's shape on the upper side seems to be over-concentrated. Therefore, Black 1 is the worst play.

Problem 17 Framework in Practice

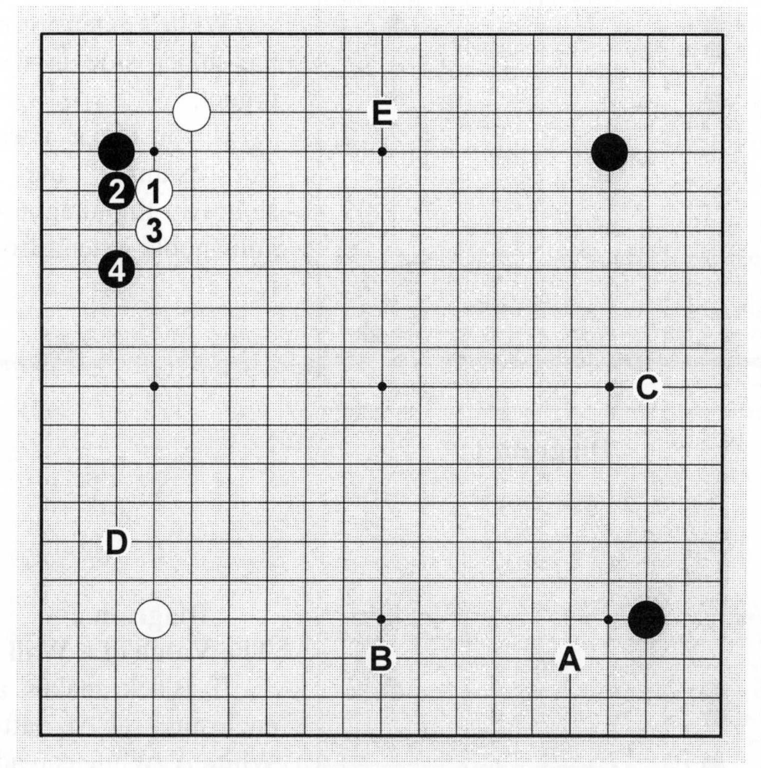

Problem Diagram – White to play

White 1 and 3 are often played when you want to make a wall. However, you inevitably allow the opponent some territory. Now you should decide whether to continue to play on the upper side or play elsewhere. Choose the correct play from **A** to **E**.

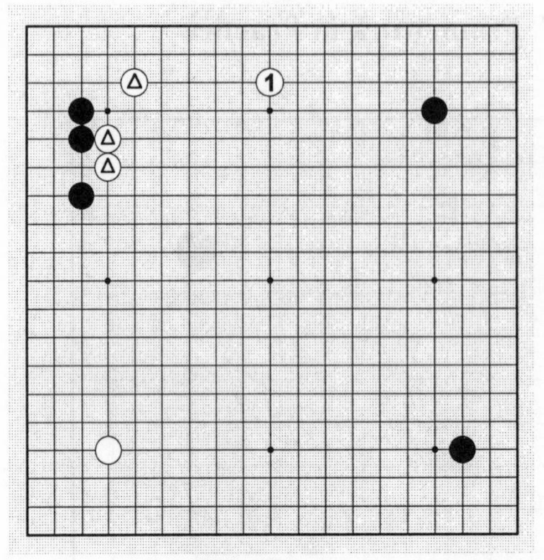

Diagram 1

Diagram 1
Correct Answer

White's extension on the upper side is very urgent.

If you make a wall (for example, the Δ stones in this diagram), you should extend from it.

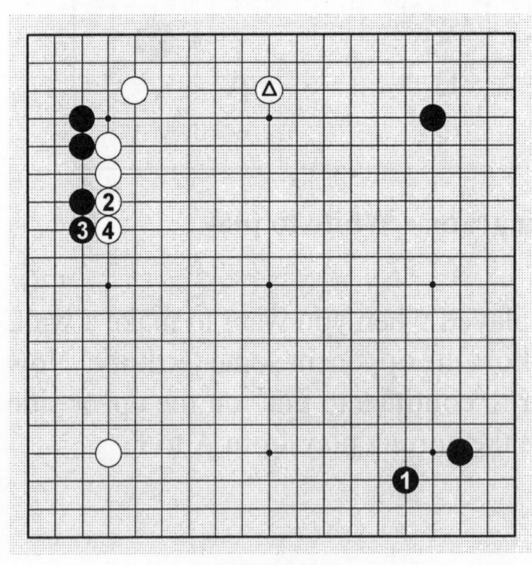

Diagram 2

Diagram 2
The Value of a Wall

If Black makes an enclosure at 1 after White Δ, White can add height to the wall by pushing at 2 and 4.

An extension made properly from a good wall gives a naturally strong territory.

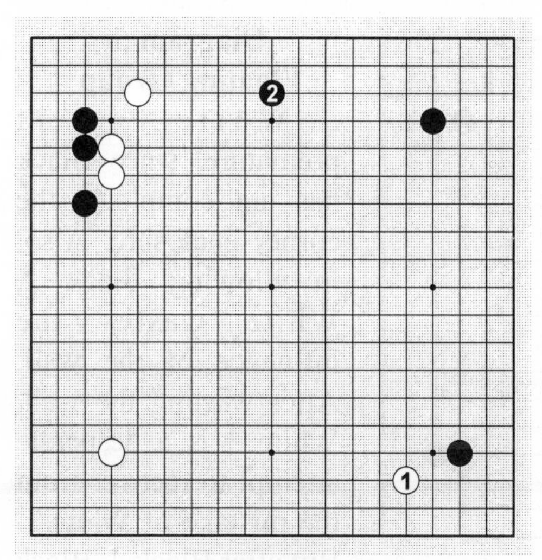

Diagram 3

Diagram 3
Wrong Direction 1

White 1 is a good play, but is not the most urgent. Black 2 is the key point, which White should have played. After Black 2, White has a wall that is almost useless. This result is not good for White.

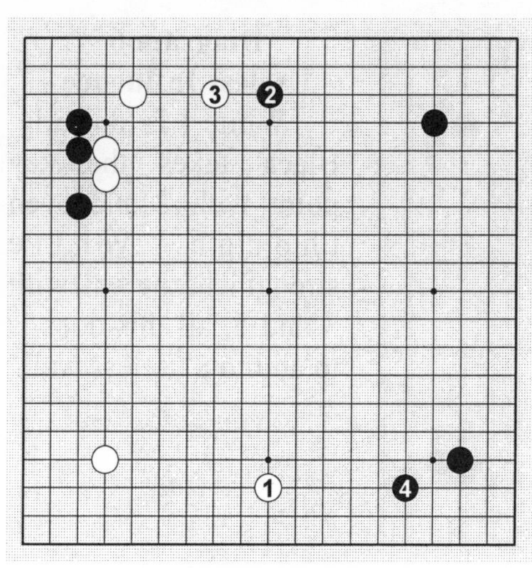

Diagram 4

Diagram 4
Wrong Direction 2

White's extension at 1 aims for influence on the lower side. It is a poor play; even White 1 in the previous Diagram is better than this. Up to Black 4, Black has taken all of the key points.

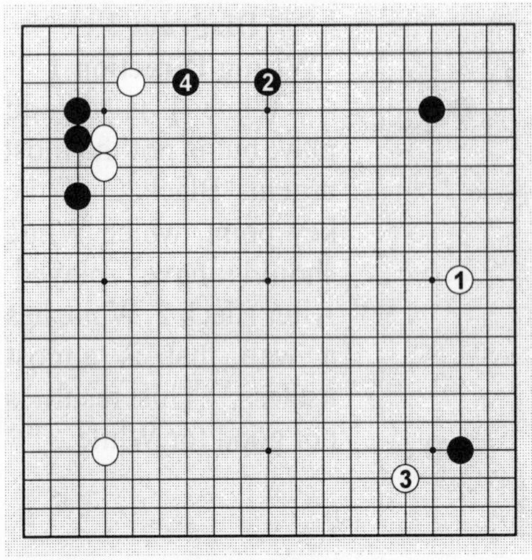

Diagram 5

Diagram 5
Floating Group

White 1 is premature, since Black has not completed the corner enclosure. Also, in allowing Black 2, White wastes the influence of the wall. After wasting the wall, White 3 is a desperate attempt to recover from the mistake of White 1. But after Black 4, Black is clearly ahead.

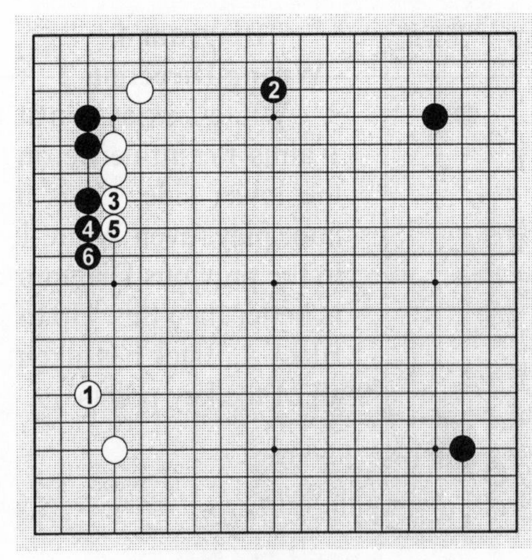

Diagram 6

Diagram 6
Useless Influence

White 1 is too early. Black takes the key point with 2 and even though White strengthens the wall with 3 and 5, all this does is to add to a useless wall.

Problem 18 The Weakness of a Higher Position

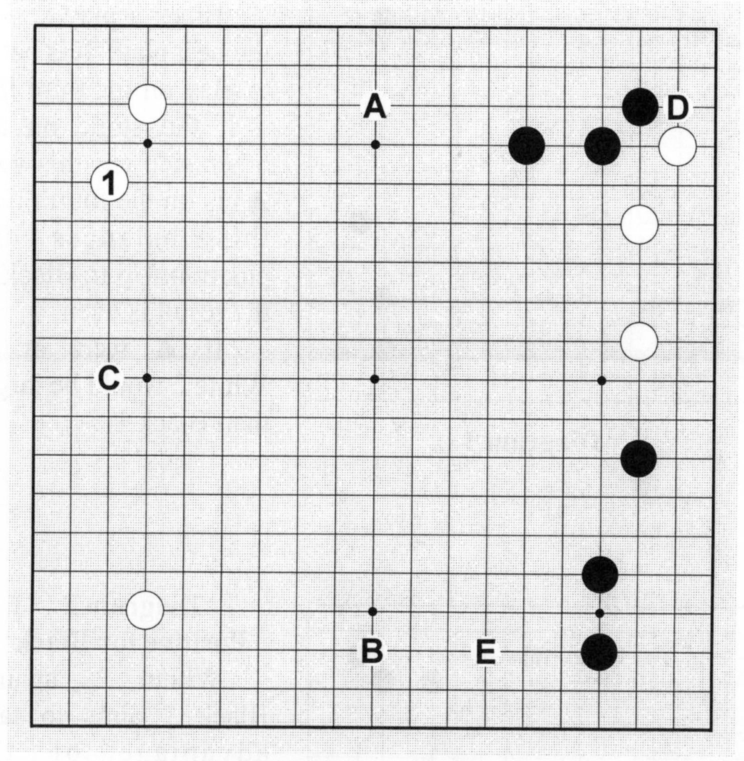

Problem Diagram – Black to play

White 1 provides a secure base from which to expand influence and make territory. Now Black should decide the next play, considering the position of the other Black stones. You should remember that the opponent's key point is also your key point. Choose the best play from **A** to **E**.

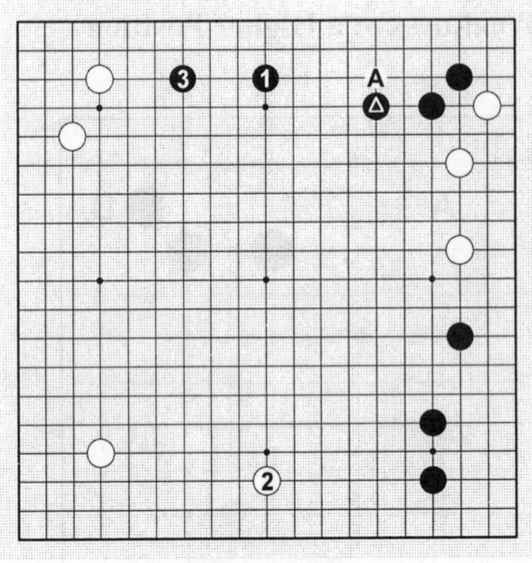

Diagram 1

Diagram 1
Correct Answer

Black's play at 1 is the best play. It is better to play on the third line – if the stone on the other side (in this case ▲) is on the fourth line, this balances the position. Up to Black 3, the result is even.

If ▲ were at **A**, White 2 would be larger than Black 1.

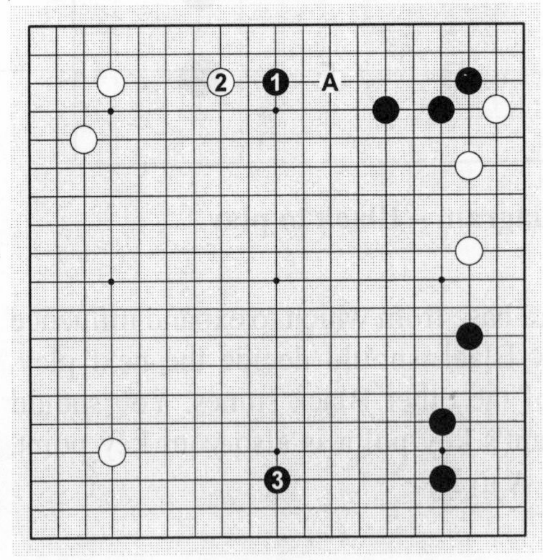

Diagram 2

Diagram 2
Positive for Black

White 2 against Black 1 aims to take advantage of the weakness at **A**. However, by allowing Black 3, White falls behind, since Black 3 rapidly develops a good position for Black. So White 2 at 3 is a more positive play.

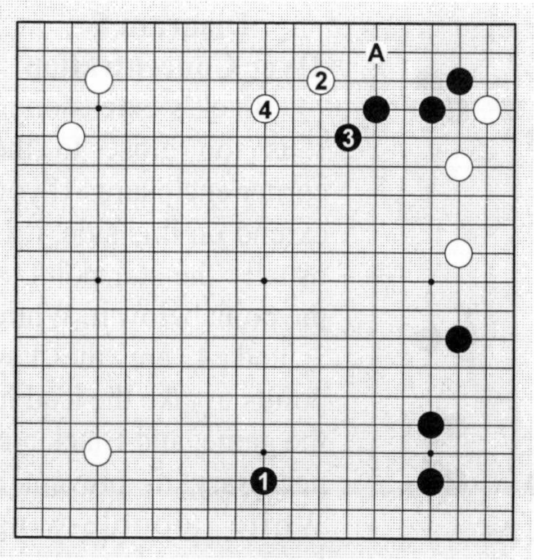

Diagram 3

Diagram 3
Open at the Side

Black 1 is the second-best play. After White's approach at 2, Black has difficulty in defending. Black 3 would be the usual response although this does not fully defend the weakness at A. Up to White 4, Black is slightly behind in the opening.

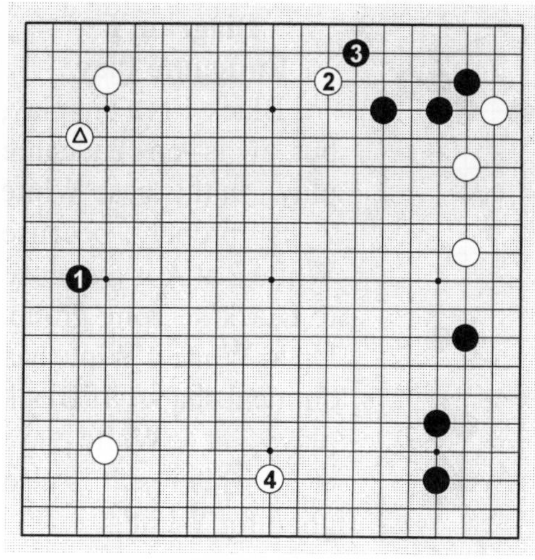

Diagram 4

Diagram 4
Limiting Black's Influence in *Sente*

The value of Black's wedge at 1 is lower than if it were played on the upper or lower sides, because the position of Δ is on the third line. White's approach at 2 is the key point. Black 3 is the play to keep the corner, but it is on the second line and *gote*. Up to White 4, White plays ahead at speed.

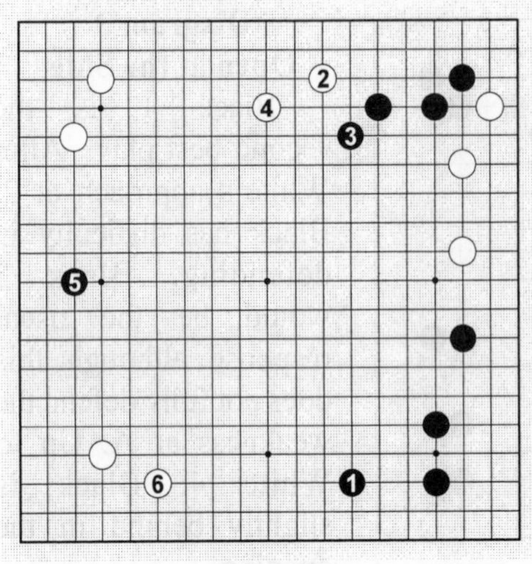

Diagram 5

Diagram 5
Over Concentration

Black's extension at 1 is too close to the corner enclosure. If you extend on this side, it is usually the star point or the point below it. White 2 and 4 are the key points to take the lead in the game, and Black 5 is necessary to prevent a White double-wing formation. Up to White 6 this result is good for White.

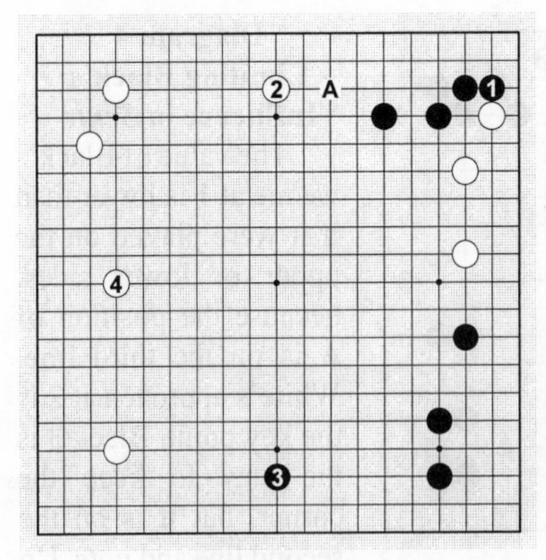

Diagram 6

Diagram 6
Endgame Play

Black 1 is a big play, but it is an endgame play. In this case White 2 is proper, because White 2 at **A** is too close to Black's strong group. Up to White 4 White has an ideal shape. If Black plays 3 at 4, White plays at 3. This result is also good for White.

Problem 19 The Counter Chinese

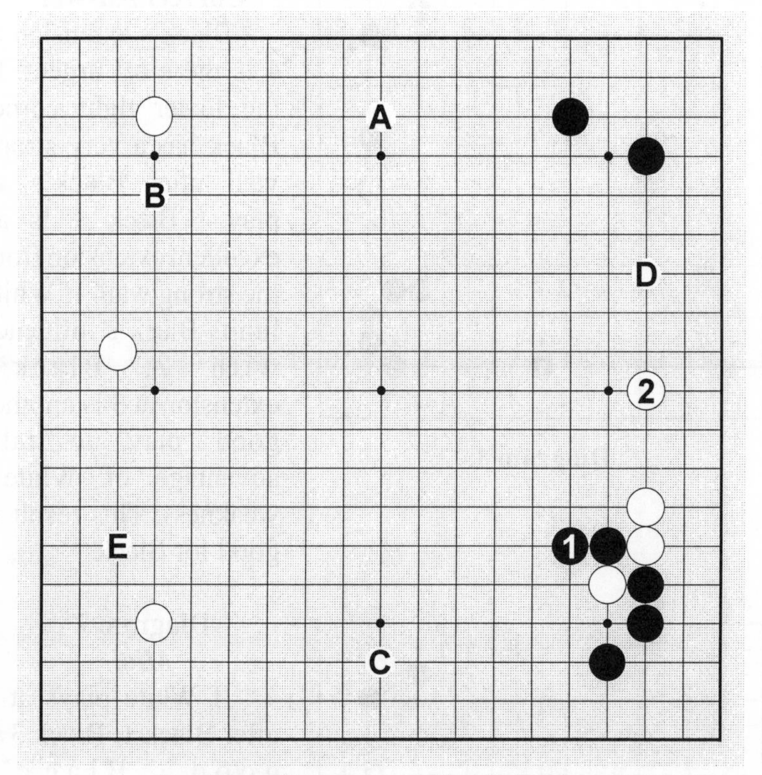

Problem Diagram – Black to play

After Black extends out at 1, White settles the right side with 2. Considering White's Chinese style on the left, and the strong wall in the lower right corner, choose the best play from **A** to **E**.

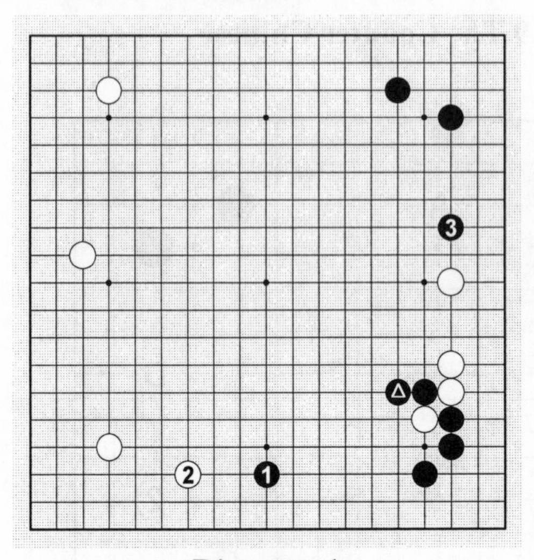
Diagram 1

Diagram 1
Correct Answer

Black's extension at 1 is the most urgent. In the lower right corner Black has a very strong wall after Black's ▲ play. Black 1 is an excellent extension from the strong wall. If White limits Black's influence with 2, Black's extension at 3 is another good play to take advantage of White's weakness. This result is good for Black.

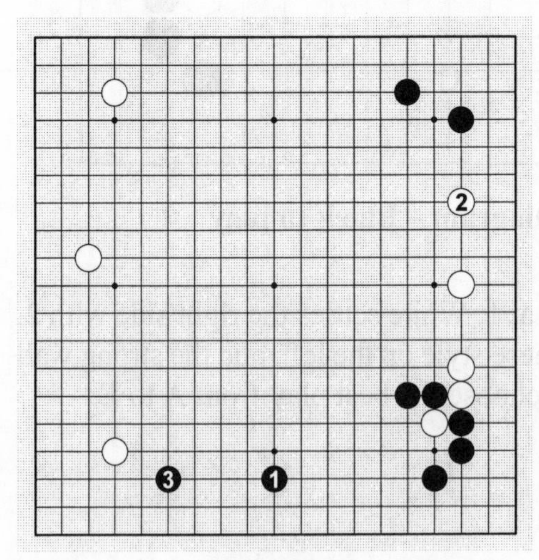
Diagram 2

Diagram 2
Miai

If White plays at 2 after Black 1, Black 3 is good. Black's framework in the lower part is very solid, because it is based on the strong wall in the lower right corner. (That is, after Black 1, the lower and right sides are *miai.*)

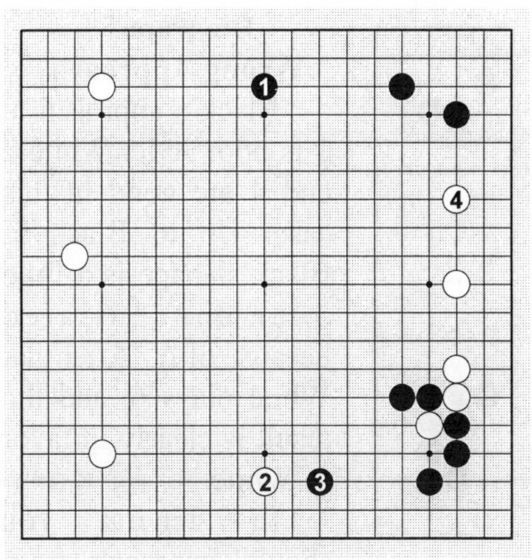

Diagram 3

Diagram 3
Positive For White

Black 1 is the tactic to limit White's Chinese style formation, and expand influence. But if Black allows White 2, Black is immediately behind. Black 3 is too close to the strong wall. Up to White 4 this result is clearly good for White.

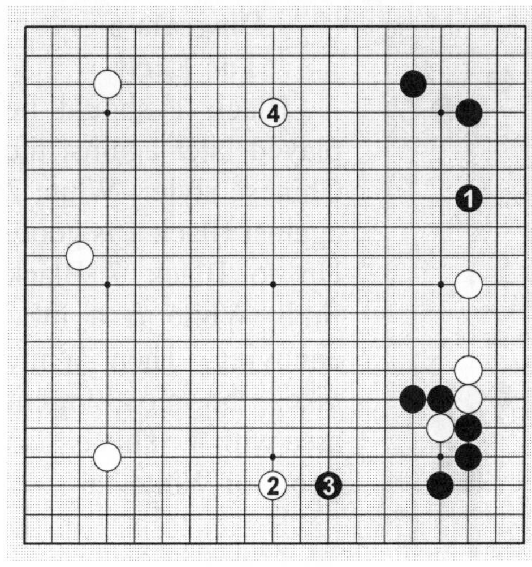

Diagram 4

Diagram 4
Wrong Direction

Black's extension at 1 is a poor play, since White immediately plays 2 and 4. Up to White 4, White has a very broad framework, while Black's shapes are a little over-concentrated.

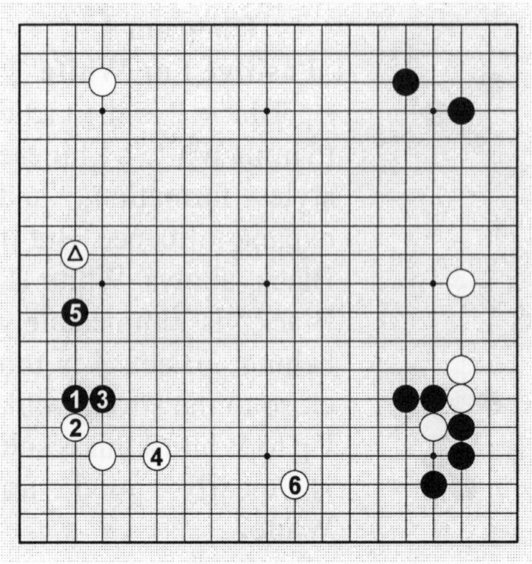

Diagram 5

Diagram 5
Wrong Approach

Black's approach at 1 is poor style. White 2 and 4 are good in this case. Up to Black 5, Black's shape is a little over-concentrated because of Δ. After that White plays 6, and the result is clearly in favor of White.

In general you should approach from the open side.

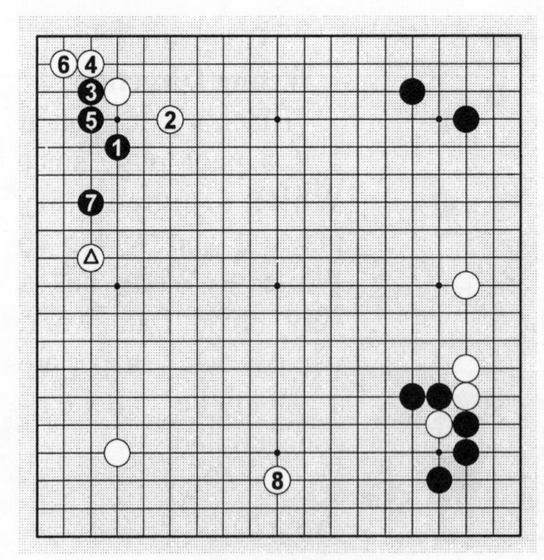

Diagram 6

Diagram 6
Too Early

Black 1 should be played later against the Chinese style. White 2 against Black 1 is good. Up to Black 7 Black finds White Δ a little annoying. Then White takes the most urgent area with 8. This is also good for White.

Problem 20 Settling the Side

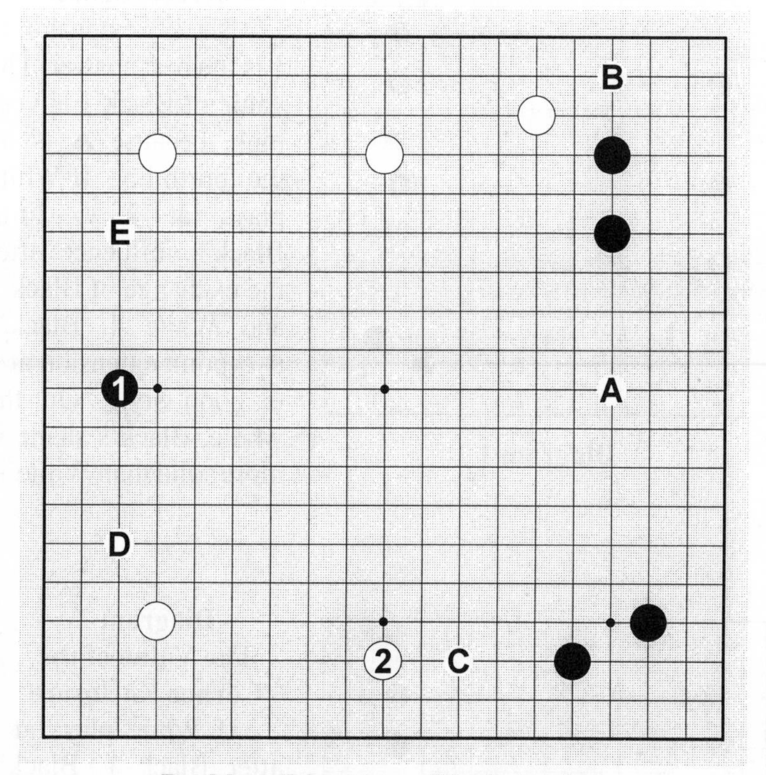

Problem Diagram – Black to play

After Black's wedge at 1, White extends at 2 on the lower side. Now you should judge whether to strengthen Black 1, or expand on the right. Choose the correct answer from **A** to **E**.

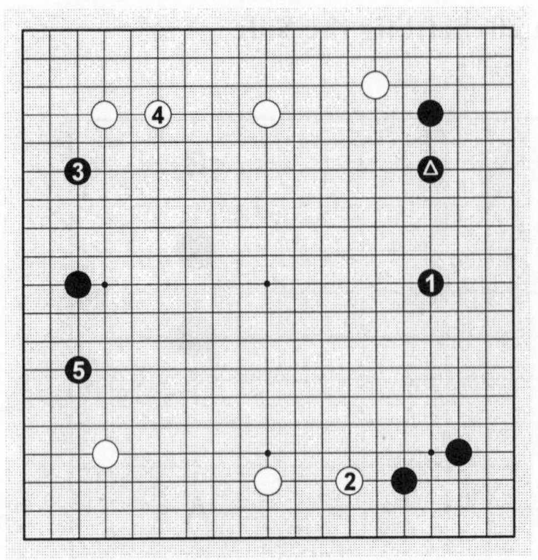

Diagram 1

Diagram 1
Correct Answer

Black's extension at 1 is the best answer. The value of Black 1 is very high, because ▲ is on the fourth line. If White plays at 2 to limit Black's influence after the exchange of Black 3 and White 4, Black's two-point extension at 5 is good style. On the whole, Black's shape is more solid than White's.

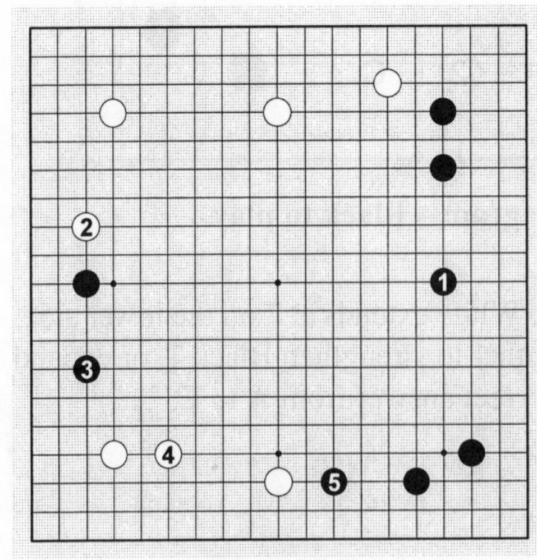

Diagram 2

Diagram 2
The Value of the Corner Enclosure

If White plays at 2 after Black 1, Black's two-point extension at 3 is good, and then White 4 is routine. Up to Black 5 Black can complete a framework.

Black's framework is better than White's, because it is based on the corner enclosure.

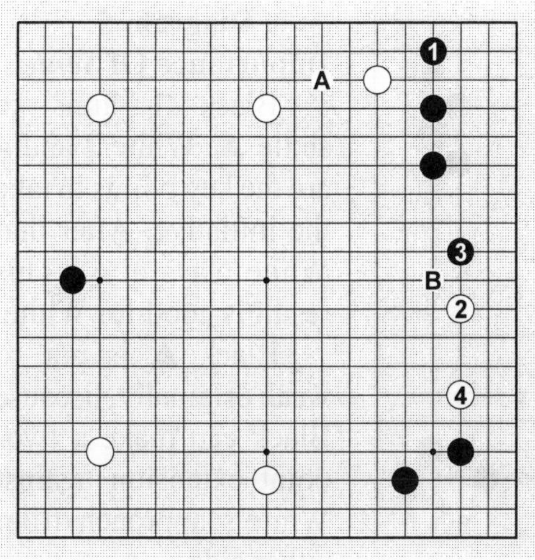

Diagram 3

Diagram 3
Too Early

Black's one-point jump at 1 is the play to keep the corner territory, and take advantage of the weakness at **A**. But it is too early, because there is no Black stone around **B**. White's wedge at 2 is very good. Up to White 4 White settles the group easily. This result is not good for Black.

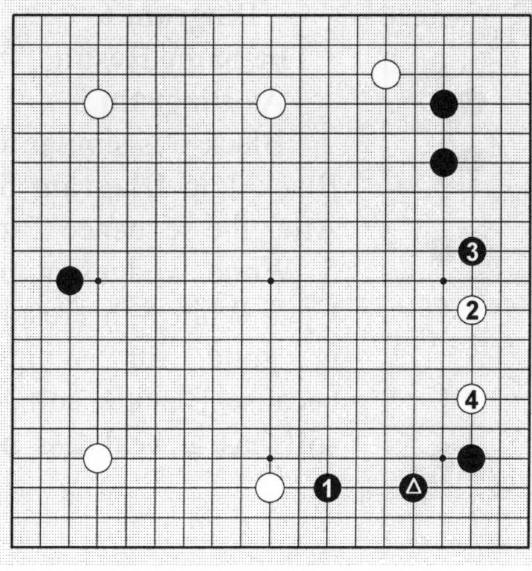

Diagram 4

Diagram 4
Poor Extension

Black's two-point extension at 1 aims to expand the lower right. But this is too small. Furthermore the position of ▲ is too low. Up to White 4 this result is clearly bad for Black.

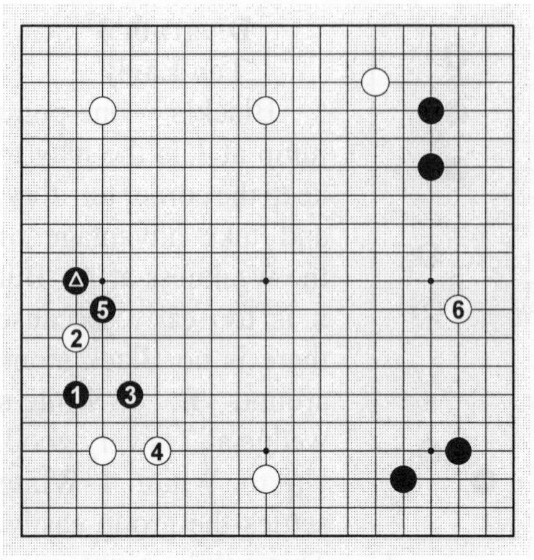

Diagram 5

Diagram 5
Importance Of *Sente*

Black 1 aims to settle ▲. White 2 and 4 are the key points to take the initiative. After that White plays at 6. This result is good for White.

Black ▲ is not so weak originally, because Black can make a two-point extension against White's approach from either side.

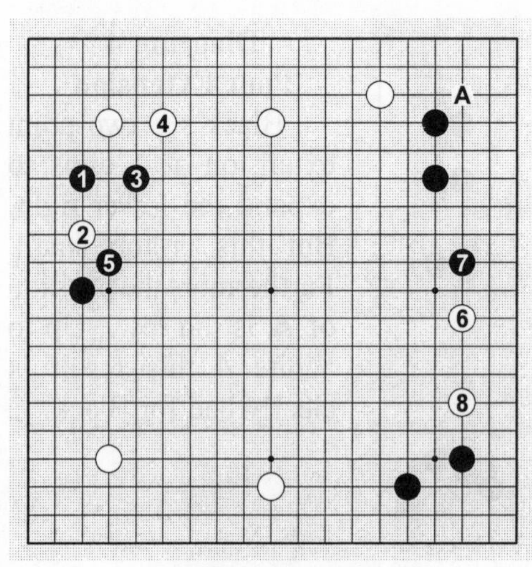

Diagram 6

Diagram 6
The Same Result
As Diagram 5

Black 1 is similar to Black 1 in **Diagram 5.** After the sequence 2 to 5, White wedges at 6. Up to White 8 this result is good for White, because Black's corner still has a weakness at **A**.

Problem 21 Restrict and Neutralize

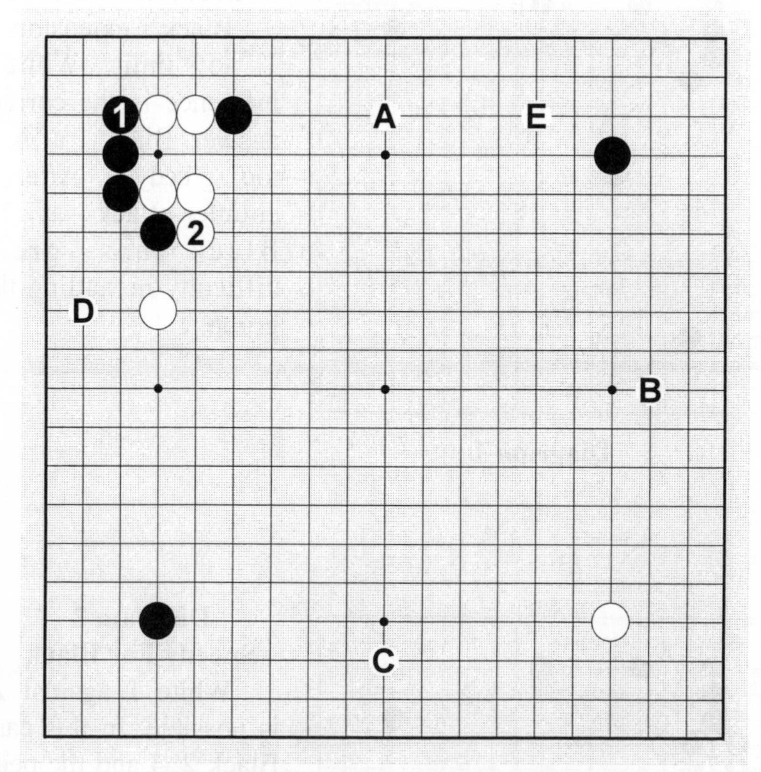

Problem Diagram – Black to play

Black takes territory with 1, while White completes the wall with 2. Now Black should judge whether to counter White's influence or play elsewhere. Choose the correct answer from **A** to **E**.

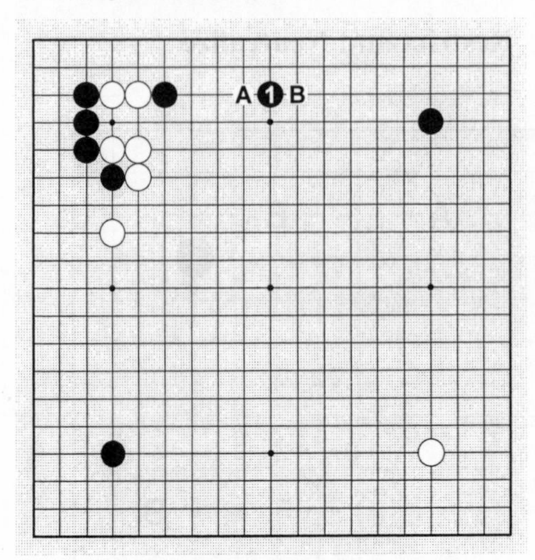

Diagram 1

Diagram 1
Correct Answer

Black's extension at 1 to limit White's influence is the correct answer. Black 1 at **A** is too greedy. After a counter-attack at **B**, Black has great difficulty in settling the group.

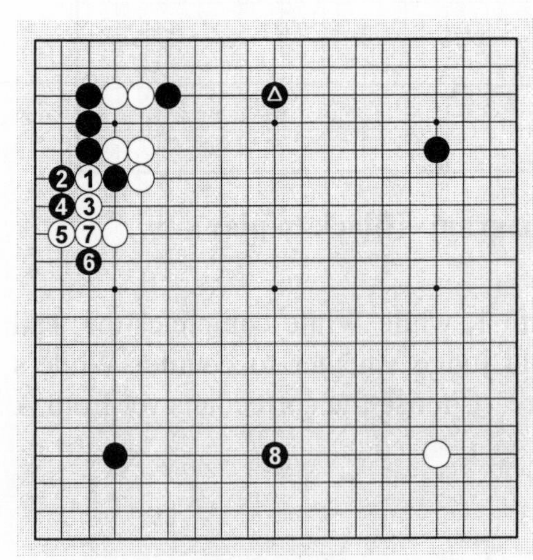

Diagram 2

Diagram 2
Speedy For Black

White 1 against ▲ is possible. In this case Black 2, 4 and the peep at 6 are good. Then Black plays at 8. Even though Black allows White a strong wall, Black's play is very speedy. This result is not bad for Black.

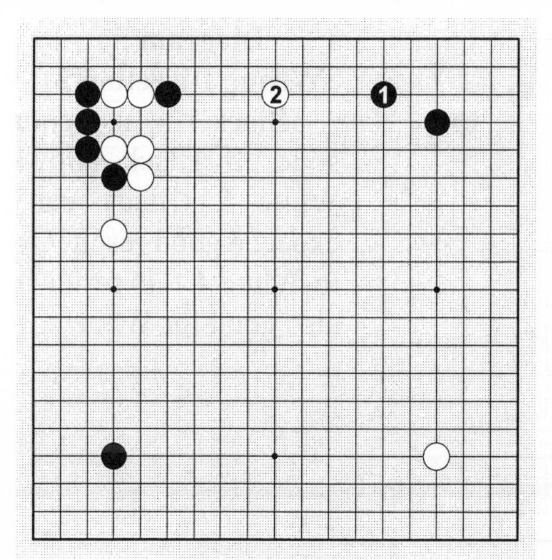

Diagram 3

Diagram 3
Passive

Black's enclosure at 1 aims to limit White's influence from a distance, but it is too passive. White 2 is a proper extension from the wall.

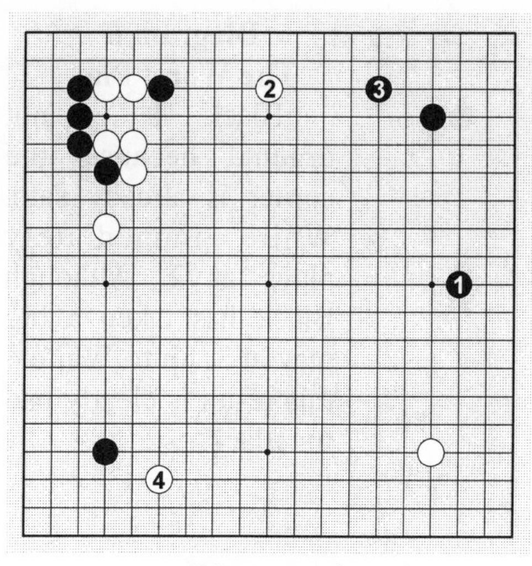

Diagram 4

Diagram 4
Wrong Direction 1

Black's extension at 1 is poor style. White 2 is the key point. Black 3 is inevitable to limit White's influence. But after White's approach at 4, White is very happy.

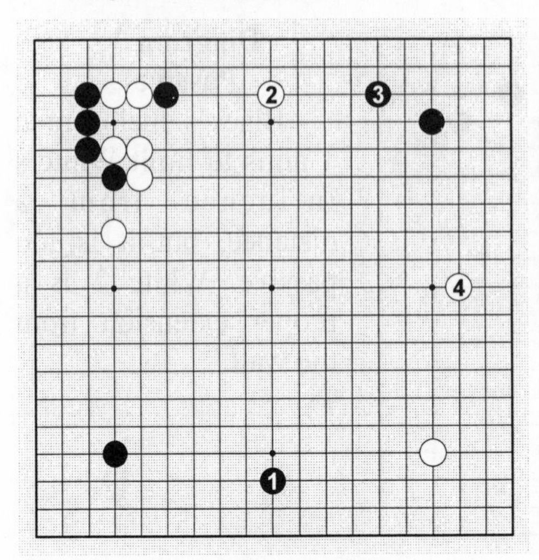

Diagram 5

Diagram 5
Wrong Direction 2

Black 1 is also poor style. If Black allows White 2, Black can't expect a good result. Up to White 4 this result is also good for White.

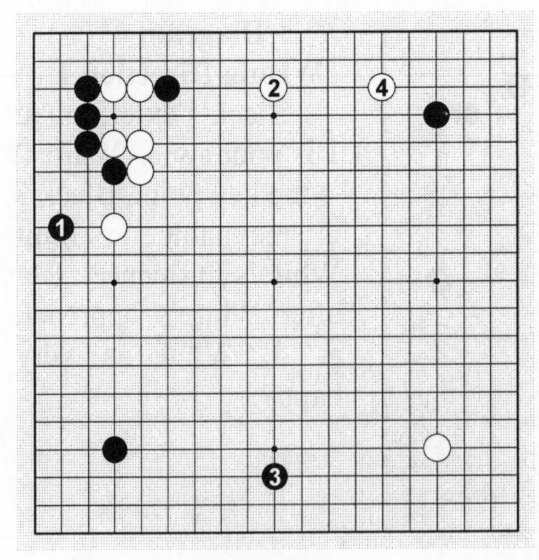

Diagram 6

Diagram 6
The Worst Play

Black 1 is not urgent, because the corner is already safe. White immediately plays at 2. Although Black has taken a big play at 3, up to White 4 this result is clearly bad for Black.

Problem 22 Against the Approach on the Closed Side

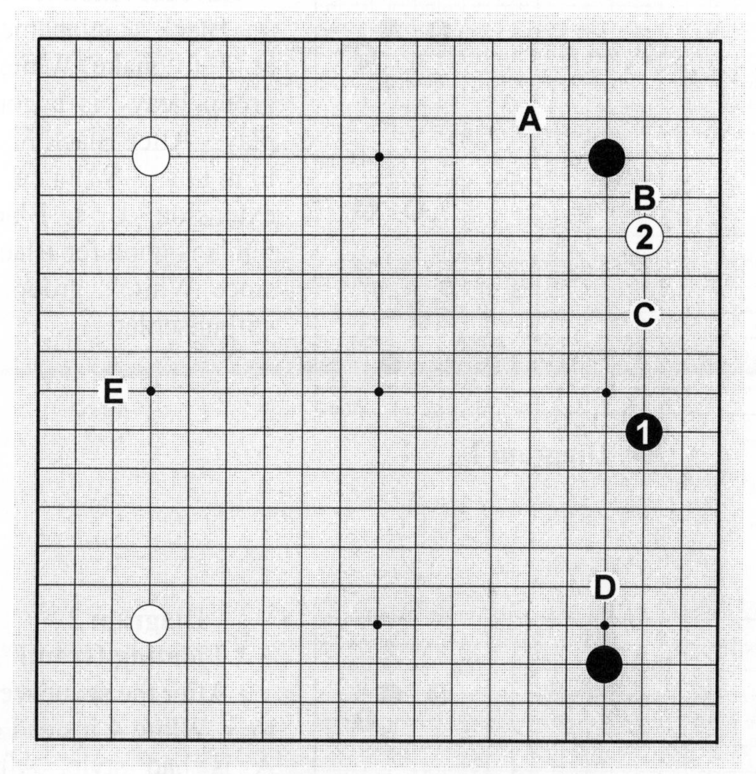

Problem Diagram – Black to play

Black 1 is the Chinese style, against which White's approach at A is usual. Black should punish White 2 fully. Choose the most appropriate play from **A** to **E**.

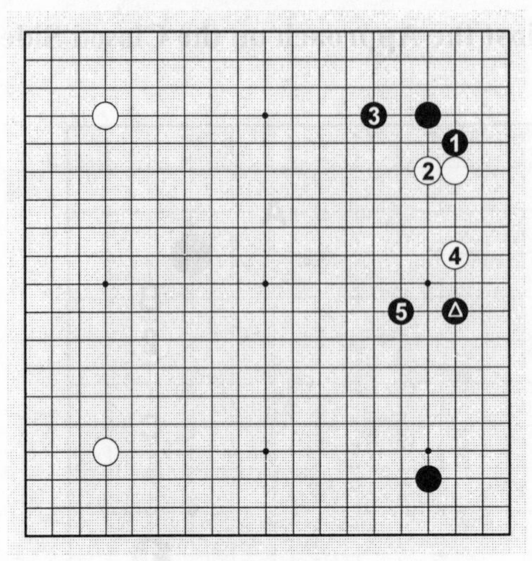

Diagram 1

Diagram 1
Correct Answer

Black's attachment at 1 to make White's group heavy is a good play. After Black 3, ▲ limits White's extension. Up to Black 5 this is good for Black, since White's group is still unsettled.

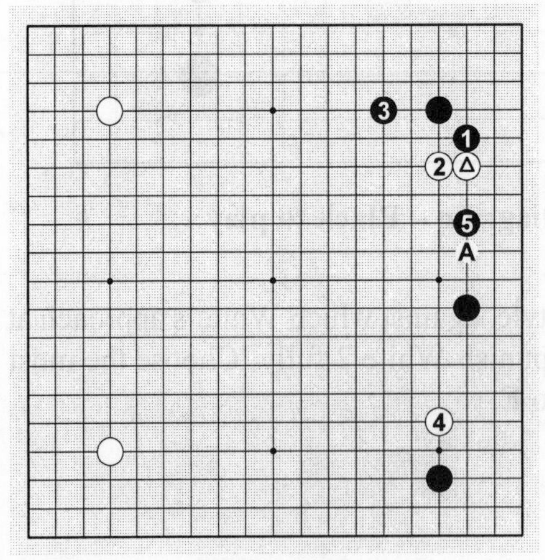

Diagram 2

Diagram 2
A Floating Group

After the sequence 1 to 3, White 4 instead of A is bad style. After Black 5, the situation looks bleak for White.

In conclusion, the approach with Δ fails.

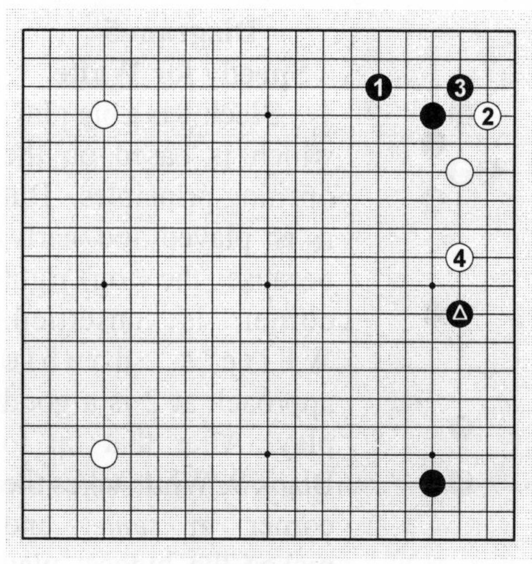

Diagram 3

Diagram 3
Settling Early

Black 1 is not fully thought through, since White's group can settle easily with the plays 2 and 4. After White 4, the position of ▲ is somewhat strange. Therefore the result is not good for Black.

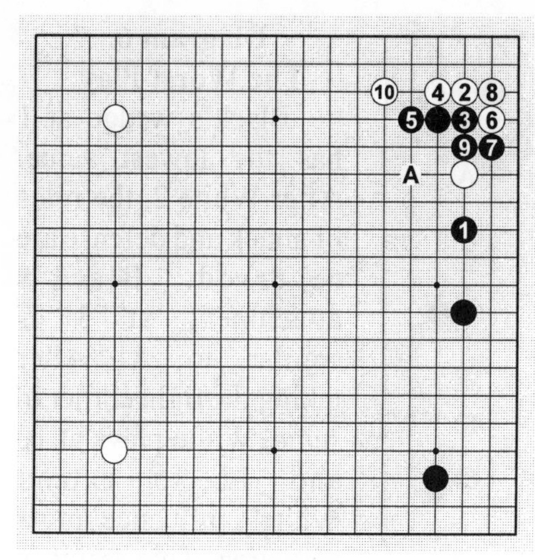

Diagram 4

Diagram 4
Bias Towards
The Right Side

Black's pincer at 1 aims to attack White's stone. Instead of escaping at **A**, White tries to take the corner. After White 2, the process up until 10 is normal. This result gains White some territory, while Black's shape shows bias towards the right side.

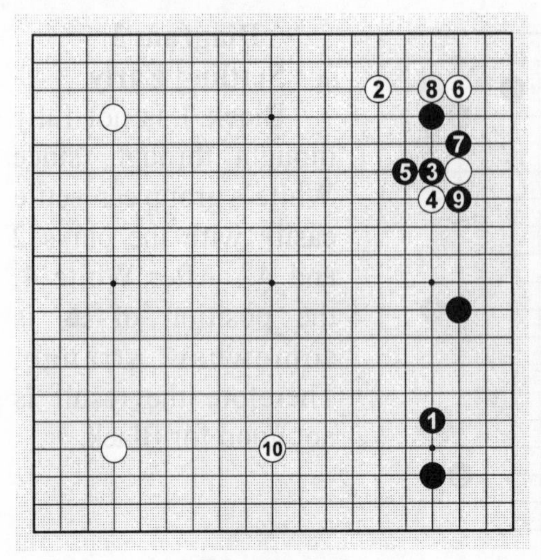

Diagram 5

Diagram 5
Speedy for White

Black 1 is a big play, which is based on the opening principles. But it is played too early, because the top right corner is unsettled. White's double approach at 2 is a good play. After that up to Black 9, White takes the corner in *sente*, and makes the biggest play left at 10. White has quickly gained a good position.

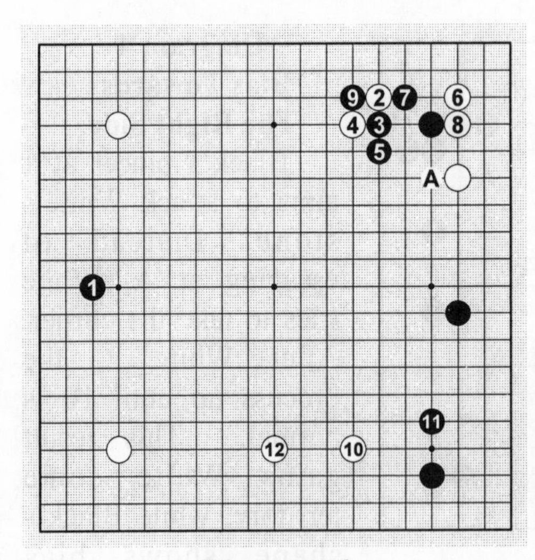

Diagram 6

Diagram 6
The Worst Play

Black's wedge at 1 has the lowest value. After White 2, the roles of attack and defense are reversed. Black's attachment at 3 is similar to **A**. After taking the right corner in *sente*, White plays at 10 and 12 to extend White's influence into a new area. This result is clearly better for White.

Problem 23 When there is only One Key Area

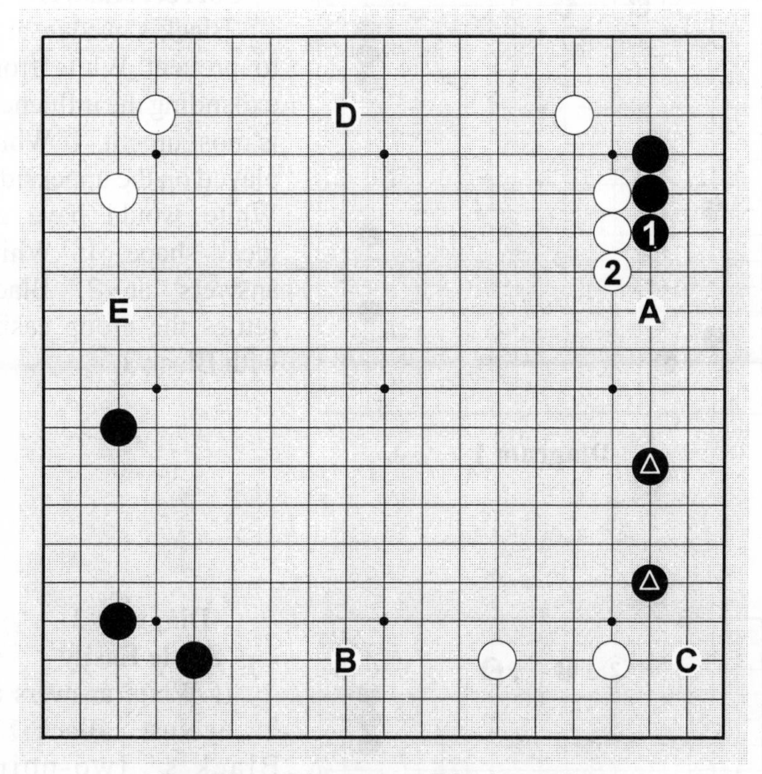

Problem Diagram – Black to play

The exchange of Black 1 and White 2 is inevitable for Black. Now Black should decide whether to maneuver in this area or to play elsewhere. Hint: the existence of Black ▲. Choose the correct answer from **A** to **E**.

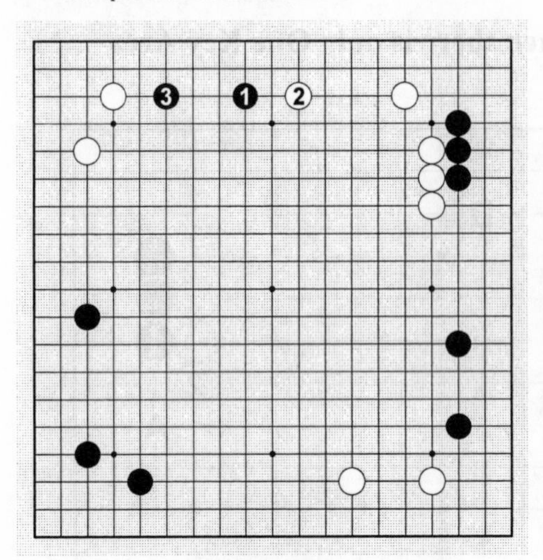

Diagram 1

Diagram 1
Correct Answer

Black's wedge at 1 to prevent White from expanding the influence, is most urgent. If White played on the upper side, White would have an ideal shape. If White answers at 2, Black settles the group easily with Black 3.

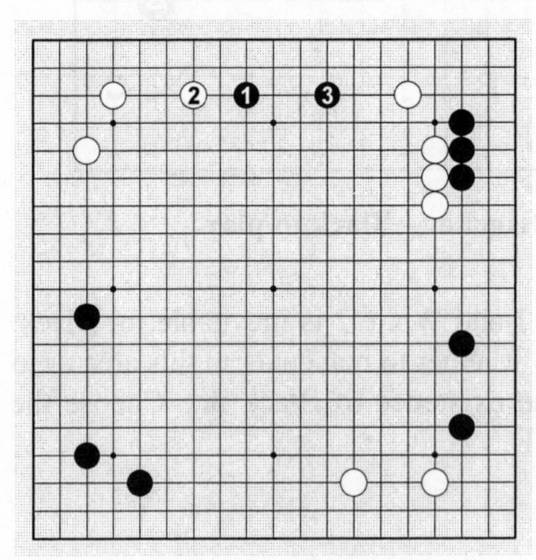

Diagram 2

Diagram 2
Settle Easily

If White answers at 2 against Black 1, Black's two-point extension at 3 is good. Now White's wall hardly works. This result is good for Black.

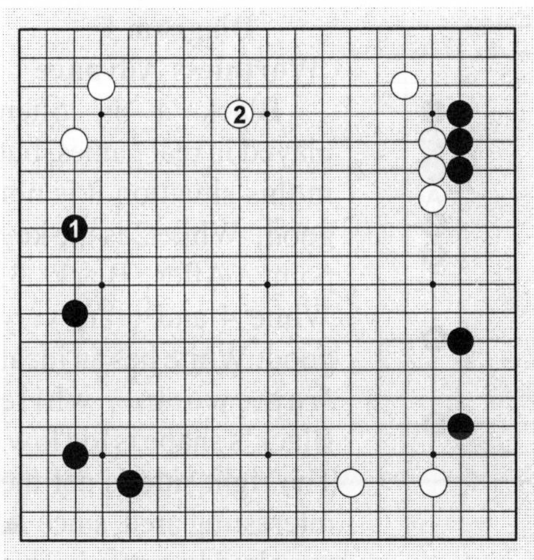

Diagram 3

Diagram 3
Wrong Direction

Black's two-point extension at 1 is poor style, but White 2 is very good. Now White has an ideal shape in the upper part of the board.

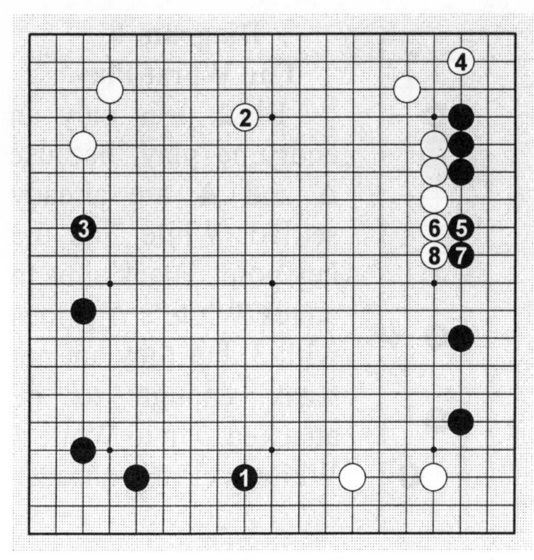

Diagram 4

Diagram 4
Too Early

Black's extension at 1 is too early. After allowing White 2, Black can't expect a good result. Black 3 is a consistent play to extend the influence. After the sequence 4 to 8, White's framework is much better.

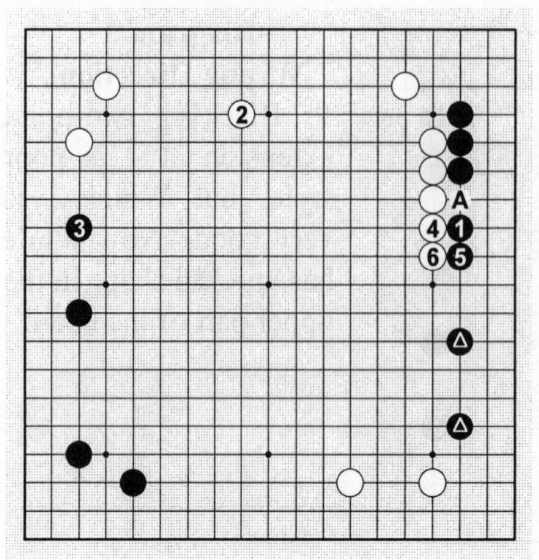

Diagram 5

Diagram 5
Worthless Advance

Black 1 is often played in real games, but in this situation it is not good. White 2 is the key point. After Black 3, White 4 and 6 are very good: White has an ideal framework, while Black's shape is too low. The right side is not the interesting area, since ▲ are already settled. This result is good for White.

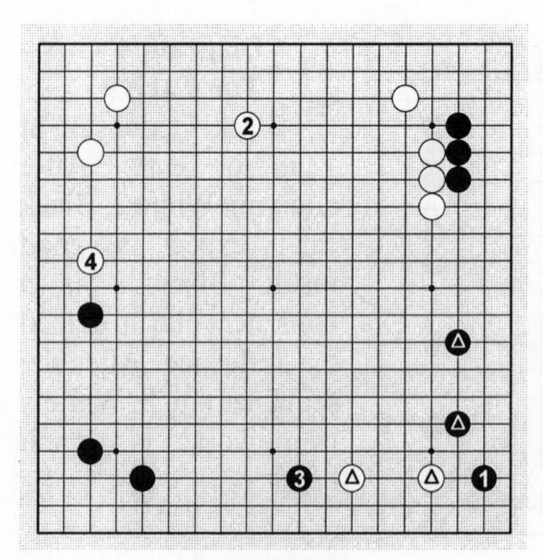

Diagram 6

Diagram 6
The Worst Play

Black 1 is only an endgame play, because Δ and ▲ are already settled. White 2 is the key point. Black aims to attack White's Δ stones with 3, but they are not weak enough to be attacked. Up to White 4 White is clearly ahead.

Problem 24 First Touch on the Brakes

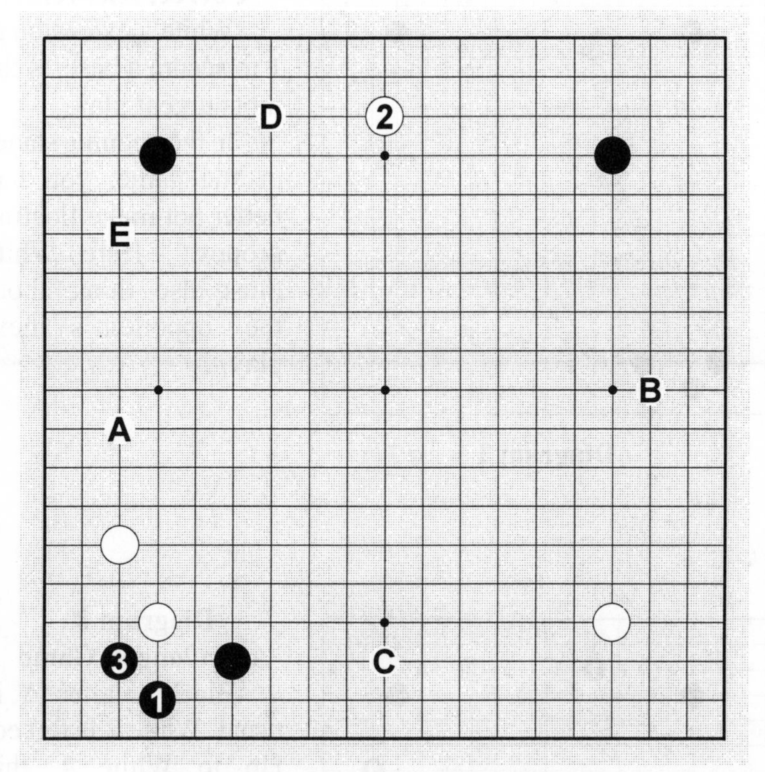

Problem Diagram – White to play

White ignored Black 1 and played at 2. Black 3 seems to slow the game down. It has taken the corner, attacking White's group. Now White should decide whether to play away again or to settle the lower left group. Choose the correct answer from **A** to **E**.

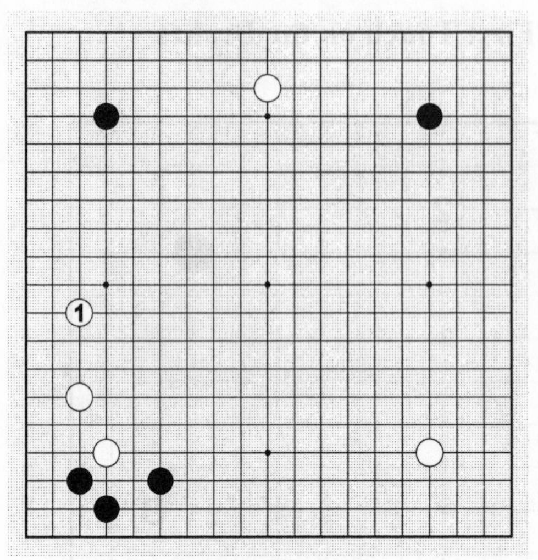

Diagram 1

Diagram 1
Correct Answer

White's extension at 1 to secure a base, is the most urgent play.

In the opening stages of the game, you had better not make floating groups. Here White must also think about the opponent's next play.

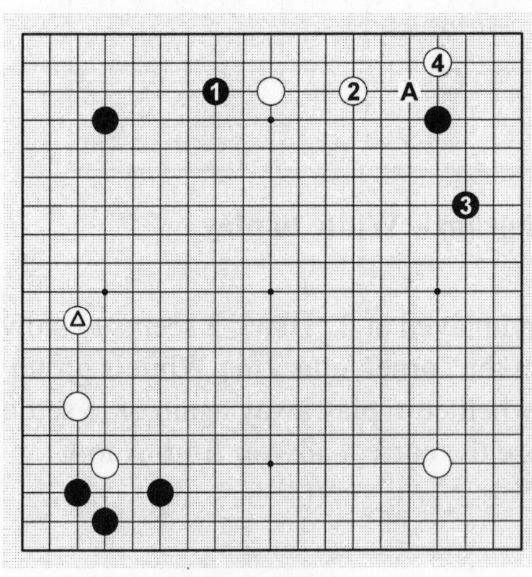

Diagram 2

Diagram 2
A Prolonged Game

Black 1 after Δ is usual. White 2 is forced. Up to White 4, this seems to be a drawn-out game. White 4 doesn't involve the base of White's group, but comparing with Black **A**, it is very big.

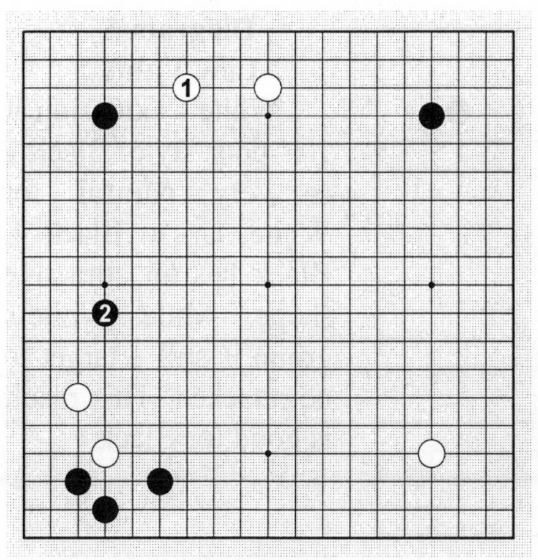

Diagram 3

Diagram 3
Floating Group

White 1 aims to settle the upper side. It is not urgent, because White can develop the group with a two-point extension at any time, against the opponent's approach from either side. After allowing Black 2, White can't expect a good result.

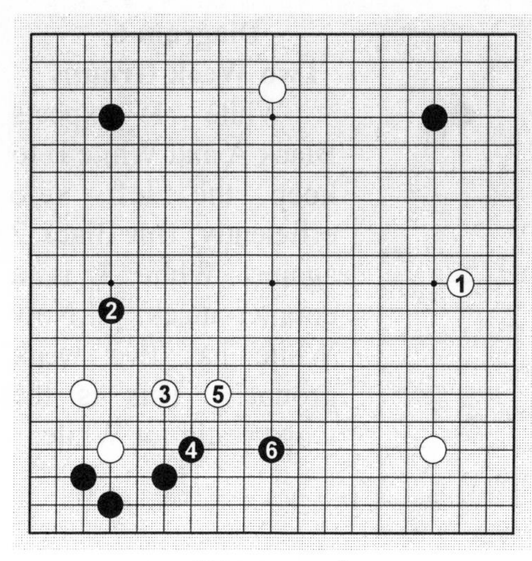

Diagram 4

Diagram 4
Wrong Direction

White 1 aims to extend the influence on the right side, but after Black 2, White can't expect a good result. Up to Black 6 White's group is still unsettled, and Black naturally takes a good territory, while attacking White's group.

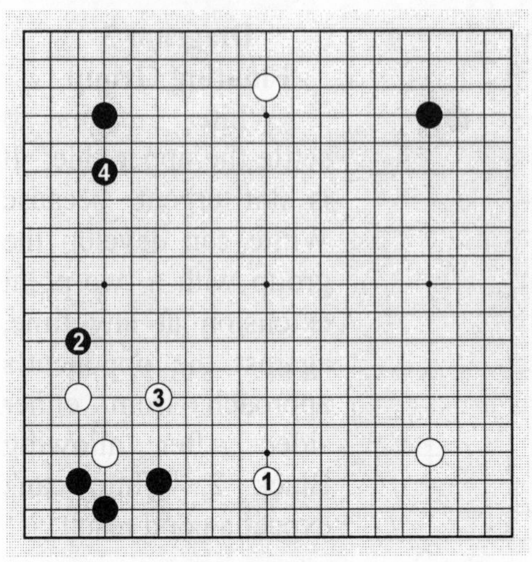

Diagram 5

Diagram 5
Low Value

White's extension at 1 is poor style. Black 2 is very painful for White. Up to Black 4, Black has an attractive shape, while White's group is still a target to be attacked. This result is good for Black.

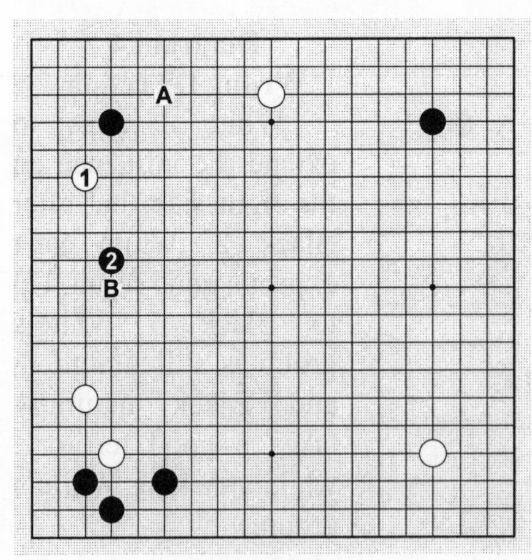

Diagram 6

Diagram 6
Two Weak Groups

White 1 expects Black A and White B to keep the left side efficiently. But Black 2 against White 1 is a counter-attack. Now White has two weak groups. This is the worst result for White.

Problem 25 After the Approach

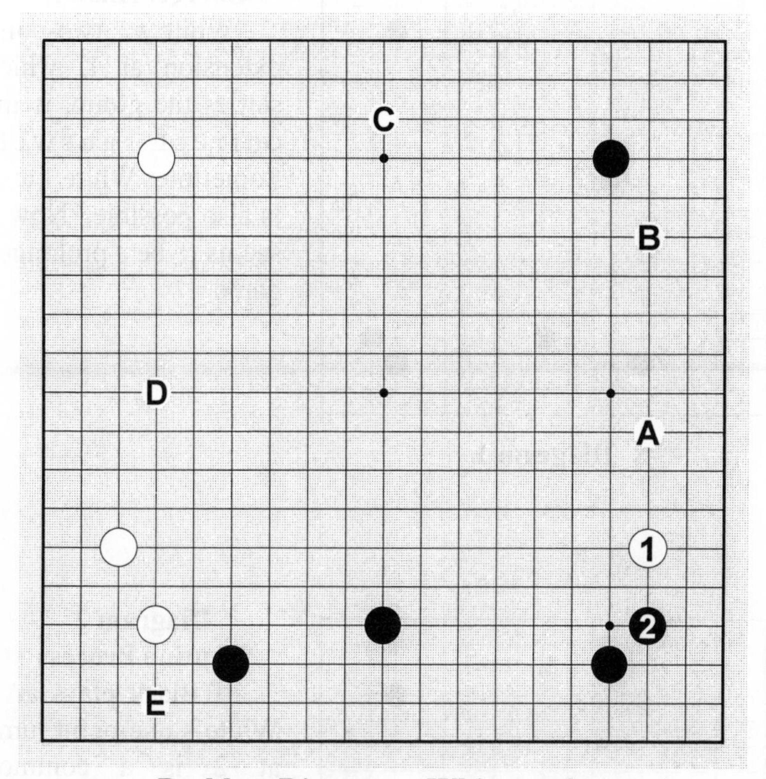

Problem Diagram – White to play

White's large knight's approach at 1 aims to avoid a pincer from around **A**. Black 2 is common to keep the corner territory. Now you should judge whether to settle the group or to play elsewhere. Choose the correct answer from **A** to **E**.

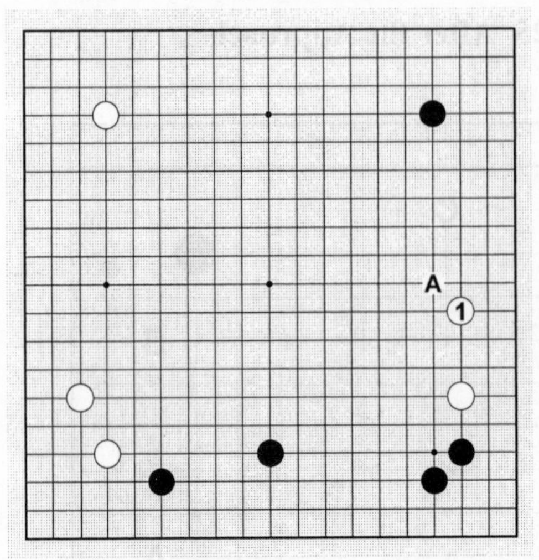

Diagram 1

Diagram 1
Correct Answer

White's two-point extension at 1, which settles the group, is the correct answer. Sometimes White 1 at **A** is also possible. Now it seems to be a prolonged game.

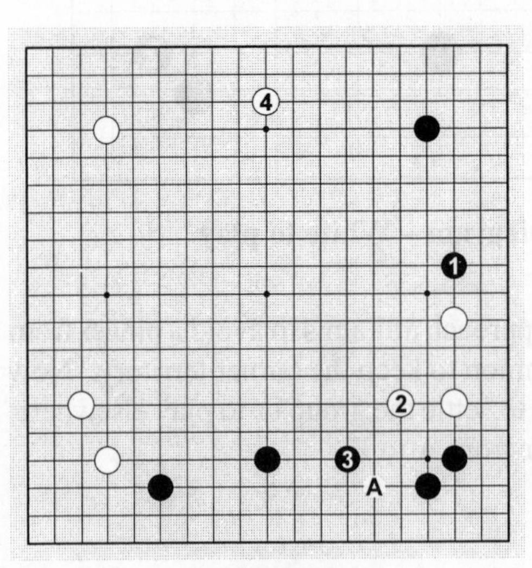

Diagram 2

Diagram 2
Routine Process

If Black plays at 1, White's one-point jump at 2 is a common response. Black 3 is forced to cover the weakness at **A**. Up to White 4 this result is quite even.

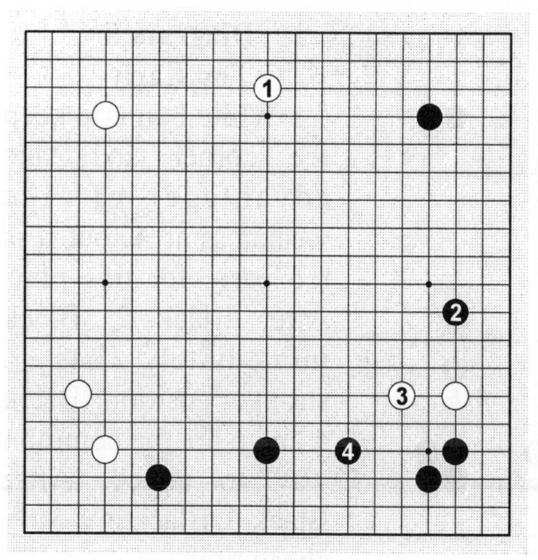

Diagram 3

Diagram 3
Floating Group

White 1 is a bad play, betraying a lack of understanding of the importance of a base. If White allows Black 2 then White has to run in the center, and allow the opponent territory. This result is bad for White.

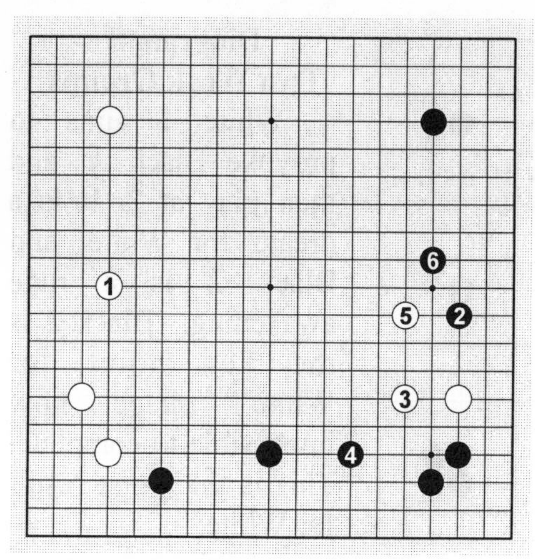

Diagram 4

Diagram 4
Wrong Direction

White 1 aims to expand on the left side. Black's pincer at 2 is dangerous for White. White 3 and 5 are necessary to strengthen the group even though they allow Black some territory. But up to Black 6 White's group is not yet safe.

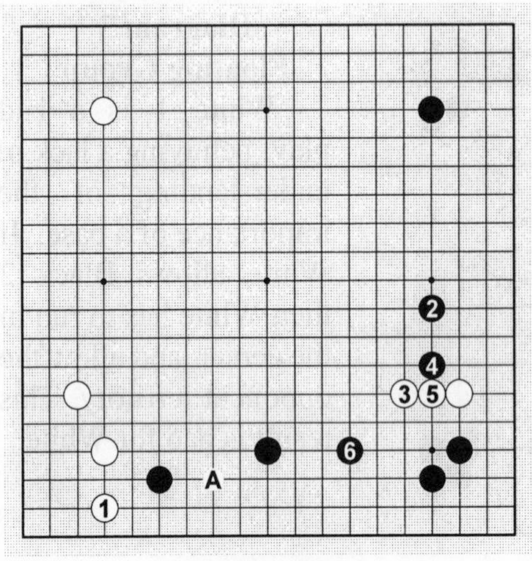

Diagram 5

Diagram 5
Too Early

White 1 aims to keep the corner and take advantage of the weakness at **A**, but it is too early for this play. After Black 2, Black immediately has a stronger position. Black 4 and 6 are the common way to attack. After Black 6, Black is clearly ahead.

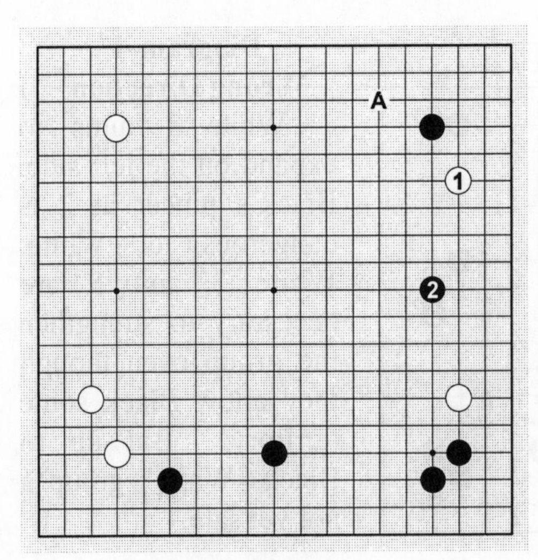

Diagram 6

Diagram 6
Two Weak Groups

White 1 aims to provoke Black **A**, and then play at 2. It is a dream for White, and Black 2 is a rude awakening. Black 2 is the key point for White's shape, now impossible to complete. This is the worst result for White.

Problem 26 Floating Lifelessly

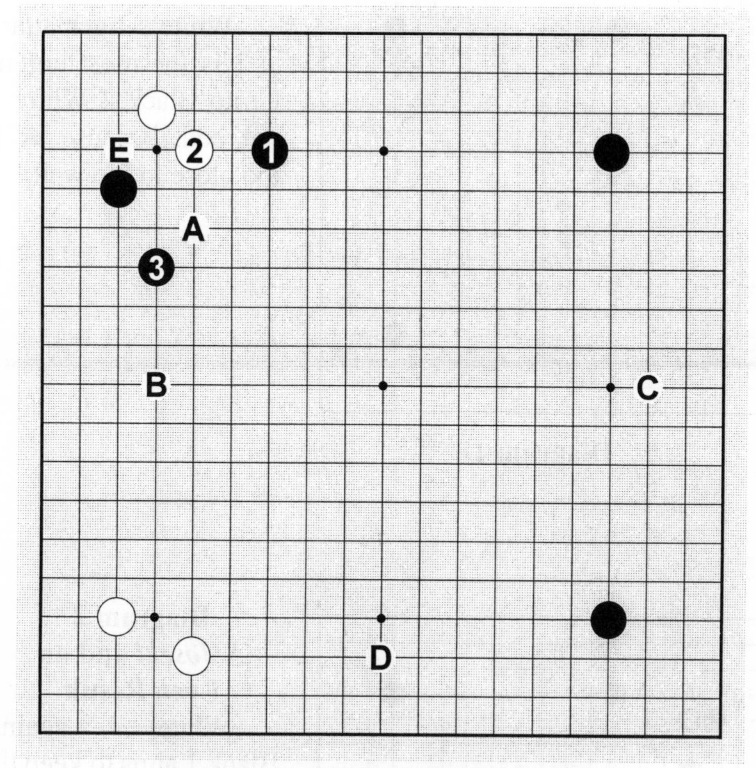

Problem Diagram – White to play

White's diagonal link at 2 against Black's pincer at 1 is common. Then Black plays at 3. Now what is the best play for White, from **A** to **E**? Hint: don't make a floating group in the opening.

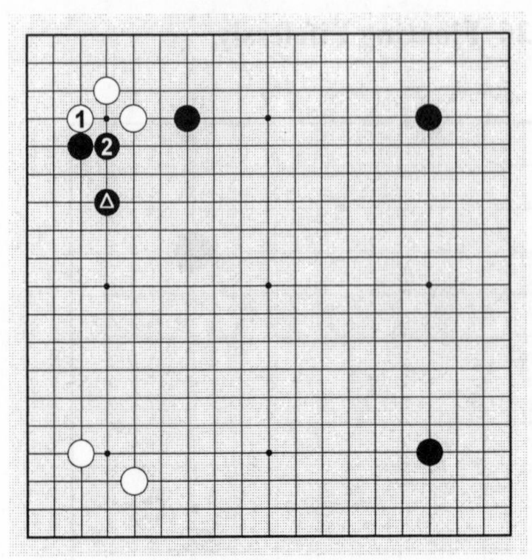

Diagram 1

Diagram 1
Correct Answer

White's tiger attack at 1 is the most urgent. Up to Black 2 White is not bad, because ▲ is too close to the wall.

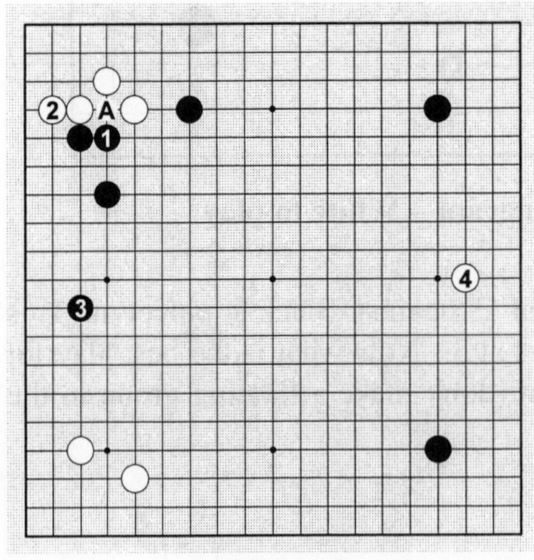

Diagram 2

Diagram 2
A *Joseki* and an Even Result

White 2 against Black 1 aims to keep the corner territory, reinforcing the weakness at **A**. After that Black's extension at 3 is necessary to secure the base. Up to White 4 this result is quite even.

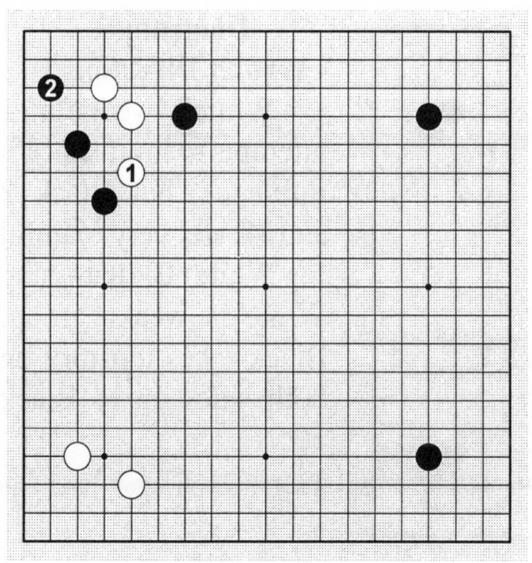

Diagram 3

Diagram 3
Poor Style

White 1 aims to play towards the center, but this is in the wrong direction. Black's slide at 2 is the key point to steal White's base. This result is good for Black.

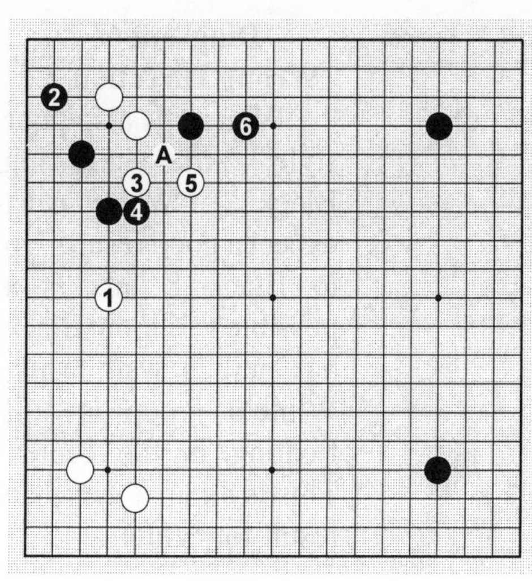

Diagram 4

Diagram 4
Key Point At Black 2

White 1 attempts to expand from the lower left, while attacking Black's group. But after allowing Black 2, White 3 and 5 are necessary to run away. After Black 6, White's group is still unsettled. Furthermore there is a weak point at **A**.

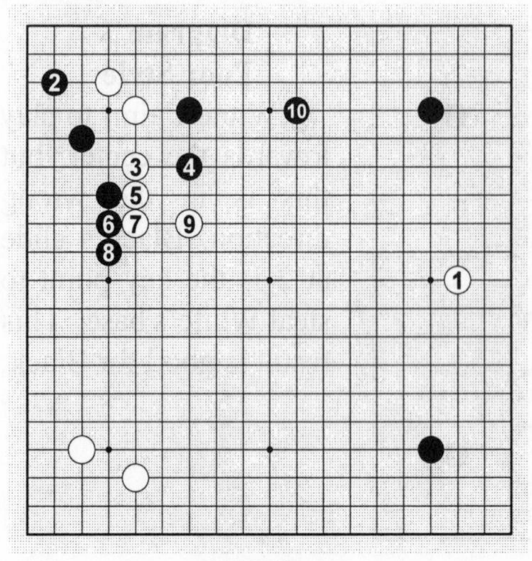

Diagram 5

Diagram 5
Wrong Direction 1

White's wedge at 1 attempts to limit Black's influence, but Black 2 and 4 are very painful for White. By harassing White's weak group, Black takes territory on both sides up to Black 10.

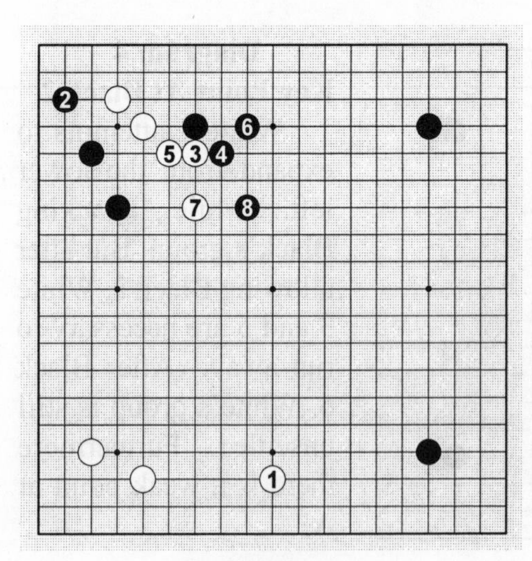

Diagram 6

Diagram 6
Wrong Direction 2

White 1 is also poor style. After allowing Black 2, White can't expect a good result. Up to Black 8 this is a possible variation: Black has built a wall, while White's group is still floating in the center. This is again a very bad result for White.

Problem 27 A Clear Priority

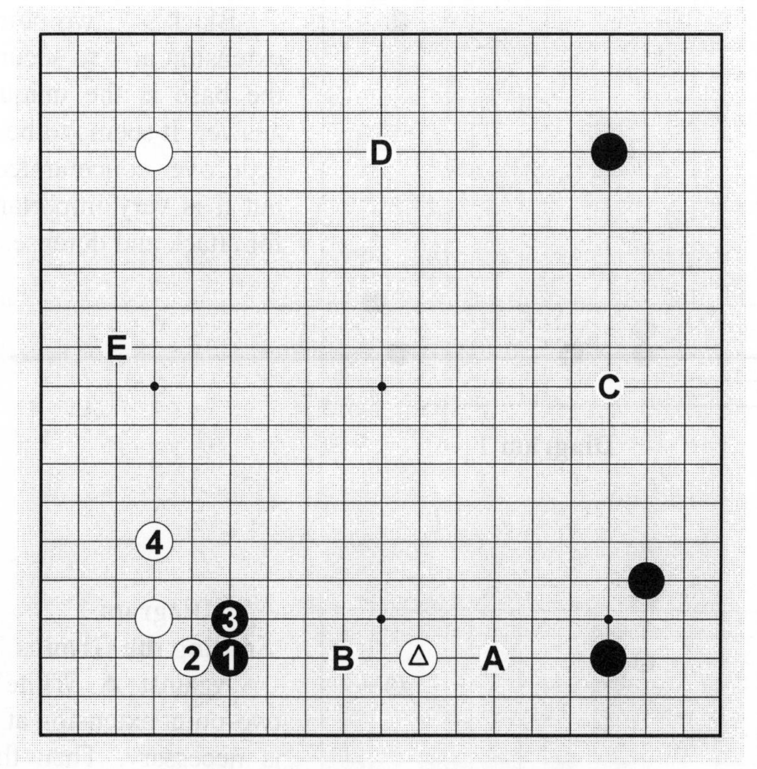

Problem Diagram – Black to play

Against Black 1, the exchange of White 2 and Black 3 is usually not good. But in this case it is possible because of White Δ. In reply to this there is a unique answer. Choose it from **A** to **E**.

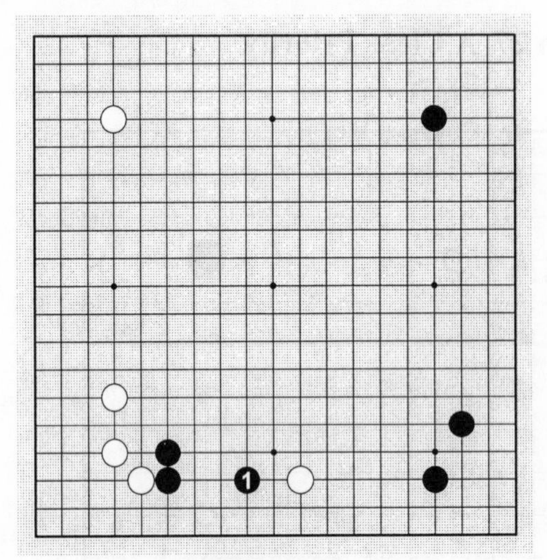

Diagram 1

Diagram 1
Correct Answer

Black's two-point extension at 1 to secure the base is the unique answer. It seems to be a little over-concentrated, but it is very important for attack and defense.

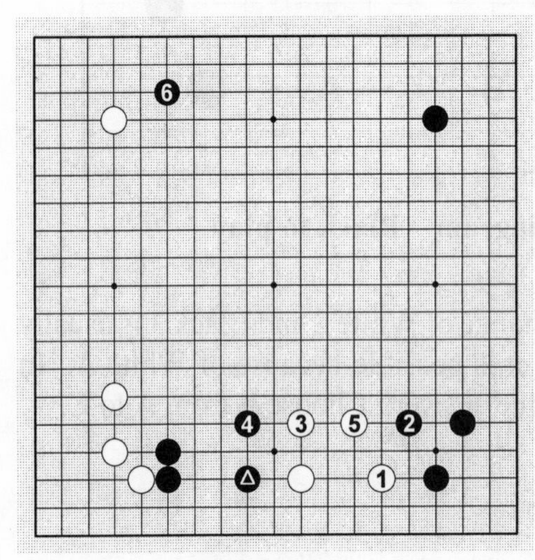

Diagram 2

Diagram 2
Settling the Groups

Against ▲ White's two-point extension at 1 is necessary. Then the sequence 2 to 5 is routine in order to settle the groups. Up to Black 6 the result is almost even.

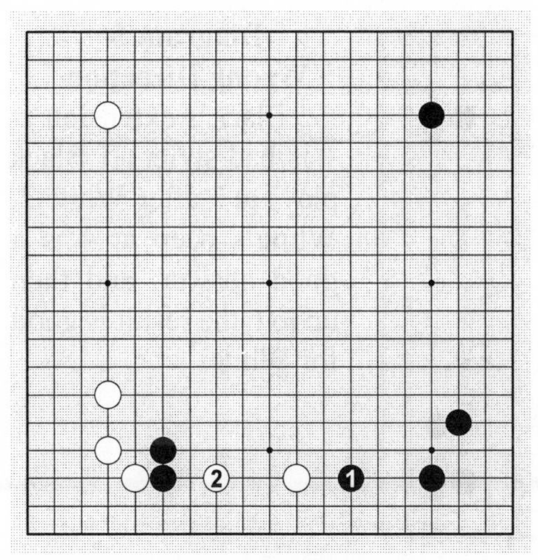

Diagram 3

Diagram 3
Black's
Floating Group

Black 1 aims to take territory, whilst attacking White's stone. White 2 kills two birds with one stone by securing a base and attacking Black's stones. The result is bad for Black.

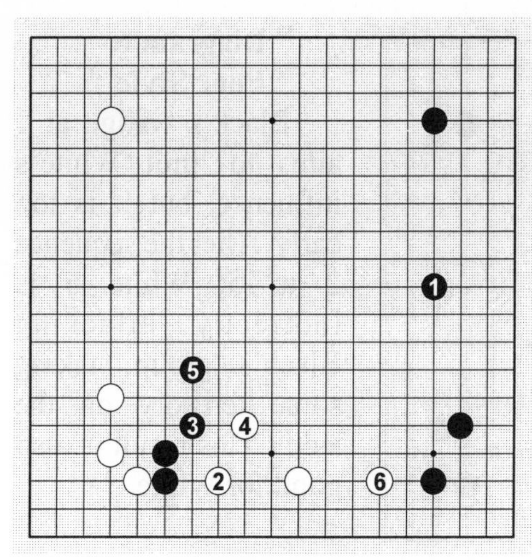

Diagram 4

Diagram 4
Too Early

Black 1 is a big play, but is made too early. After allowing White 2, Black must run away with 3 and 5. Up to White 6, White naturally takes territory, while Black still has an unsettled group in the center.

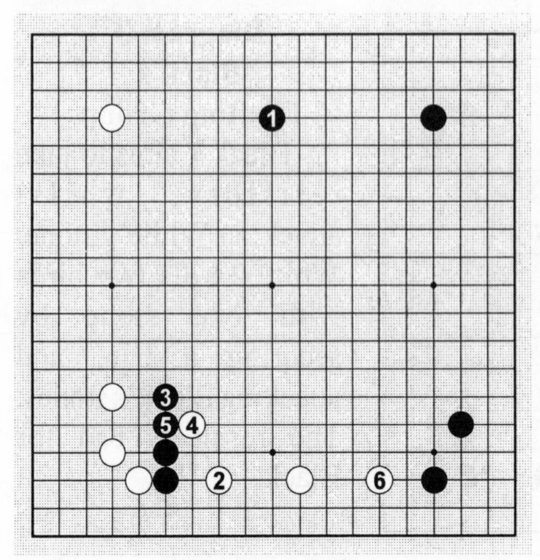

Diagram 5

Diagram 5
Wrong Direction

Black's extension at 1 is bad style. If Black plays at 3 after White 2, White's peep at 4 is a good answer, and then up to 6 the result is good for White.

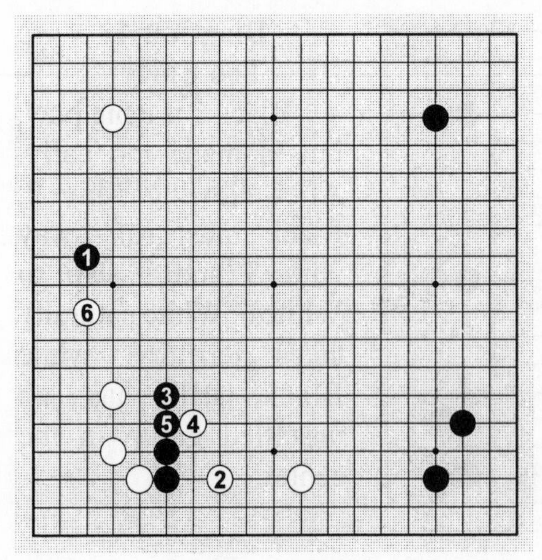

Diagram 6

Diagram 6
Poor Style

Black's wedge at 1 aims to limit White's influence, but it is too early. After the sequence 2 to 5, White 6 is indirectly attacking Black's group, taking some territory on the side. This result is also good for White.

Problem 28 A Double Purpose Play

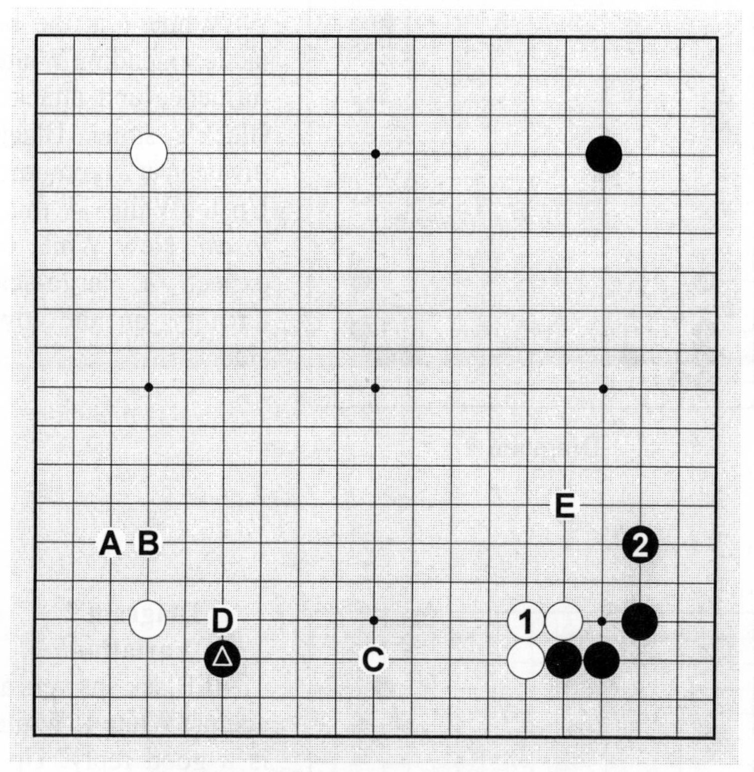

Problem Diagram – White to play

The exchange of White 1 and Black 2 has just taken place. White must decide how to treat ▲. Choose the most efficient play from **A** to **E**.

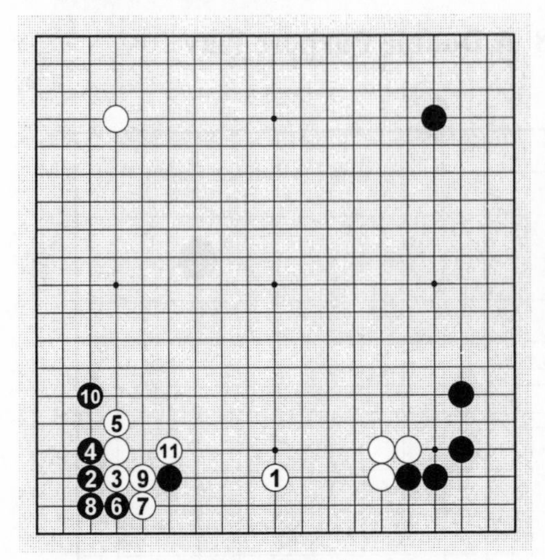

Diagram 1

Diagram 1
Correct Answer

White 1 is the best tactic, extending White's influence and attacking Black's stone. Black's invasion at 2 is common. Up to White 11 this is *joseki*. Now White can expect a large-scale territory on the lower side.

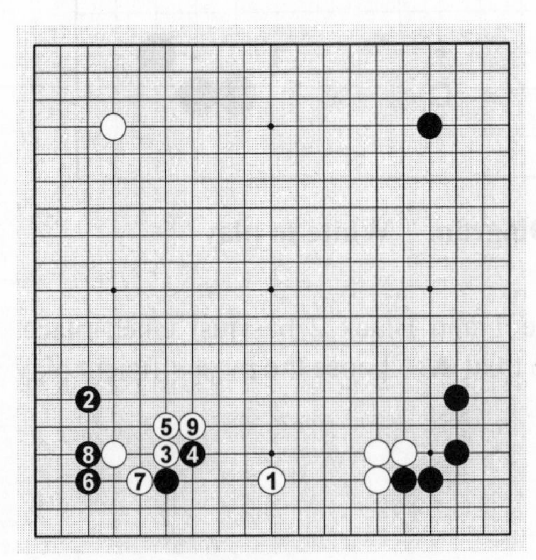

Diagram 2

Diagram 2
Variation

If Black answers at 2 against White 1, White 3 is a good reply. Up to White 9, Black takes the corner in *sente*, while White has a large-scale framework. This result is well-balanced.

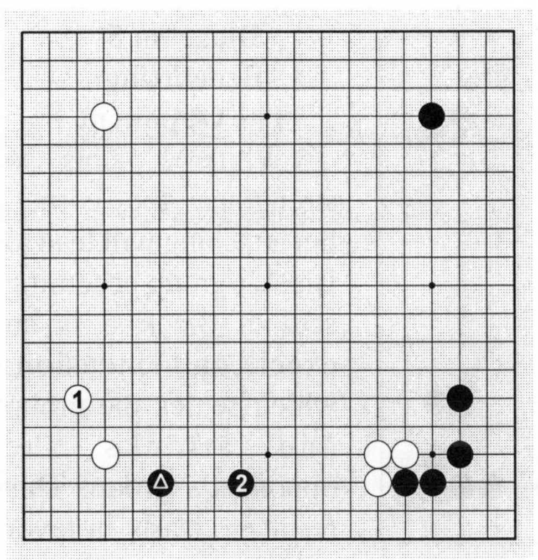

Diagram 3

Diagram 3
Careless Reply

White 1 against ▲ is too passive. Black 2 is an excellent play in this situation, which settles Black's group and attacks White's group.

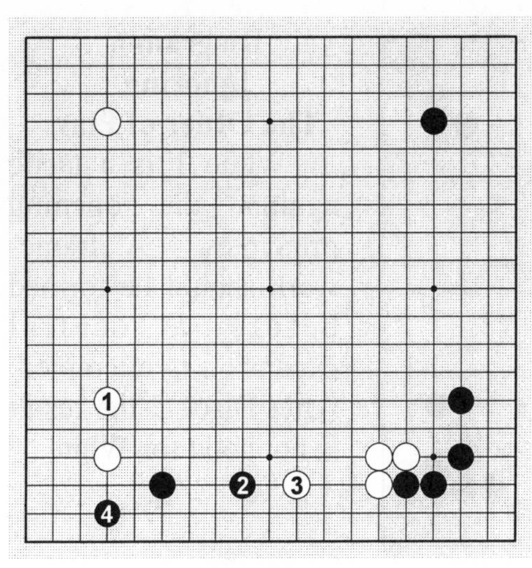

Diagram 4

Diagram 4
Too Passive

White 1 is also careless. Up to Black 4 Black has ideal shape, while White's group is a little over-concentrated. This result is also good for Black.

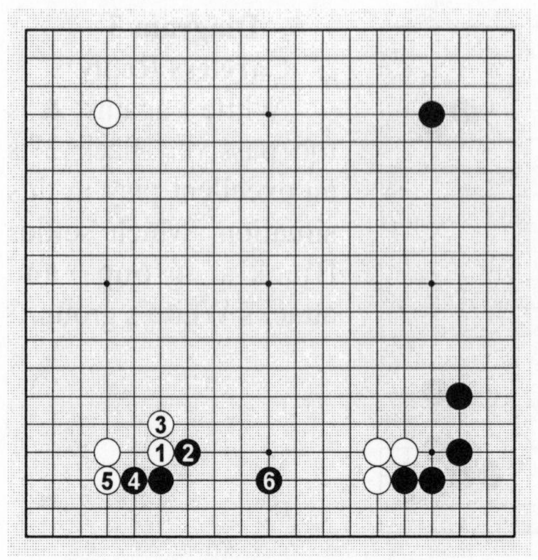

Diagram 5

Diagram 5
Benefitting
The Opponent

White 1 aims to strengthen the corner, but attaching will lead to Black's group becoming settled. Black 6 is an excellent extension, which settles the group and attacks the opponent's group. This result is clearly in favor of Black.

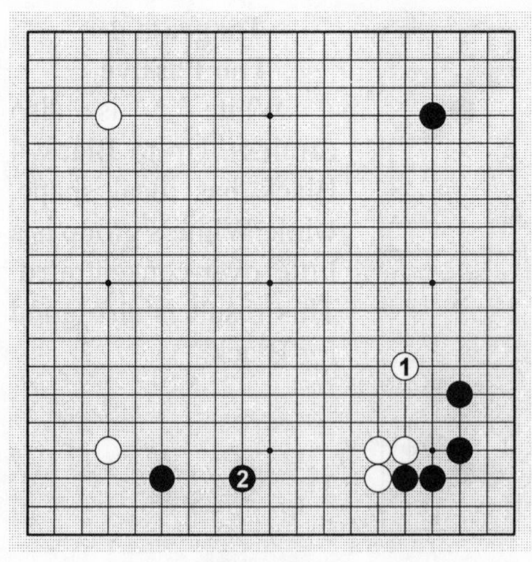

Diagram 6

Diagram 6
Ignoring
The Order of Play

White 1 is a tactic against the opening principles. A framework should be formed before a central expansion is attempted. After Black 2 the result is not good for White.

Problem 29 Take Advantage of a Slip

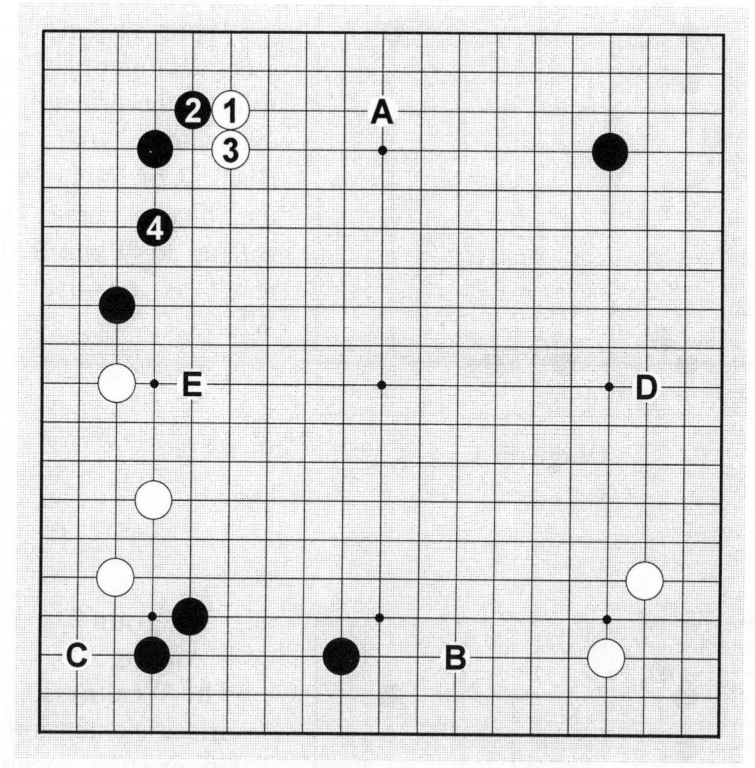

Problem Diagram – White to play

Black 2 against White 1 is a bad tactic. After Black 4, White should decide whether to settle the group or to play elsewhere. Choose the correct answer from **A** to **E**.

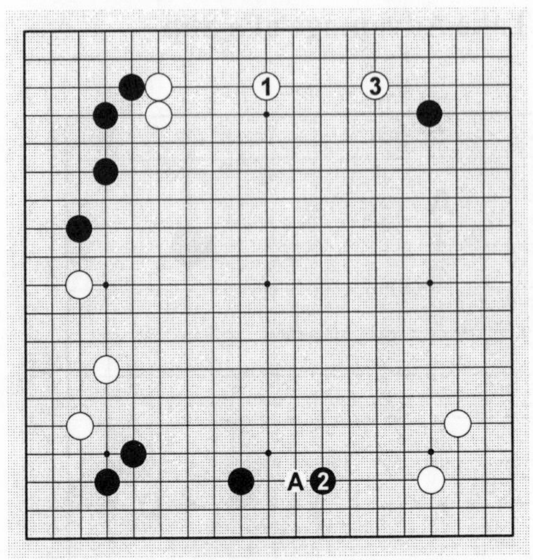

Diagram 1

Diagram 1
Correct Answer

White's extension at 1 is the proper play, and follows the principle of extension. After that Black 2 or White **A** is the biggest area left. But up to White 3 the result is positive for White.

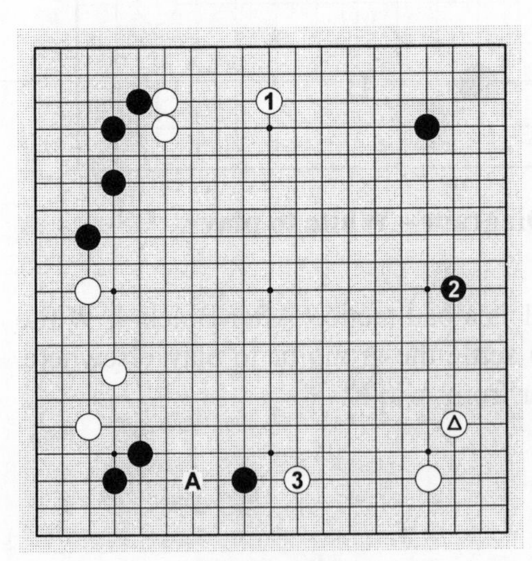

Diagram 2

Diagram 2
Aiming At
The Weakness

Black's extension at 2 is poor style, because White Δ is on the third line. Then White 3 is a good play to extend influence and takes advantage of the weakness at **A**. This result is clearly good for White.

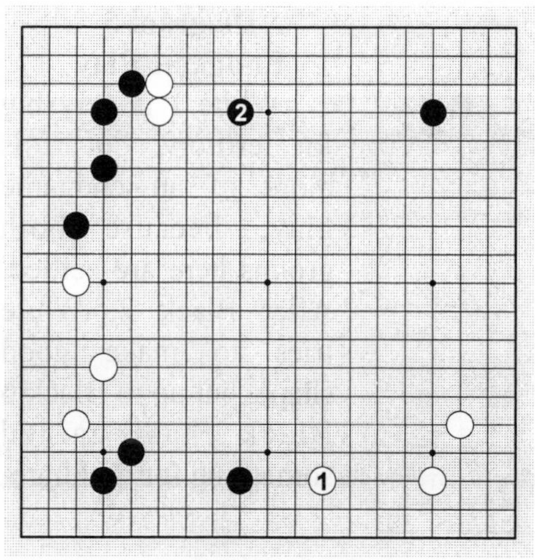

Diagram 3

Diagram 3
Floating Group

White 1 attempts to expand from the corner enclosure. But Black's pincer at 2 is painful for White. Now White has to run away without a base. This result is bad for White.

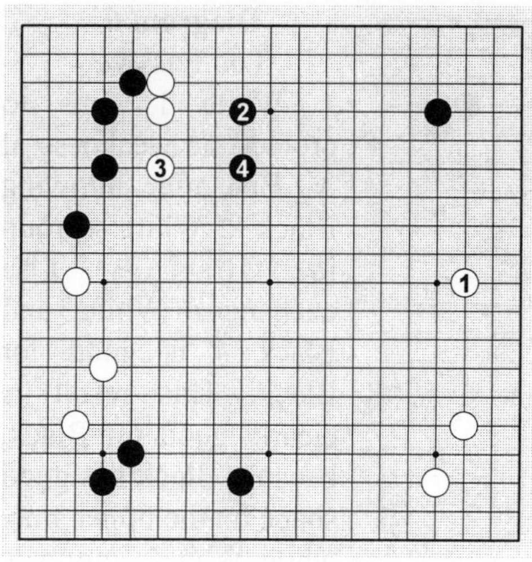

Diagram 4

Diagram 4
Wrong Direction

White 1 here is similar to White 1 in **Diagram 3.** After allowing Black 2 and 4, White can't expect a good result. Up to Black 4 Black is definitely ahead.

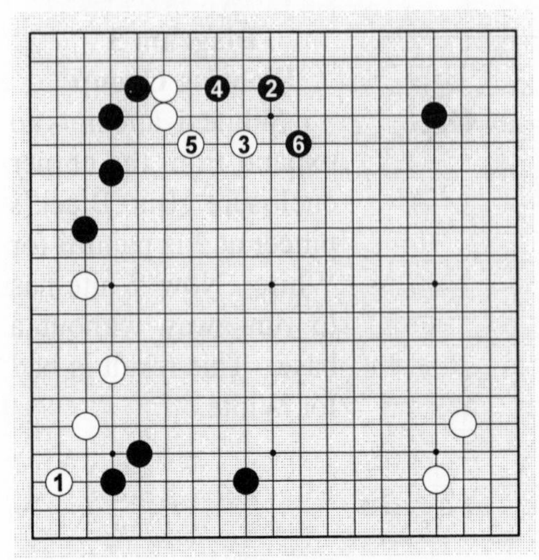

Diagram 5

Diagram 5
Endgame Play

White 1 is very big for territory, but it is more of an endgame play, because both groups here are settled. After Black 2, White tries to make good shape, but up to Black 6 Black has gained something for nothing.

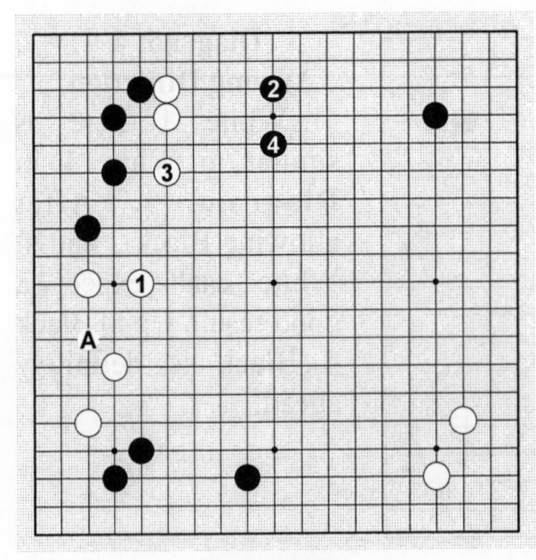

Diagram 6

Diagram 6
Too Passive

White 1 aims to protect the weakness at **A**. But after allowing Black 2, White's group is floating. The exchange of White 3 and Black 4 is good for Black. This result is clearly good for Black, because Black has good shape on the upper side, while White's group is still not settled.

Problem 30 Which Way to Safety?

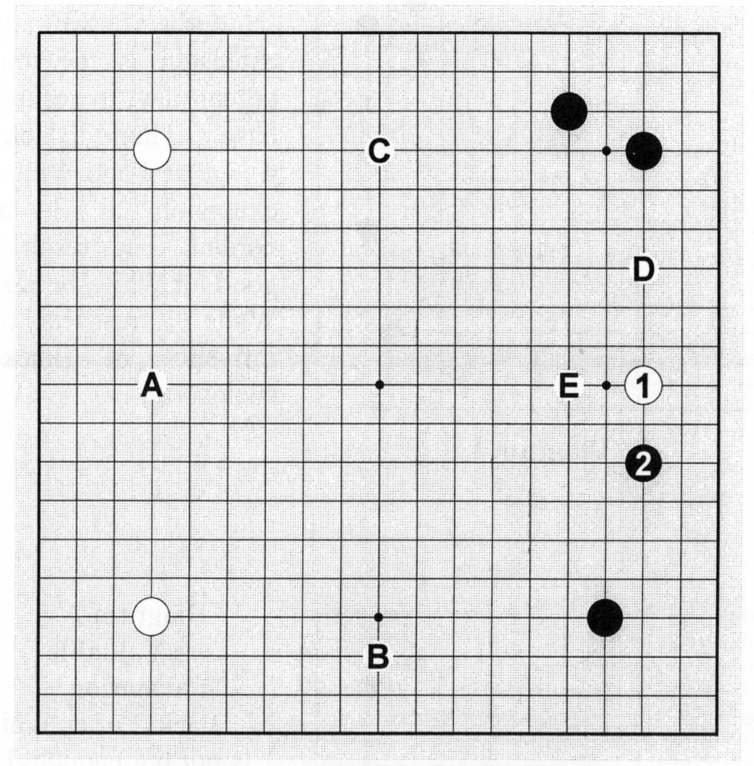

Problem Diagram – White to play

White 1 aims to stop Black from extending influence. Now Black 2 from the lower side stops White's extension that way. The next play is very important. Choose the best one from **A** to **E**.

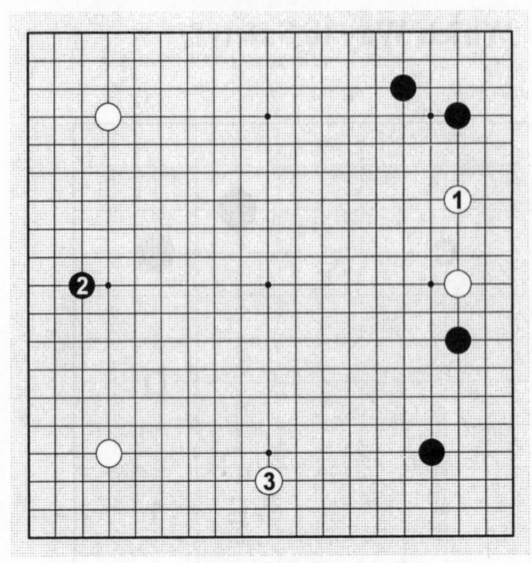

Diagram 1

Diagram 1
Correct Answer

White's two-point extension is the most urgent play, to secure a base. Then Black's wedge at 2 and White's extension at 3 are normal. The result is good for White, because White 1 restricts the influence of Black's enclosure.

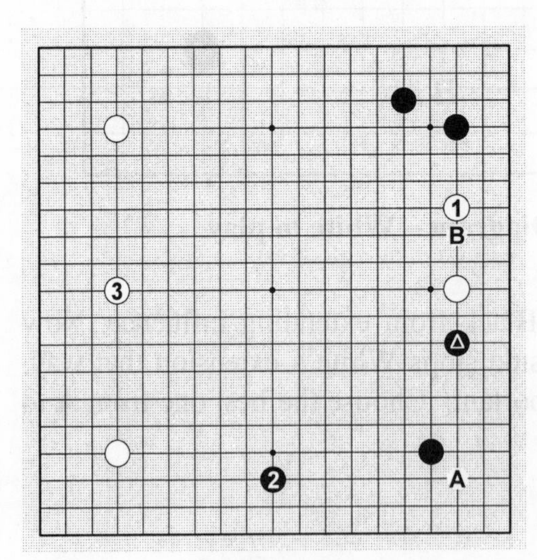

Diagram 2

Diagram 2
Less Valuable Formation

Black 2 after White 1 is not big enough. Up to White 3, White's three-star formation is better than Black's framework, because the corner has a weak point at **A**. Black should have played at **B** originally, instead of ▲.

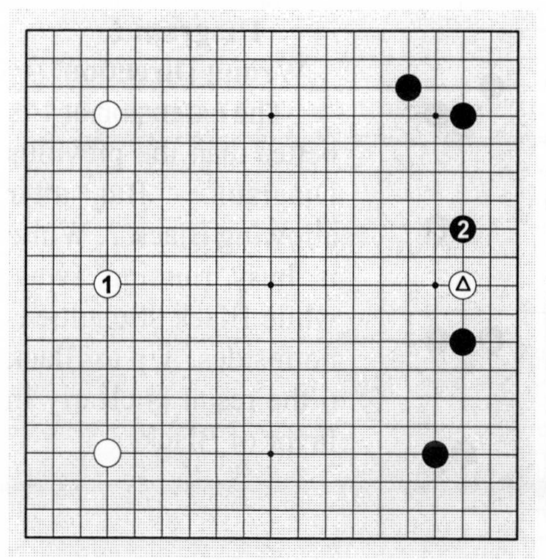

Diagram 3

Diagram 3
Cost of a Floating Group

White 1 aims to build a framework, but Black 2 is painful for White. Now White Δ has no base. This result is very bad for White.

If White's original plan was to expand on the left, Δ should not have been played.

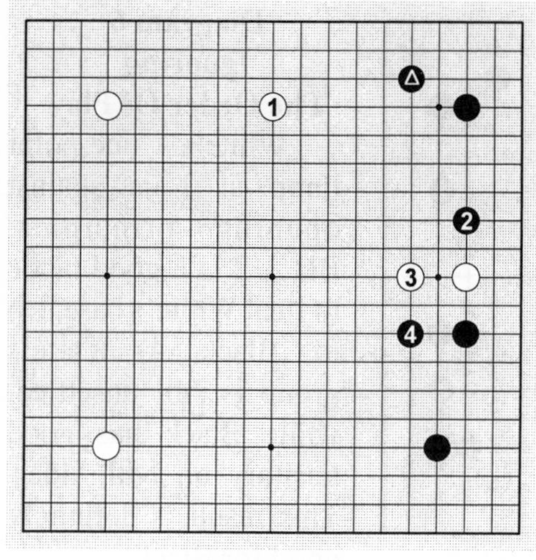

Diagram 4

Diagram 4
Too Passive

The value of White's extension at 1 is even lower than that on the left side, because ▲ is on the third line. After allowing Black a one-sided attack, White cannot expect a good result. Up to Black 4 Black is definitely ahead.

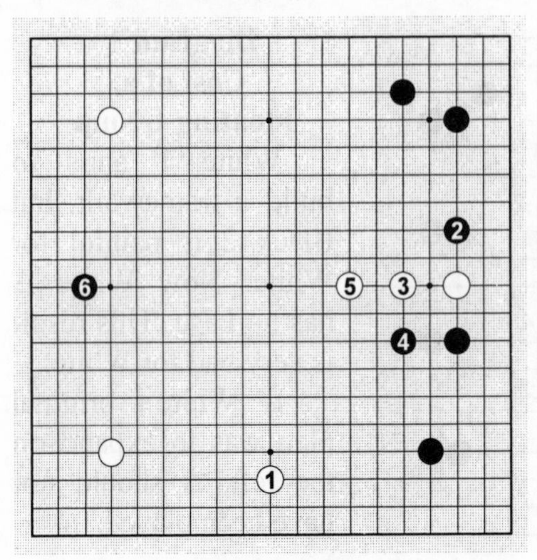

Diagram 5

Diagram 5
Wrong Direction

The extension at 1 is better than the previous Diagram. But after allowing Black 2, White is busy running away, while Black strengthens both sides. Up to Black 6 the result is clearly in favor of Black.

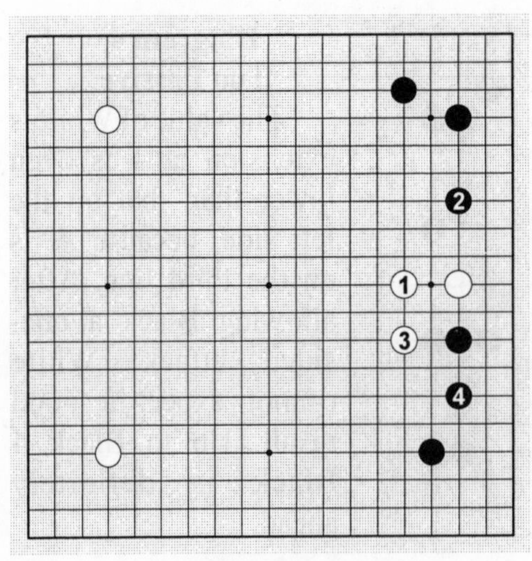

Diagram 6

Diagram 6
Ignoring
The Order Of Play

White's one-point jump at 1 is against opening principles. Black 2 is a good tactic to steal White's base. Up to Black 4 White's group is still unsettled, while Black has good territory on both sides. This result is definitely good for Black.

Problem 31 Establishing a Formation

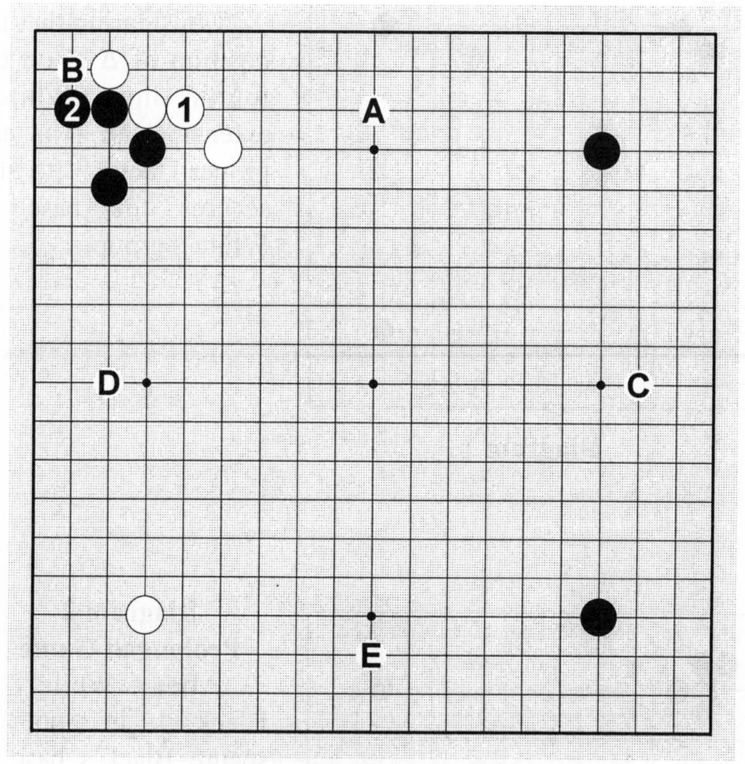

Problem Diagram – White to play

In the top left corner there is a *joseki* in progress. Black 2 is the key point to secure the base. Now what is White's most urgent play? Choose it from **A** to **E**.

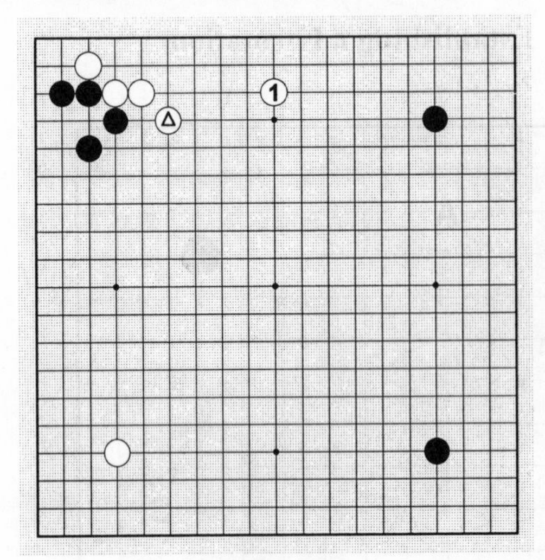

Diagram 1

Diagram 1
Correct Answer

Considering that the position of Δ is on the fourth line, White's extension at 1 is the proper tactic. It also secures the base of White's group.

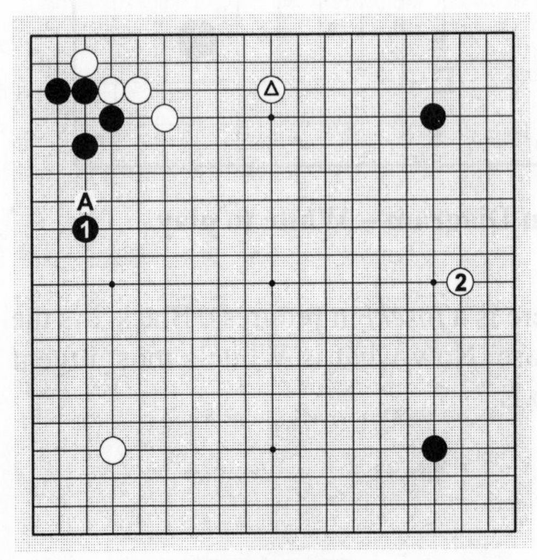

Diagram 2

Diagram 2
Prolonged Game

After White Δ, Black 1 is good to secure Black's base. If White played at **A**, Black's group in the top left corner would be attacked. Up to White 2 the result is almost even.

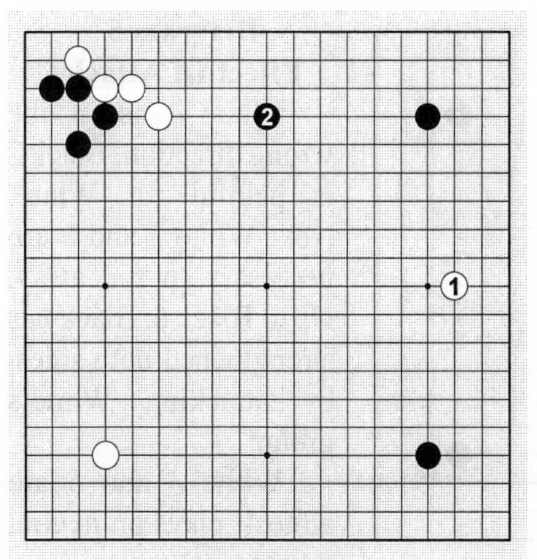

Diagram 3

Diagram 3
Base of
White's Group

White 1 attempts to limit Black's influence. But after allowing Black 2, White can't hope for a good result, because White's group is too heavy to sacrifice.

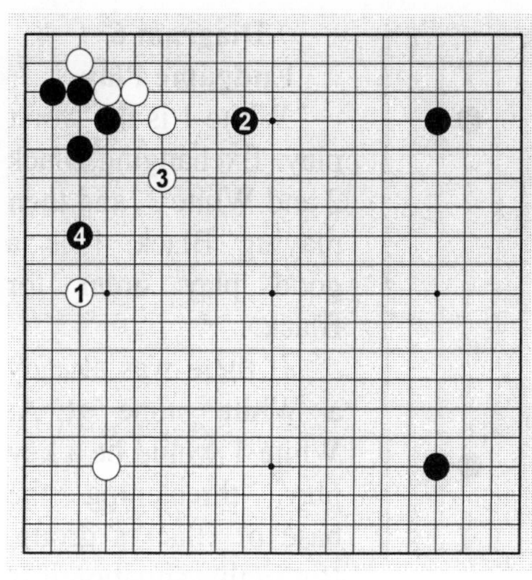

Diagram 4

Diagram 4
White 1 is a
Low Value Extension

White 1 aims to limit Black's influence, but Black 2 is uncomfortable for White. If White runs away with 3, Black extends at 4, aiming to keep up the attack on White's group. This is a successful opening for Black.

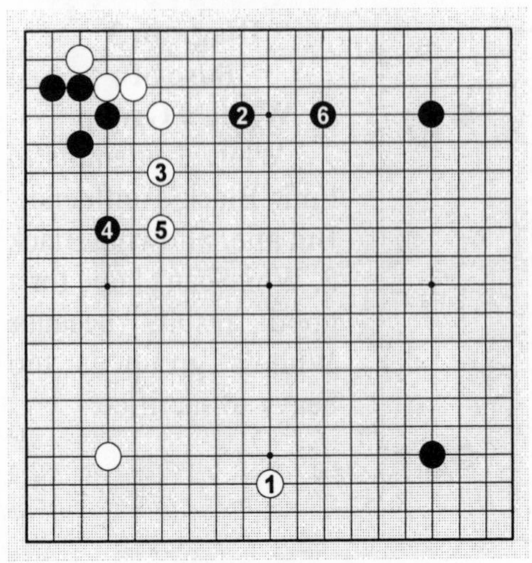

Diagram 5

Diagram 5
Effect Of Attack

White 1 is in the wrong direction. Black 2 is painful for White. Next White 3 and 5 are necessary to run away. Up to Black 6, Black has strengthened both sides, by attacking White's group.

White 3 and 5 are almost plays on neutral points.

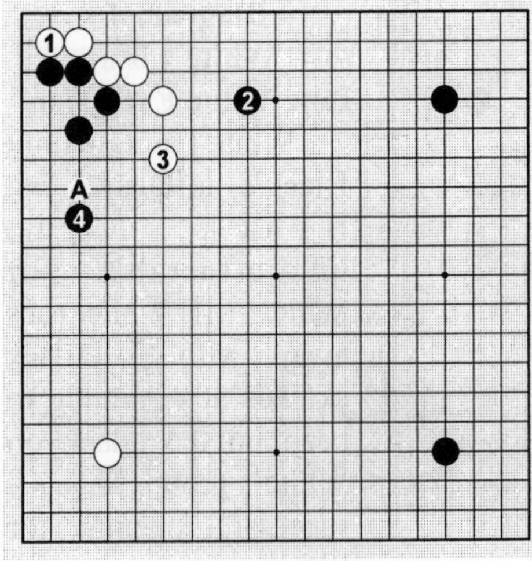

Diagram 6

Diagram 6
Endgame Play

White 1 is the worst play. Exchanging Black 2 and White 3, and then playing Black 4 is a good play order for Black.

If there was already a White stone at **A**, White 1 would be a key play, threatening the base of Black's group. But in this situation it is a mere endgame play.

Problem 32 Response to a Soft Play

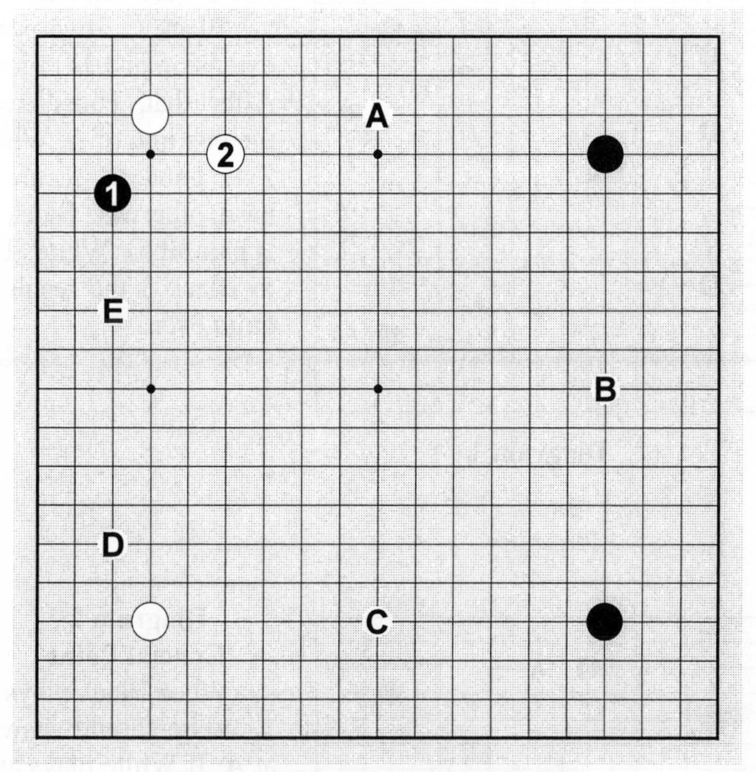

Problem Diagram – Black to play

White 2 against Black 1 is a soft answer. Now you should decide whether to reinforce in this area or to play elsewhere. Choose the best from **A** to **E**.

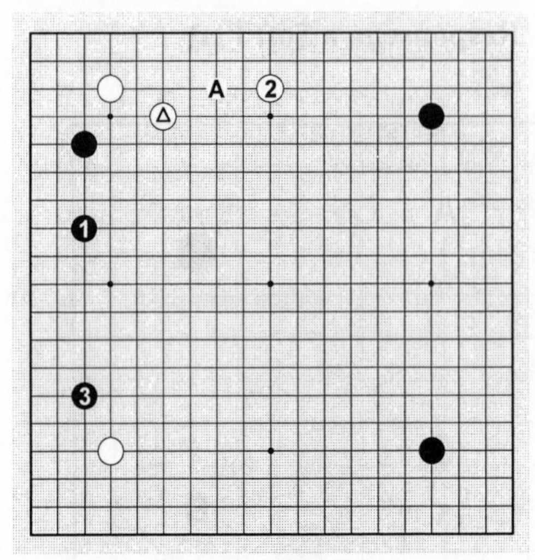

Diagram 1

Diagram 1
Correct Answer

Black's two-point extension at 1 is urgent. After that, considering the position of Δ, White 2 is good to secure a base: otherwise Black **A** is painful for White. Up to Black 3 the result is quite even.

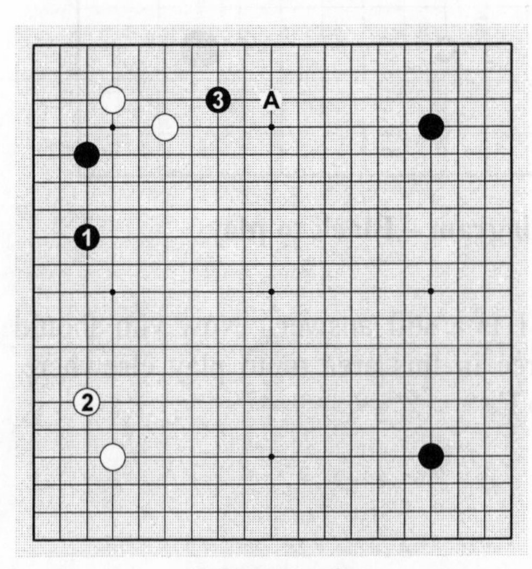

Diagram 2

Diagram 2
Crucial Point

When Black plays at 1, White should answer at **A**. If White plays at 2 instead of **A**, Black 3 to threaten White's base is severe on White. This result is very bad for White.

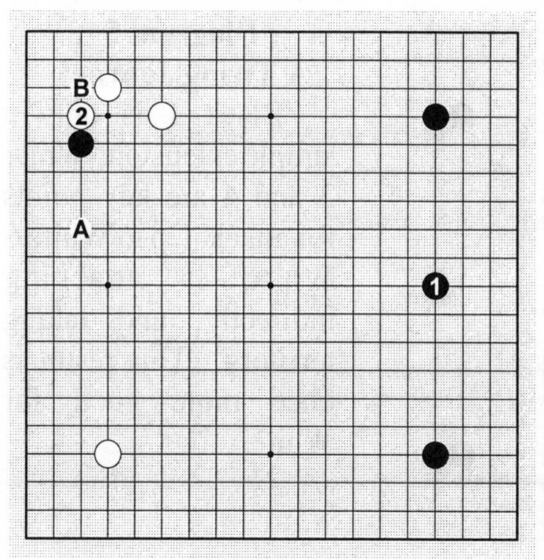

Diagram 3

Diagram 3
Key Point For Attack

Black 1 aims to build up the right, but White's diagonal attachment at 2 is the key point for attack, keeping the corner territory. This is good for White. If White plays 2 at **A**, Black **B** is a good resource to handle the attack.

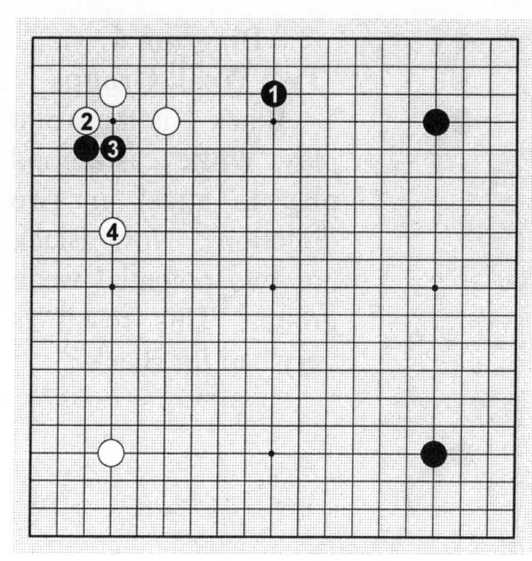

Diagram 4

Diagram 4
Settling The Group

Black 1 aims to prevent White's extension. But after being attacked by White 2 and 4, Black can't expect a good result.

Settling a weak group is prior to anything else.

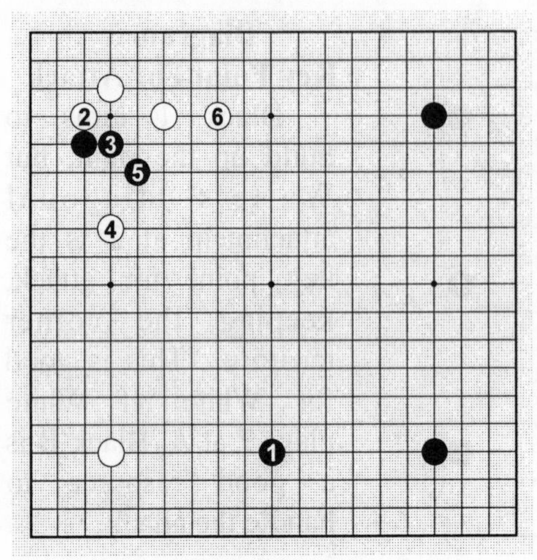

Diagram 5

Diagram 5
A Tiring Journey

Black 1 is only a simple extension; White 2 and 4 are key points for attack. Up to White 6 White is attacking indirectly, and taking territory. This result is once more good for White.

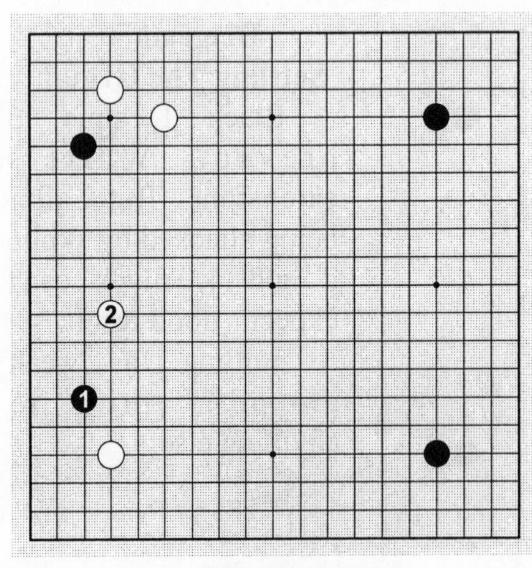

Diagram 6

Diagram 6
Two Weak Groups

Black 1 is the worst play. White 2 is a good play to attack in two directions. Now Black has two potential weak groups. This result is very bad for Black.

Problem 33 Key Point for Attack

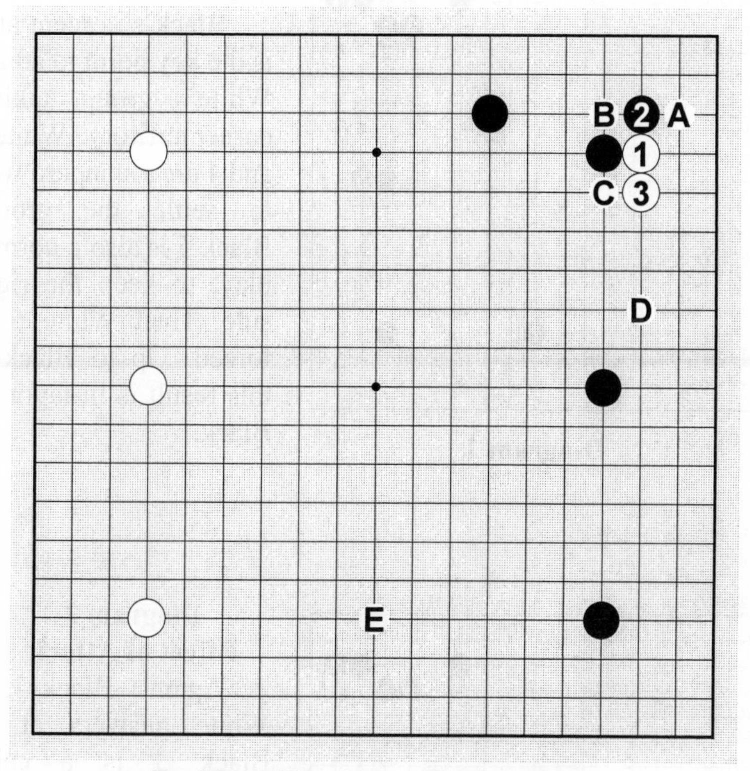

Problem Diagram – Black to play

White 1 is a standard invasion tactic, but in this case is too early. Black 2 and White 3 have just been played. What is the best play to attack White's group? Choose the answer from **A** to **E**.

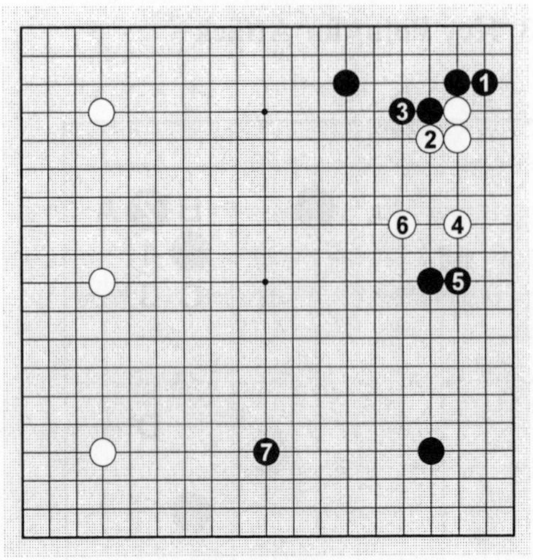

Diagram 1

Diagram 1
Key Point of the Base

Black's descent at 1 is the key point to attack White's group, taking corner territory. White 2 and 4 are a standard way to settle the group. Black 5 is also a normal play, to keep the right side. Then White 6 is forced. Up to Black 7 this result is in favor of Black.

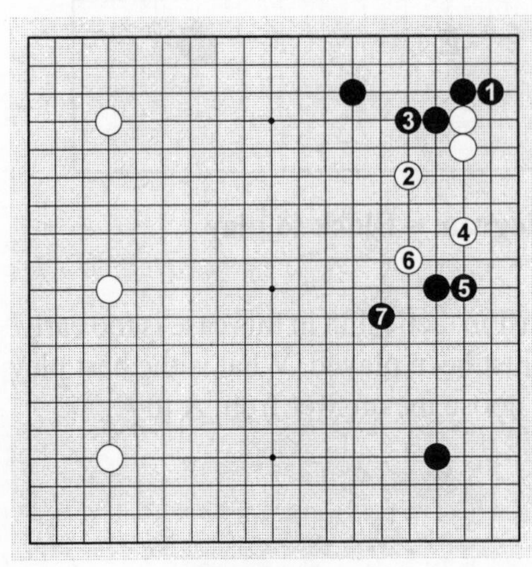

Diagram 2

Diagram 2
Effect of Attack

Against Black 1, if White answers at 2, Black 3 is a calm response, and then White 4 is forced. Up to Black 7 Black gets something for nothing.

It is not a good idea to make a floating group in the opening.

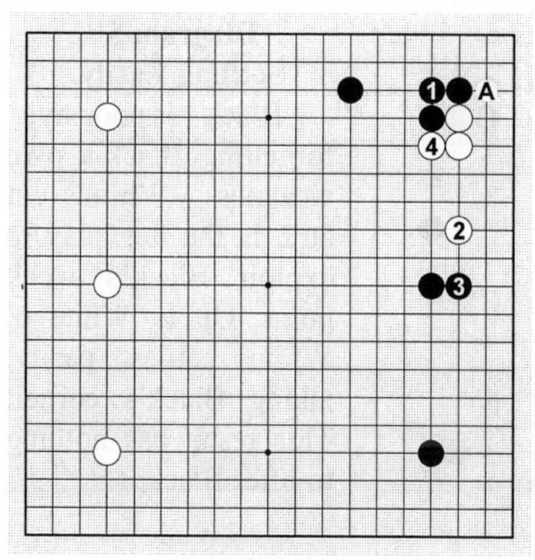

Diagram 3

Diagram 3
Big Difference

Black's connection at 1 is not good in this situation. Compared with Black **A**, this is smaller in territory; and also after White 2 and 4, it is impossible for Black to continue to attack White's group, since there is no Black stone at **A**.

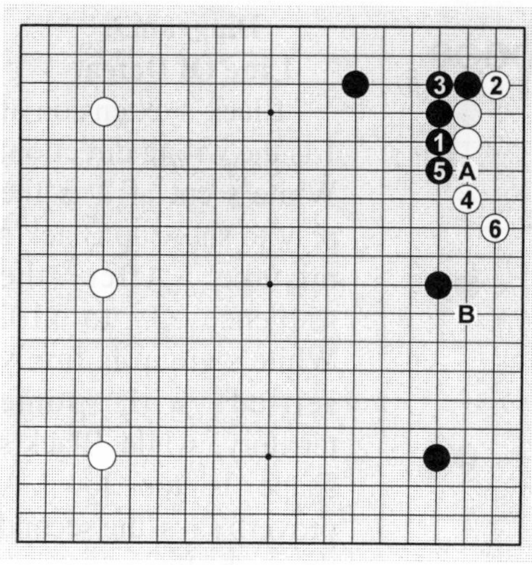

Diagram 4

Diagram 4
Efficient Reinforcement

Black 1 aims to make a strong wall. But after the exchange of White 2 and Black 3, White 4 and 6 are very good; White 6 is an especially good reinforcement to cover the weakness at **A**. After White 6, White **B** and moving into the center are *miai*. This result is clearly good for White.

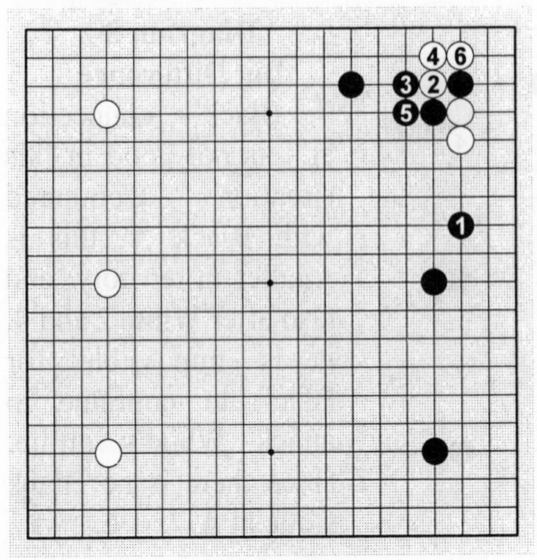

Diagram 5

Diagram 5
Settling Easily

Black 1 is poor style, forgetting Black's own weakness. White's cut at 2 is the key play to exploit Black's weak point. Up to White 6, White settles easily, taking Black's corner. This result has nothing to offer Black.

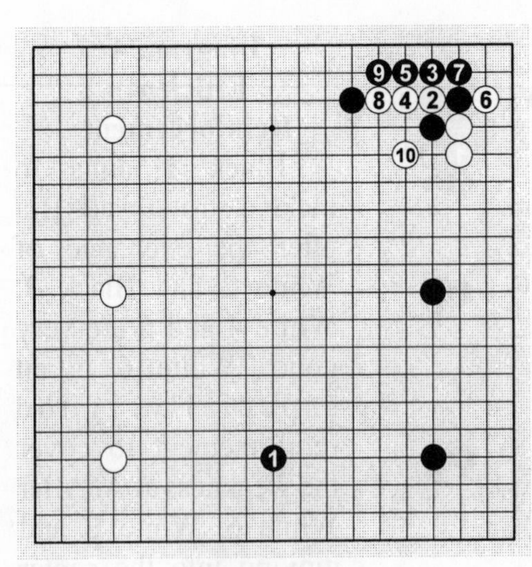

Diagram 6

Diagram 6
Line Of Defeat

Black's extension at 1 is the wrong direction. White's cut at 2 is the play to show up Black's mistake. After the sequence 3 to 10, White's group is firmly settled with some territory, while Black's shape is too low. A proverb says 'the second line is the line of defeat'. This result is therefore good for White.

Problem 34 Simple Defensive Style

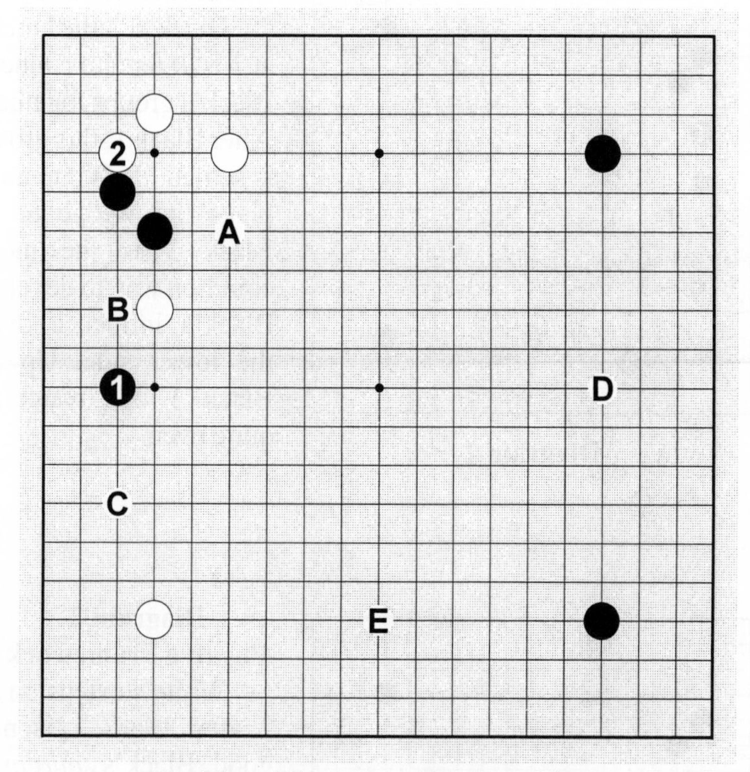

Problem Diagram – Black to play

If Black plays at 1 instead of sliding in the corner, White 2 is natural to keep the corner and steal the opponent's base. Now Black has two weak groups. Choose Black's best answer from **A** to **E**.

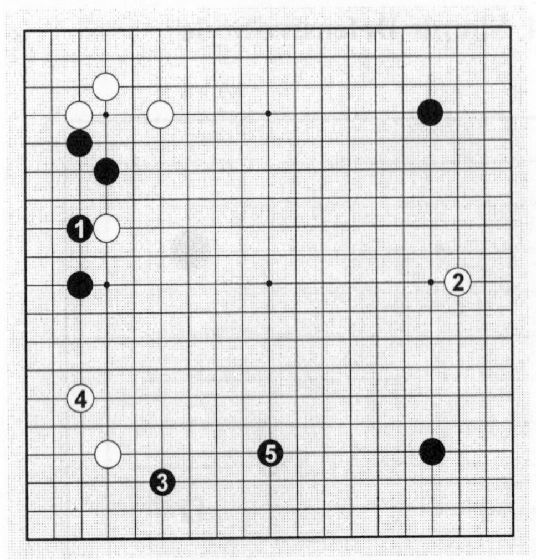

Diagram 1

Diagram 1
Correct Answer

Black's attachment at 1 is urgent, to connect Black's groups together. After Black 1, this group is settled. If White now plays the wedge at 2, Black 3 is the most common way to develop Black's influence over the lower side. Up to Black 5 this result is quite even.

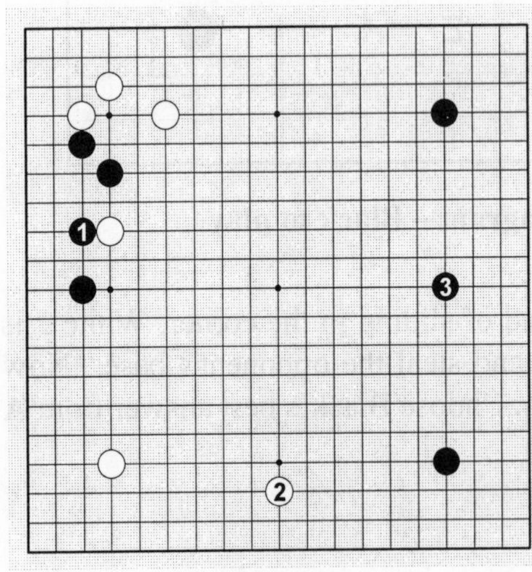

Diagram 2

Diagram 2
Positive Framework

White's extension at 2 after Black 1 is not good. Black's *sanrensei* at 3 is very good. Overall Black's shape is much more positive. Black 3 in this situation is successful, because the Black group on the left side is already settled.

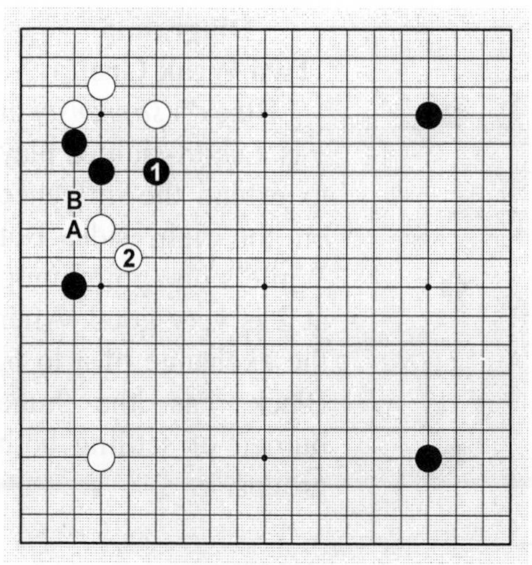

Diagram 3

Diagram 3
Divided into
Two Groups

Black's one-point jump at 1 emphasizes the center. But White 2 is an excellent play. Now Black has two weak groups to settle.

Black **A** is not successful, as White **B** will prevent Black connecting the two groups together.

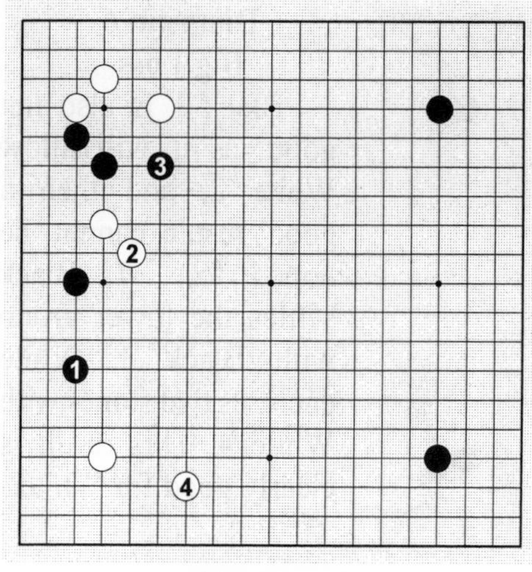

Diagram 4

Diagram 4
Wrong Direction

Black 1 attempts to settle the lower group. But after White, 2 Black's upper group is unsettled. If Black plays at 3 to escape to the center, White plays at 4. This result is good for White, because after Black 3, Black's group is still unsettled.

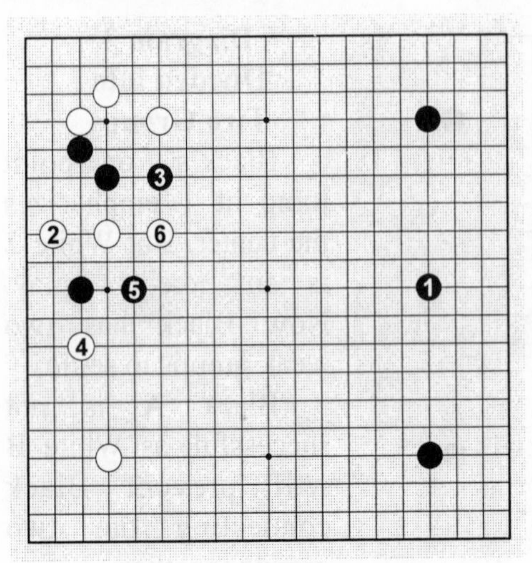

Diagram 5

Diagram 5
Two Weak Groups

Black's *sanrensei* at 1 is a short-sighted play to extend the influence on the right side. But White's one-point jump at 2 is very good. After the exchange of 3 to 6, Black has the huge burden of settling both groups.

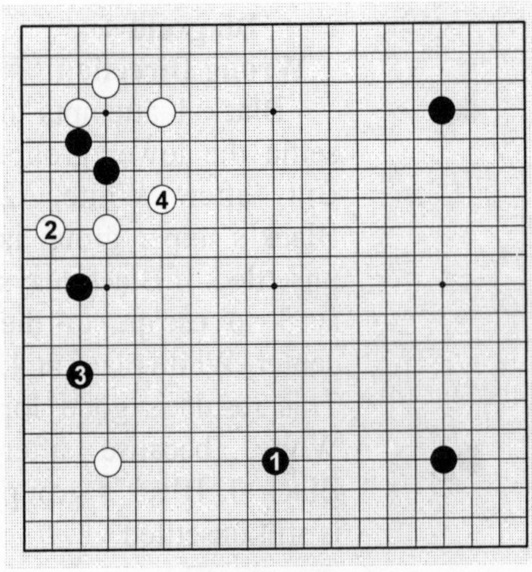

Diagram 6

Diagram 6
Big Loss

Black 1 is also not good, as it will allow White 2, and then a good result cannot be hoped for. If Black settles the lower group with Black 3, White encloses two stones with White 4. This result is clearly good for White.

Problem 35 Side Effects of a Running Fight

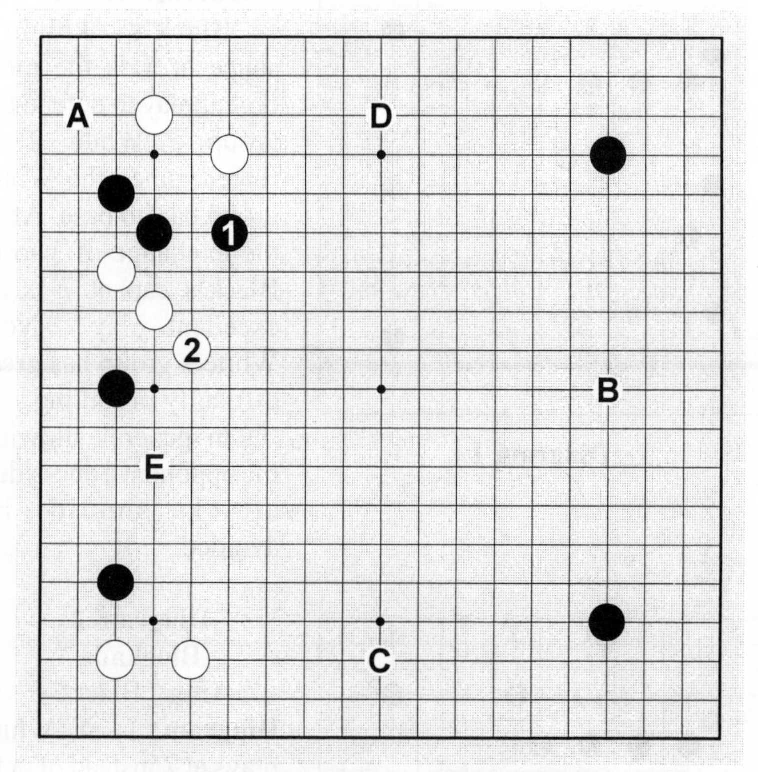

Problem Diagram – Black to play

Black 1 and White 2 focus on the center. It is not easy to decide the next play for Black. But if you understand the side effects of the floating group, you can solve this one readily. Choose the correct answer from **A** to **E**.

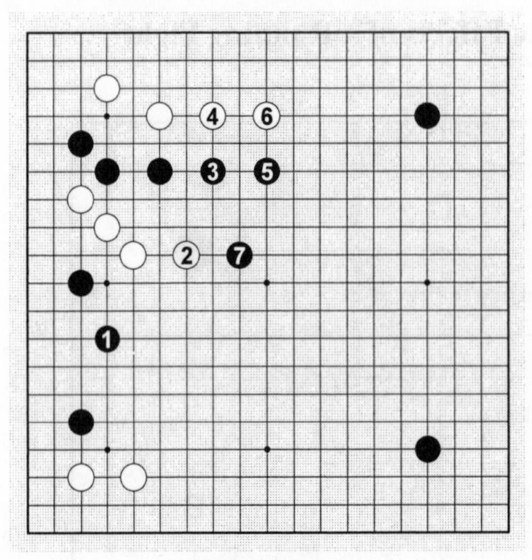

Diagram 1

Diagram 1
Correct Answer

Black's knight's shape at 1 is the most urgent play to defend the group. White 2 is forced, since the White group has no base. After the exchange of 3 to 6, Black's cap at 7 is an excellent play. Now White's group has great difficulty in settling.

In general allowing the opponent a one-sided attack should be avoided.

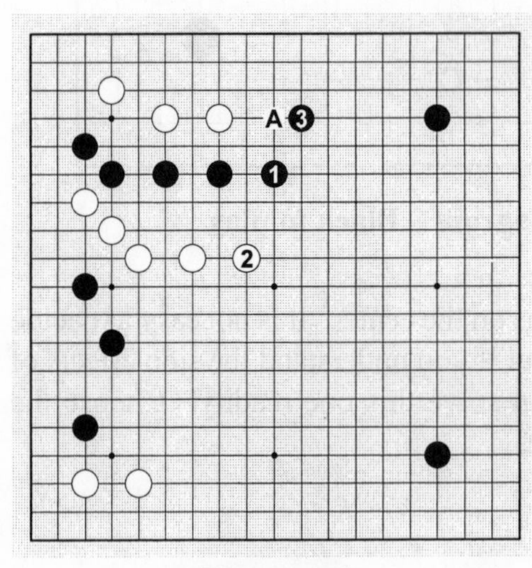

Diagram 2

Diagram 2
Blockade

After Black 5 in **Diagram 1**, if White plays at 2 instead of **A** to avoid Black's cap at 1, Black stops White's advance on the upper side with Black 3. This result is good for Black too, because Black's wall on the upper side is quite strong, while White's group is still unsettled.

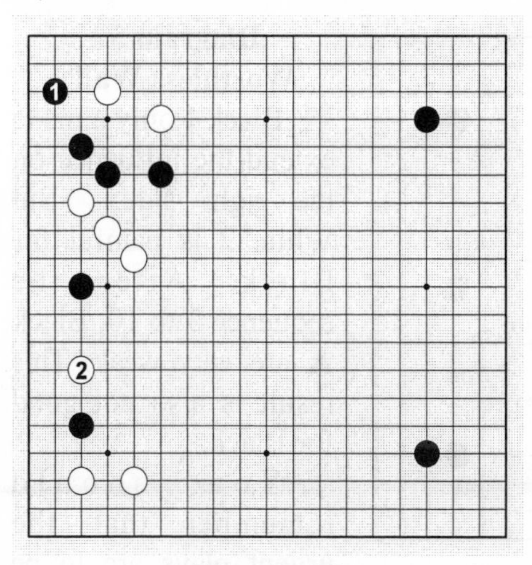

Diagram 3

Diagram 3
Defensive Principles

Black 1 aims to secure a base and steal White's base, but it is too early. If Black allows White 2, then immediately Black's group is divided into two. This is a very bad result for Black.

If you want to attack the opponent, you should settle your own weak group first; otherwise you will meet a counter-attack.

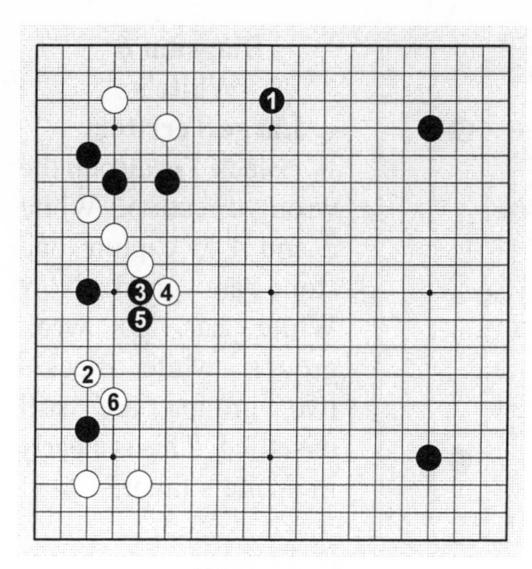

Diagram 4

Diagram 4
Poor Style

Black's extension at 1 is poor style. After allowing White 2, Black can't anticipate a good result. If Black plays at 3 and 5, White's diagonal link at 6 is a good maneuver. Now Black's one stone is almost captured, and also Black's group on the left side is still unsettled. This result is not good for Black.

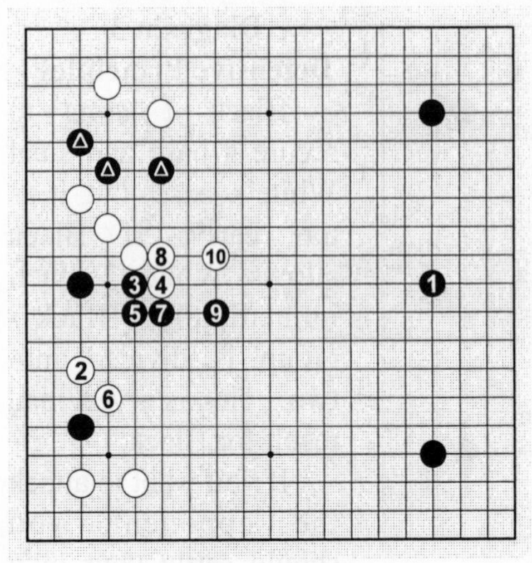

Diagram 5

Diagram 5
Worthless Wall

Black 1 only aims to extend the influence on the right side. But White 2 is painful for Black. After the sequence 3 to 10, Black ▲ are very weak. This result is also not good for Black.

You should remember that the urgent plays are to be made before the big plays.

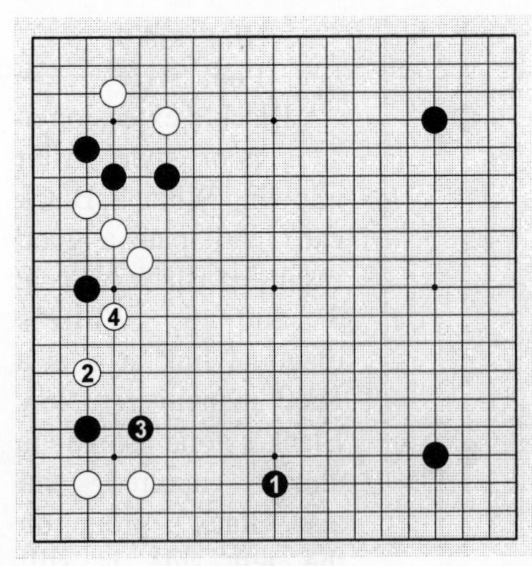

Diagram 6

Diagram 6
White's Large Territory

Black 1 is also in the wrong direction. White 2 and 4 to capture one stone are good. Now White has no weak groups, while Black's two groups are still unsettled. This is clearly in White's favor.

Problem 36 After One Side is Settled

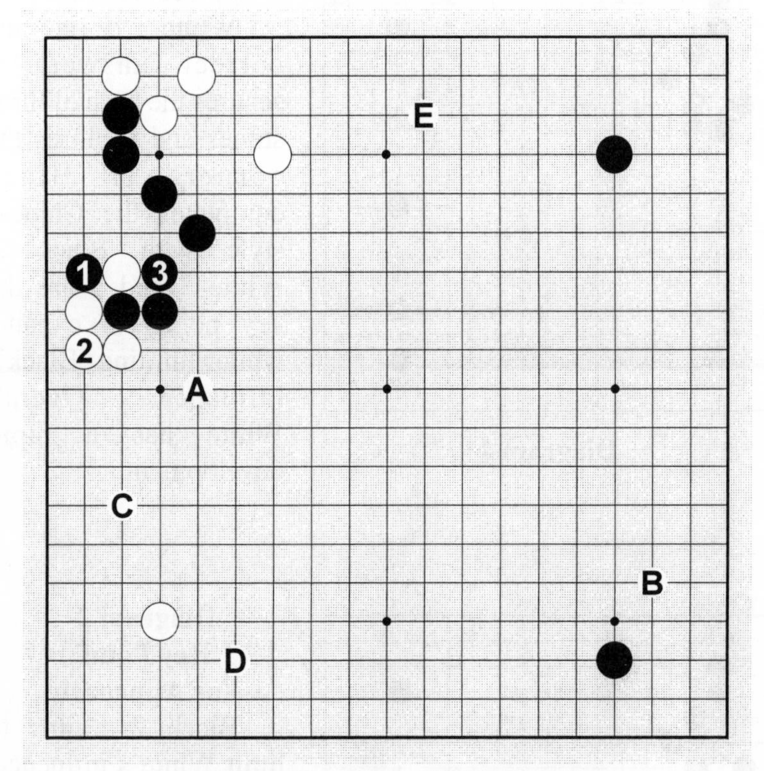

Problem Diagram – White to play

In the top left corner there is a *joseki* in process. Up to Black 3 Black has settled the group, capturing one stone. There are many big plays, but only one correct answer. Choose it, out of **A** to **E**. Hint: don't make a floating group.

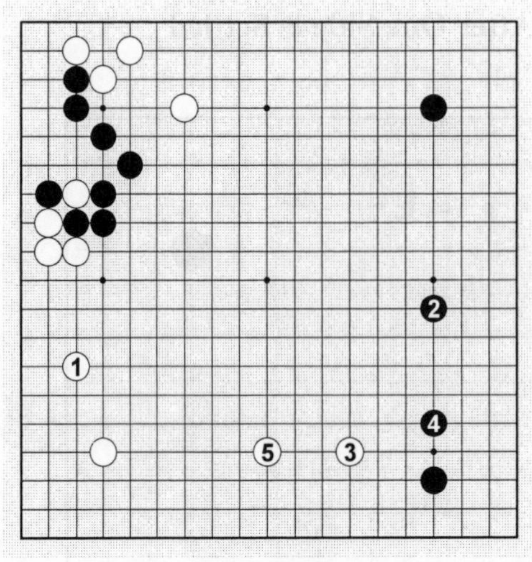

Diagram 1

Diagram 1
Correct Answer

White 1 is the correct answer: it secures the base of three stones and encloses the corner. If Black completes the Chinese style with Black 2, White 3 and 5 are the key points to expand, while limiting Black's influence. Overall White has a rapid development.

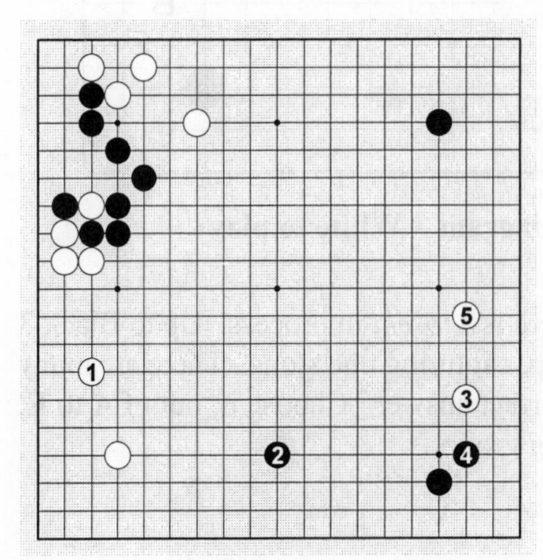

Diagram 2

Diagram 2
Key Point
For Approach

Black 2 aims to limit White's influence. White's approach at 3 is good to keep Black's corner small. Up to White 5, there seems to be a prolonged game in prospect.

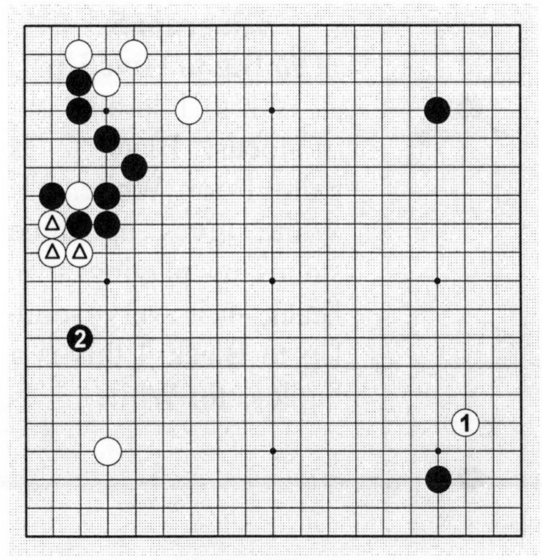

Diagram 3

Diagram 3
Floating Group

White's approach at 1 is a big play, but Black's pincer at 2 is too severe on White. Now Δ have great difficulty in settling. This result is clearly good for Black.

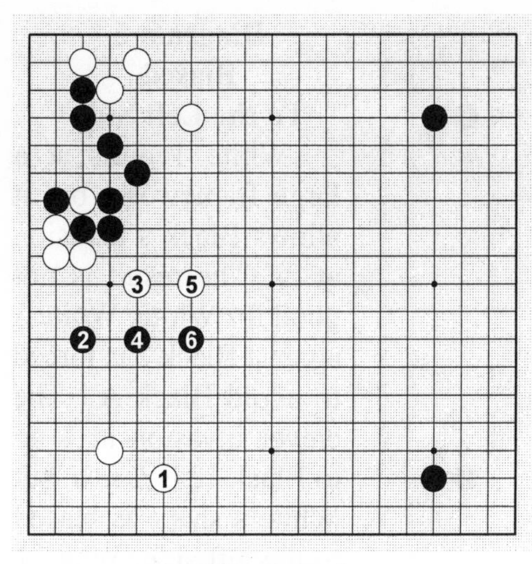

Diagram 4

Diagram 4
Painful Pincer

White 1 is the wrong direction. After allowing Black's pincer at 2, White can't expect a good result. Up to Black 6 White's group is still under threat. The result is disastrous for White.

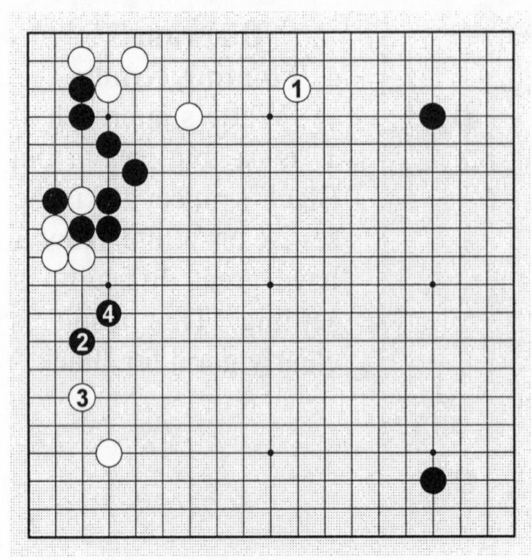

Diagram 5

Diagram 5
Too Big to Give Up

White 1 is also out of focus. Black 2 is painful for White. If White gives up three stones by playing at 3, Black 4 is very solid. Up to Black 4 this is a big loss for White.

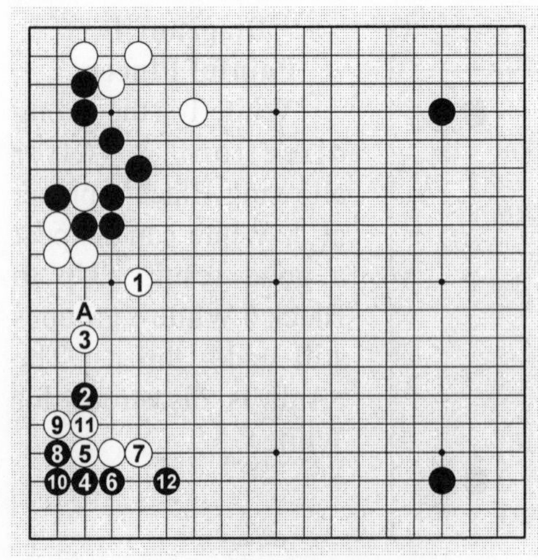

Diagram 6

Diagram 6
Biased
To the Left Side

White 1 aims at a large framework, but it allows Black's invasion at 2. The result is not good for White. White 3 against Black 2 is forced to avoid Black **A**. The clever invasion at 4 up to Black 12 is *joseki*, but White's shape is biased to the left side. White 1 is bad, since Black's territory is better than White's framework.

Problem 37 Saving Face

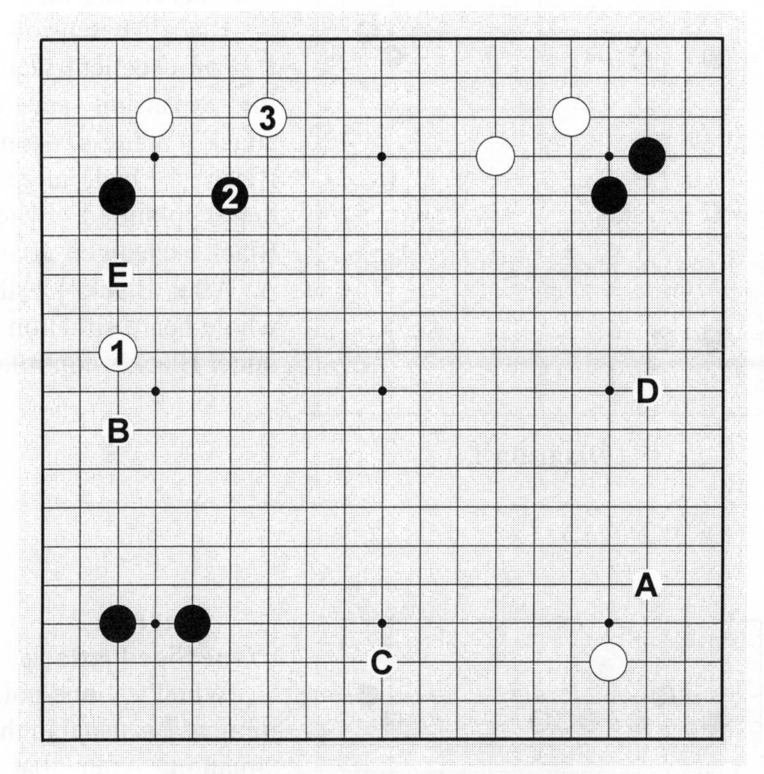

Problem Diagram – Black to play

When White pincers at 1, and Black jumps out two points, White's two-point extension at 3 on the upper side is natural. Now you should find the most efficient play, considering the position of the stones, to take the lead in the game. Choose it from **A** to **E**.

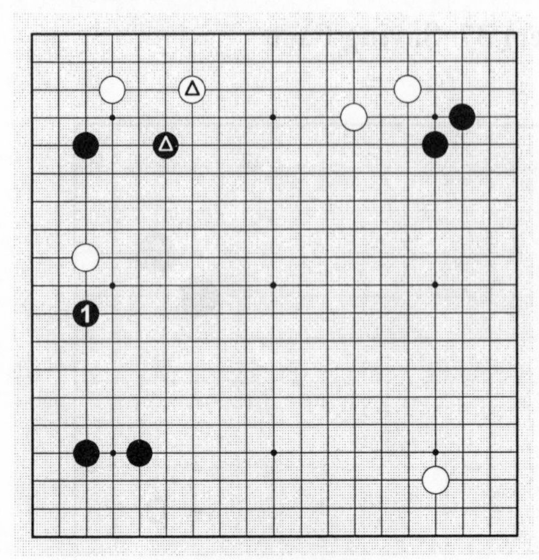

Diagram 1

Diagram 1
Correct Answer

Black's extension at 1 is an excellent tactic, for expansion and to attack White's stone. Black 1 had already been planned when Black exchanged ▲ and Δ. After Black 1, the whole board situation is under Black's control.

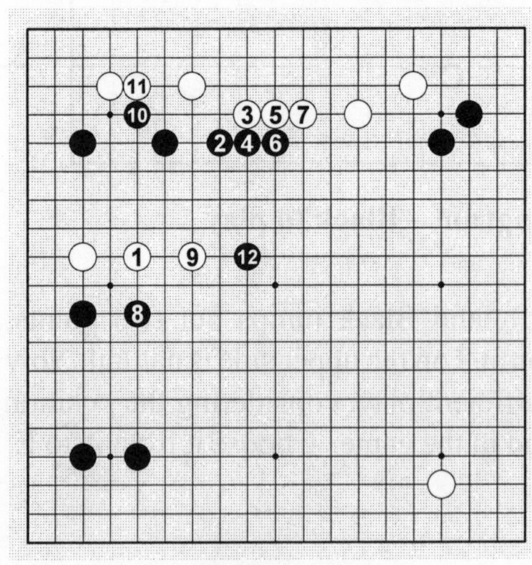

Diagram 2

Diagram 2
One Sided Attack

White's one-point jump at 1 is usual in this situation. After that a wall is formed with Black 2 to 6 and then White's group is attacked with Black 8. Up to Black 12, globally speaking, Black controls the entire board.

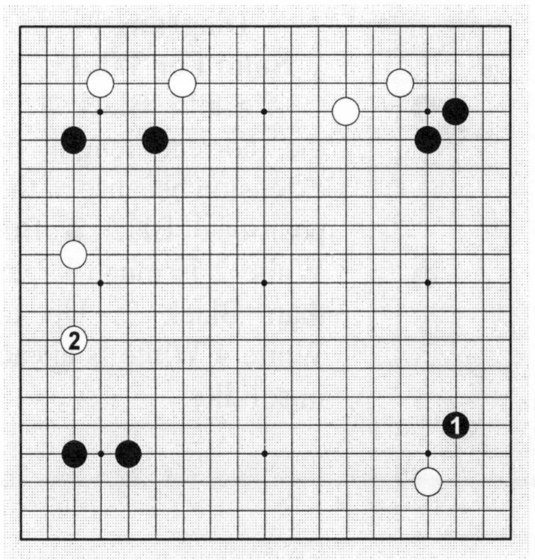

Diagram 3

Diagram 3
Missing The Chance

Black's approach at 1 is a big play. But White's two-point extension at 2 is very good. Now Black's two stones are relatively weak because White's two stones on the left side are already settled.

In general urgent points should be played before big points.

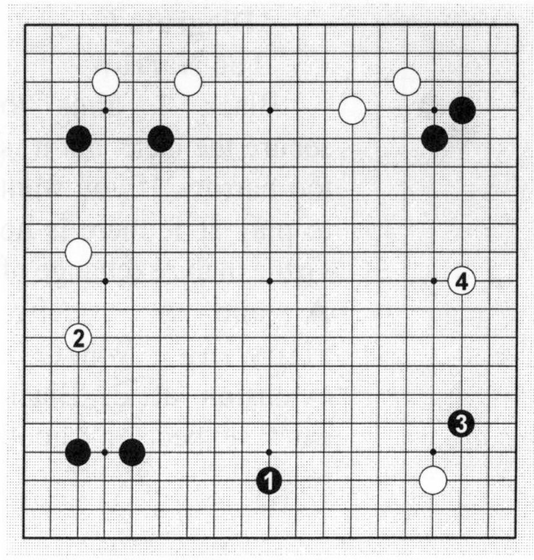

Diagram 4

Diagram 4
Wrong Direction

Black 1 is also out of focus. It is a mere extension. On the other hand White 2 settles White's group, limiting Black's influence also. Up to White 4 this result is in White's favor. You should consider the efficiency of the stones when you choose the next play.

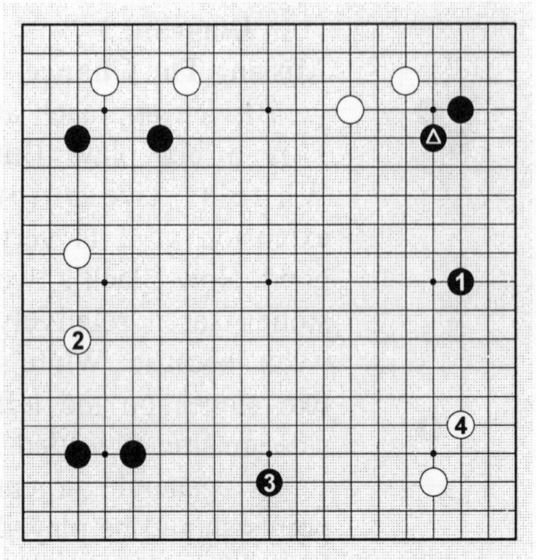

Diagram 5

Diagram 5
Solid For White

Locally Black 1 is the correct length of extension because of the position of Black ▲. But White 2 is much larger than Black 1. Up to White 4 White is ahead in solidity.

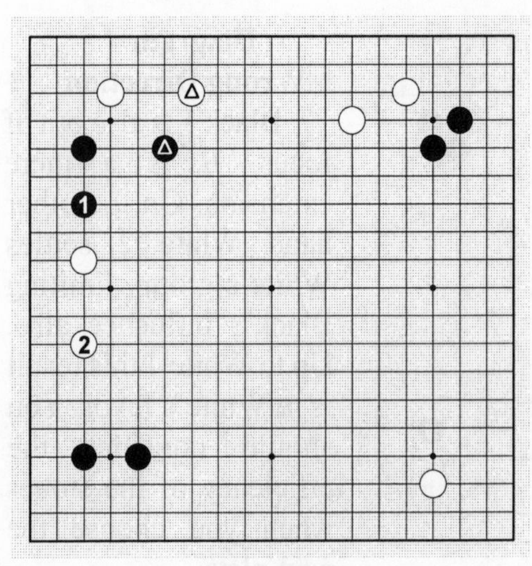

Diagram 6

Diagram 6
Too Narrow

Black 1 aims to secure the base, but it is too narrow. If you want to play at 1, there is no virtue in the exchange of ▲ and Δ. After allowing White's extension at 2, Black can't expect a good result.

Problem 38 Two Birds with One Stone

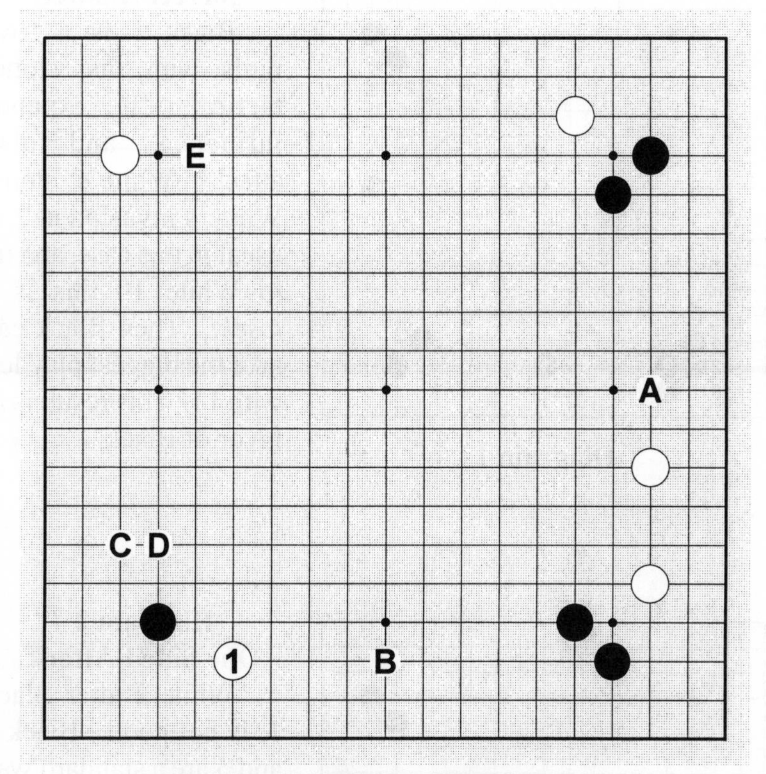

Problem Diagram – Black to play

White has just approached at 1. Overall the shape of Black's groups is very solid. The key point is how to use this type of thickness. Choose the best answer from **A** to **E**. Hint: two birds with one stone.

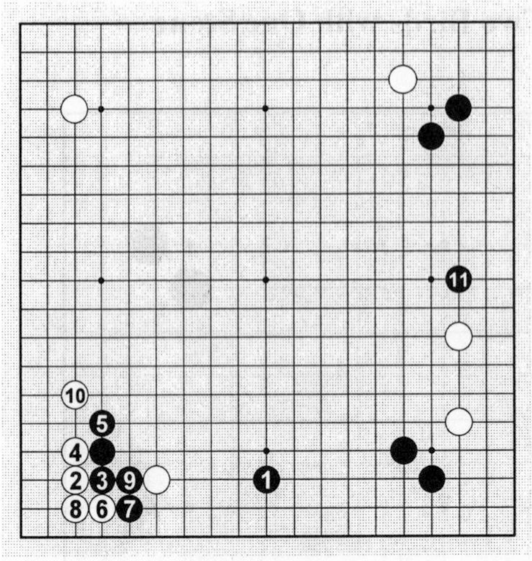

Diagram 1

Diagram 1
Correct Answer

Black 1 is a 'two birds with one stone' tactic. It expands influence, and also attacks White's stone. White's invasion at 2 is usual in this case, and up to White 10 this is a *joseki*. Then Black can take the biggest play left with 11. This result is in favor of Black.

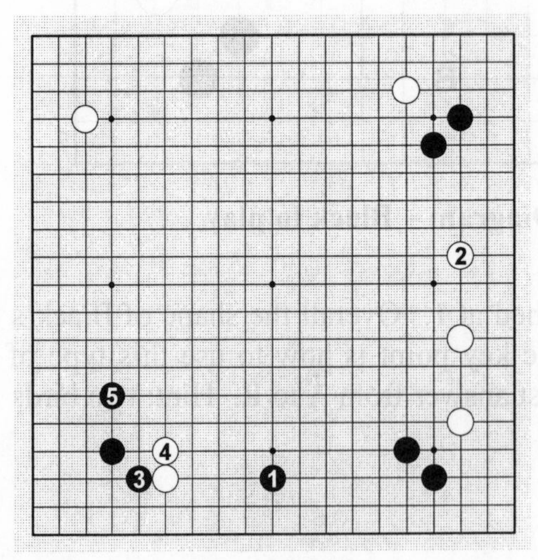

Diagram 2

Diagram 2
One Sided Attack

White 2 after Black 1, is not good. Black 3 and 5 are a standard way to attack. Now White's lower group is a little heavy, so White will have to pay something to settle it. This result is not good for White.

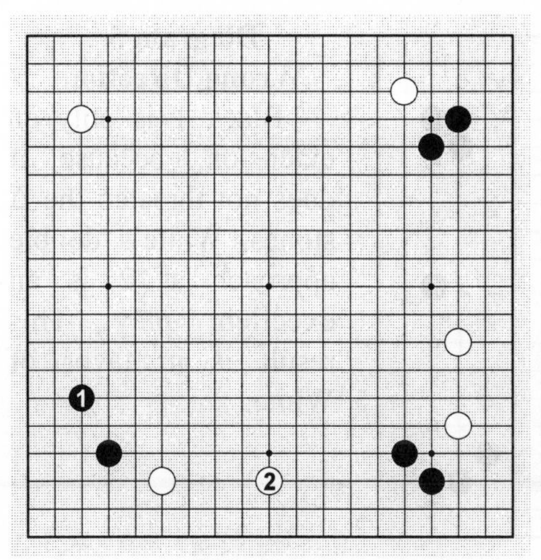

Diagram 3

Diagram 3
Careless Response 1

Black's knight's shape enclosure at 1 is poor style. White's extension at 2 is a good play to settle the group, and to prevent Black's expansion. This result is good for White.

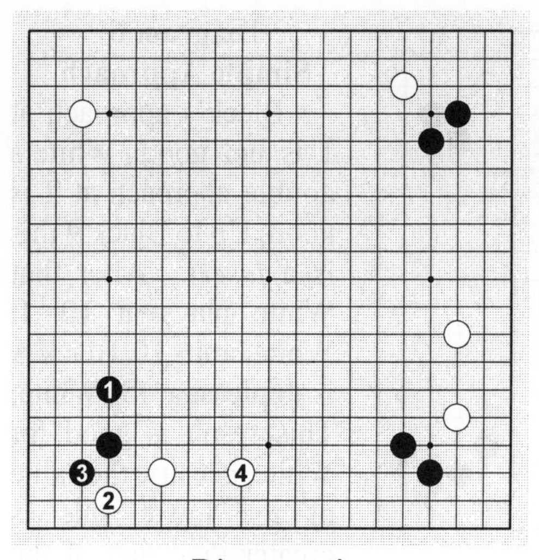

Diagram 4

Diagram 4
Careless Response 2

Black's one-point answer at 1 is also not good. White's 2 and 4 are routine to settle White's group. Up to White 4, the result is good for White.

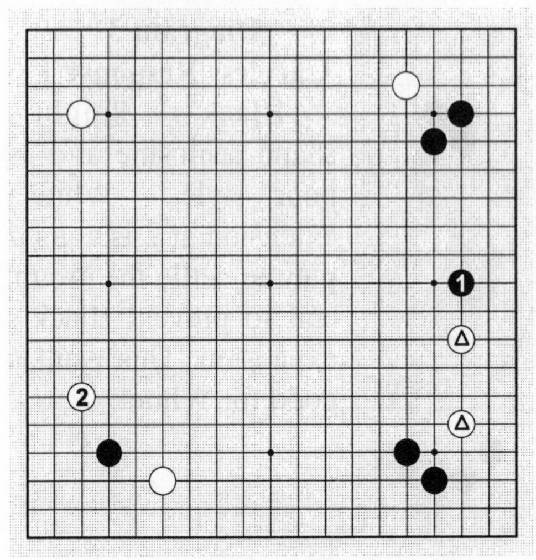

Diagram 5

Diagram 5
Wrong Direction

Black 1 is only an extension, because it does not threaten the Δ stones. White's double approach at 2 is an excellent play. This result is in favor of White.

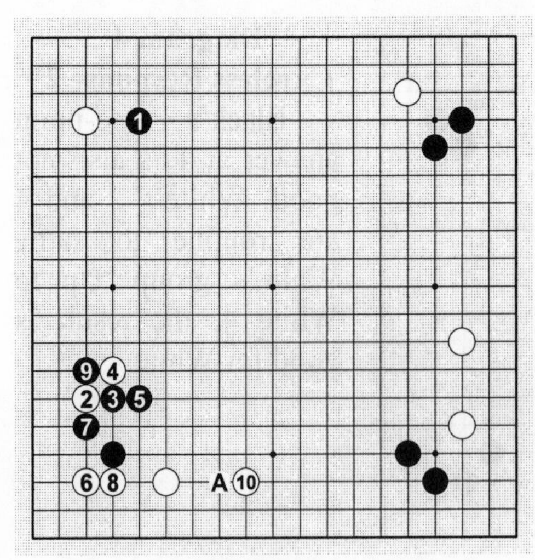

Diagram 6

Diagram 6
Simple Approach

Black's approach at 1 is not good. White's double approach at 2 is good. Up to Black 9 this is a *joseki*. After that White plays at 10. If White omits 10, Black **A** is unpleasant for White. This result is good for White, because the value of the lower side is greater than that of the upper side.

Problem 39 A Hardworking Play

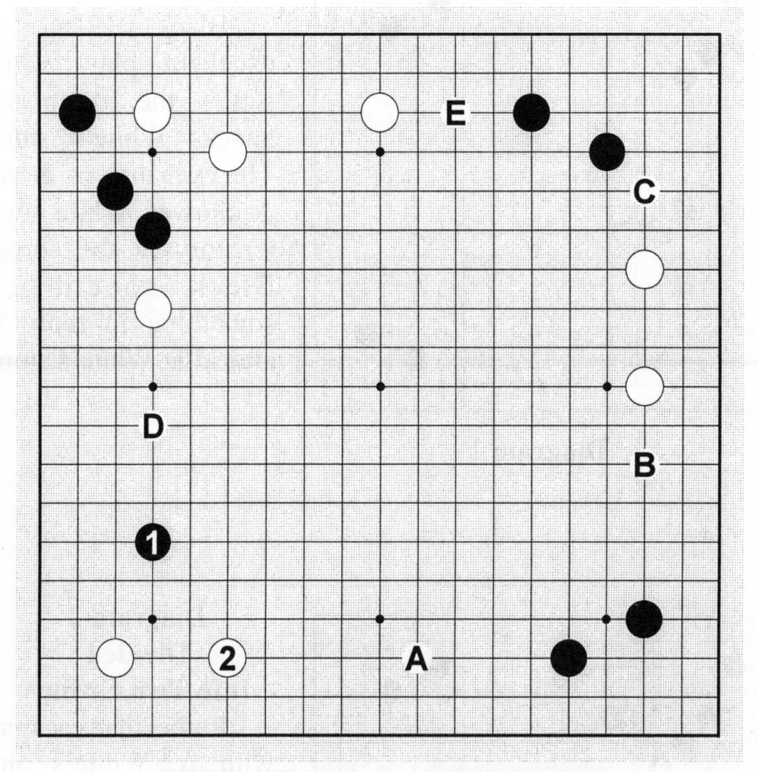

Problem Diagram – Black to play

Black's approach at 1 to White's 3-3 point is a common idea. White 2 is also a standard response. Now there is a tactic to kill two birds with one stone. Choose the correct play, out of **A** to **E**.

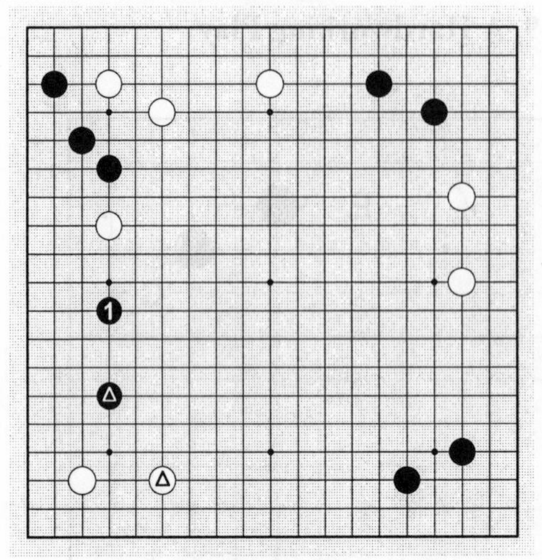

Diagram 1

Diagram 1
Correct Answer

Black 1 is an excellent play, which settles the group and attacks White's stone. The exchange of ▲ and Δ allowed White some territory in the corner. Black should get something in reply by attacking White's stone.

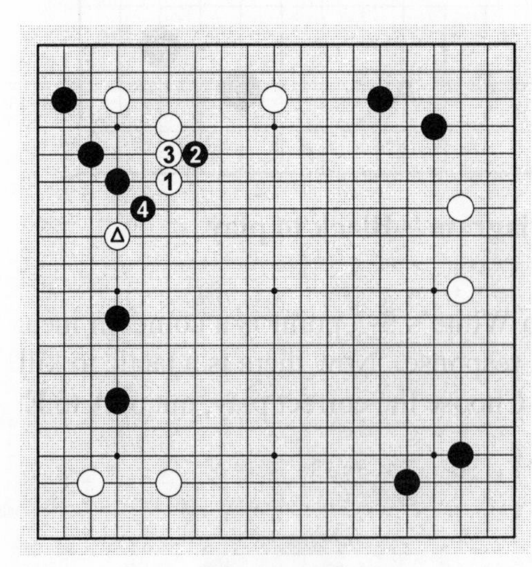

Diagram 2

Diagram 2
Divided
Into Two Groups

Rather than escaping with Δ, White's one-point jump at 1 is good. From White's point of view, it is better to give up Δ, because White has already earned some territory on the top side. After the peep at 2, Black 4 is good to divide White's forces into two. Up to Black 4 the result is quite even.

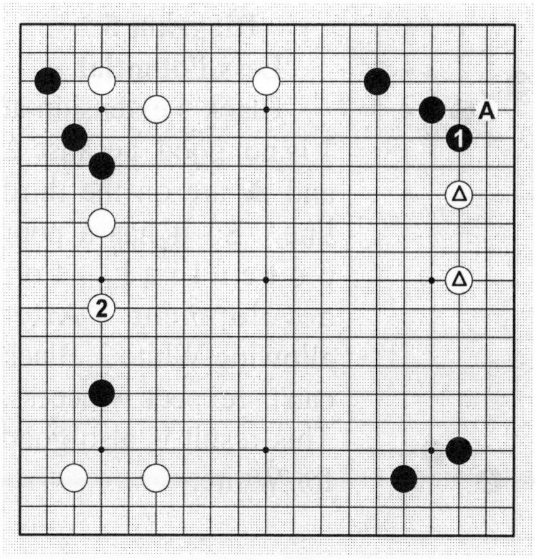

Diagram 3

Diagram 3
Too Early

Comparing with White **A**, Black 1 to keep the corner territory is a big play. But here it is played too early and its value is not high, as the Δ stones are settled. White 2 is an excellent extension, which settles the group and attacks Black's stone. This result is good for White.

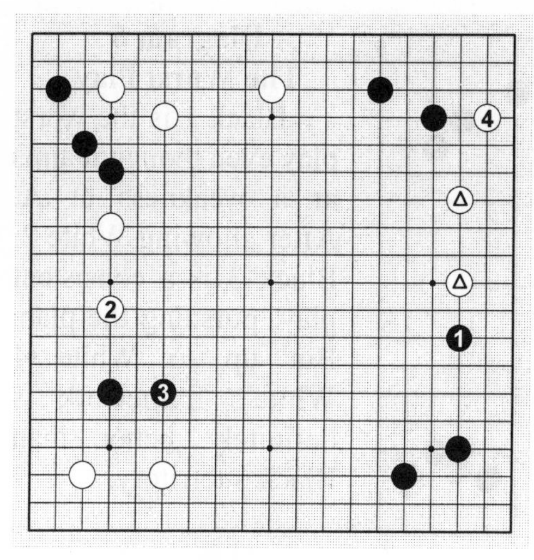

Diagram 4

Diagram 4
Wrong Direction

Black 1 attempts to expand the corner, but it is not big enough, because the Δ stones are already settled. After that White 2 is unpleasant for Black. Up to White 4 the result is good for White.

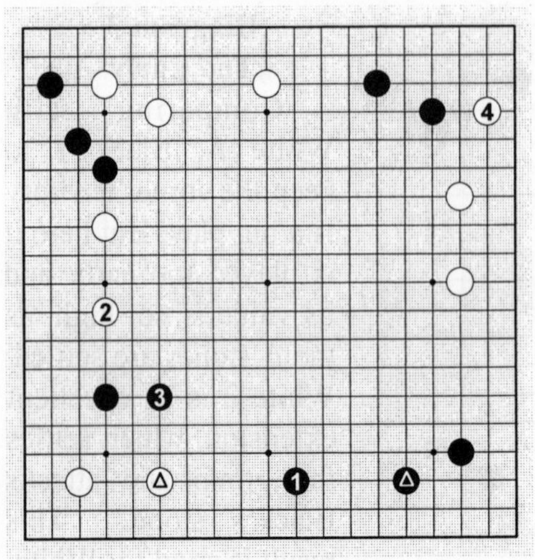

Diagram 5

Diagram 5
Less Potential

Black's extension at 1 is not good, because Δ and ▲ are on the third line. So it has a poor potential for development. After allowing White 2, Black can't expect success. This result is also good for White.

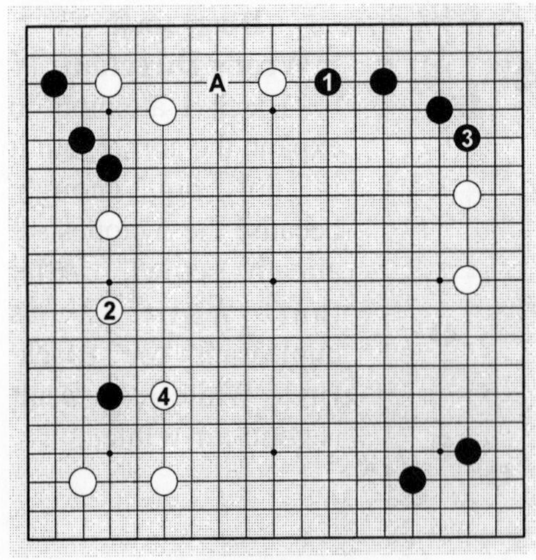

Diagram 6

Diagram 6
The Worst Play

Black 1 is the worst play even though it aims at a weakness at **A**. After allowing White 2, Black 3 is a consistent play, pursuing the plan. But up to White 4 White's framework is definitely better than Black's territory.

Problem 40 Awareness of One's Surroundings

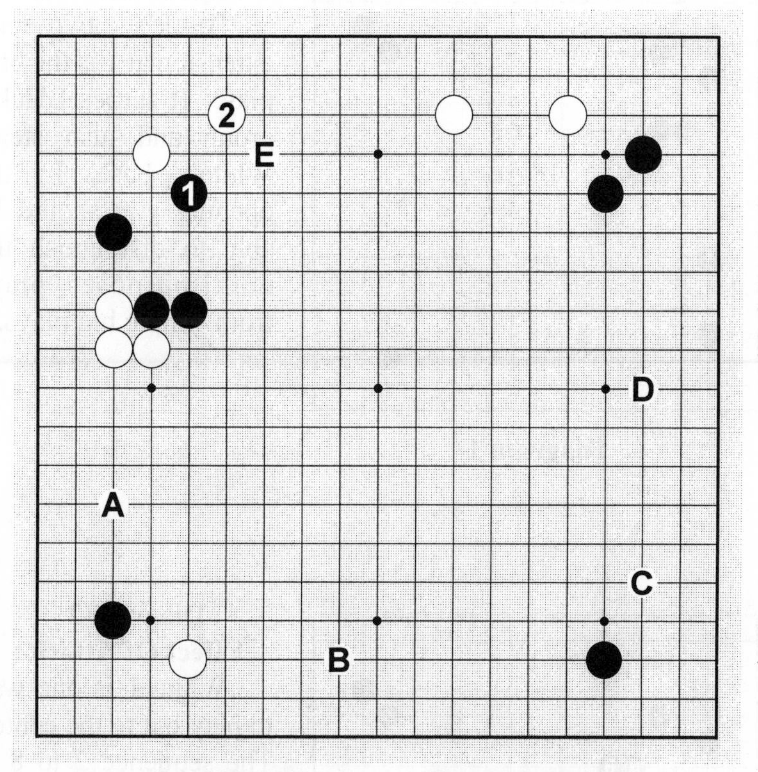

Problem Diagram – Black to play

Black 1 is inevitable to reinforce the group, even though the exchange of Black 1 and White 2 strengthens White's corner territory. Now Black should be able to find the most efficient play, by considering the surroundings. Choose the best answer from **A** to **E**.

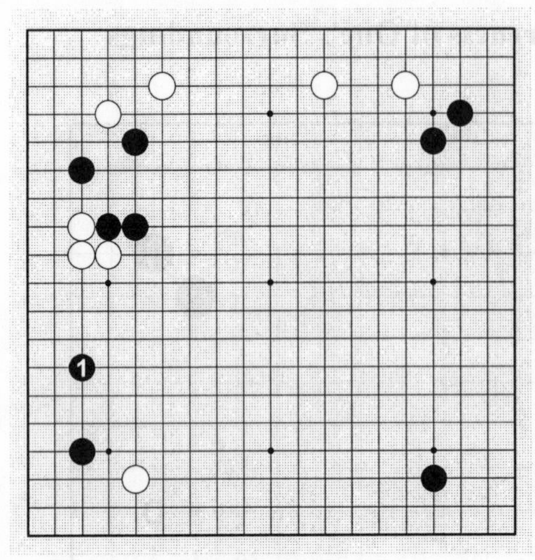

Diagram 1

Diagram 1
Correct Answer

Black's two-point extension at 1 is the best play. It settles Black's group and also steals White's base. In the opening you should be able to distinguish the multi-purpose plays from simple big plays.

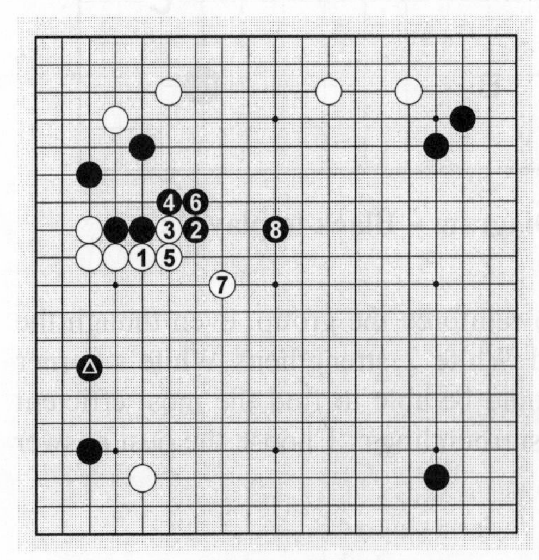

Diagram 2

Diagram 2
Effect Of Attack

White 1 is one way to play out to the center. The sequence 2 to 8 is routine. Up to Black 8 Black earns something, while White's wall is almost worthless because of Black ▲.

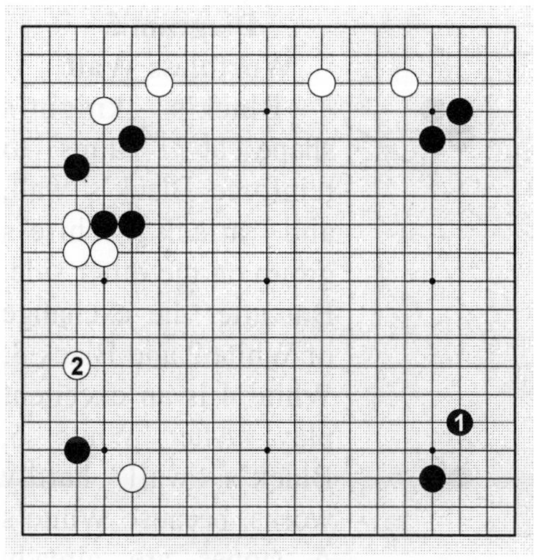

Diagram 3

Diagram 3
Back To Front?

Black's corner enclosure at 1 is a big play, but it is too early, because the left side is not settled. White's extension at 2 kills two birds with one stone: it extends White's influence, whilst it also attacks Black's stone. Comparing with the previous Diagrams, the situation is totally reversed.

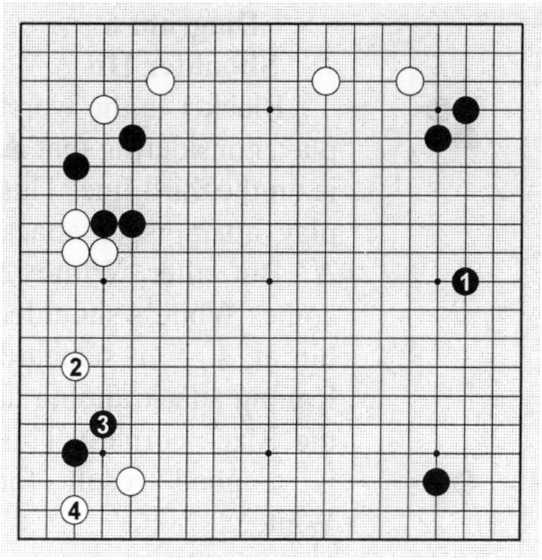

Diagram 4

Diagram 4
Key Point For Attack

Black's extension at 1 is not good. White 2 is very severe on Black. Black aims to run out into the center. White 4 is the key point to attack Black's group and steal the base. Now Black will have to pay to settle the floating group.

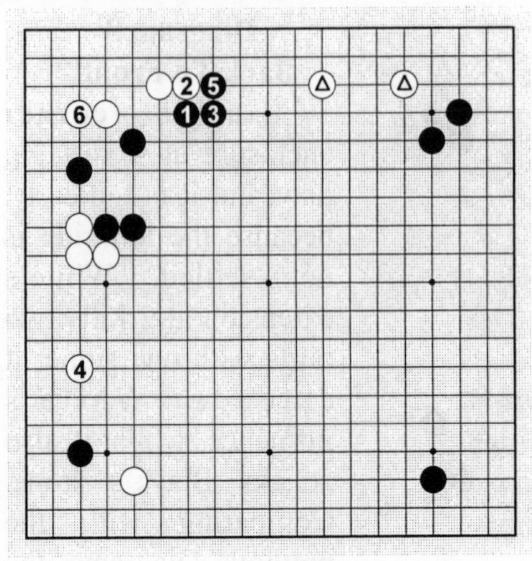

Diagram 5

Diagram 5
Worthless Wall

Black's knight's shape at 1 aims to reinforce Black's wall, and attack White's group on the other side. But after the exchange of White 2 and Black 3, White 4 is an excellent play. After White 6, Black's wall hardly works, because White's Δ stones are already settled. This result is in favor of White.

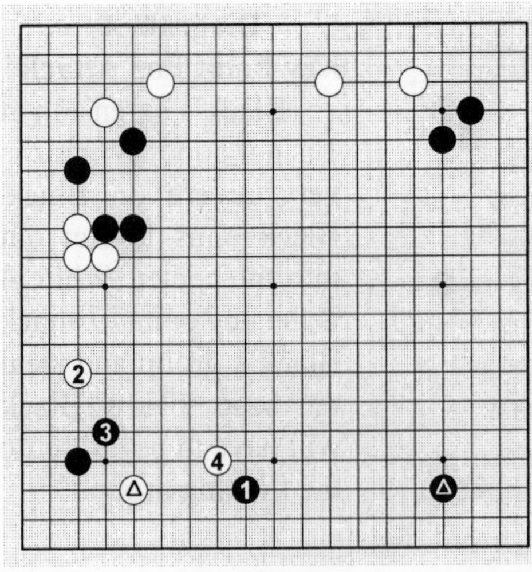

Diagram 6

Diagram 6
Shoulder Hit

Black 1 is the worst play, considering that ▲ is on the third line. This play attempts to attack Δ. But after White 2 comes White's shoulder hit at 4 – a standard leaning attack aiming at the Black corner. This is a good result for White.

Problem 41 Protect Your Investment

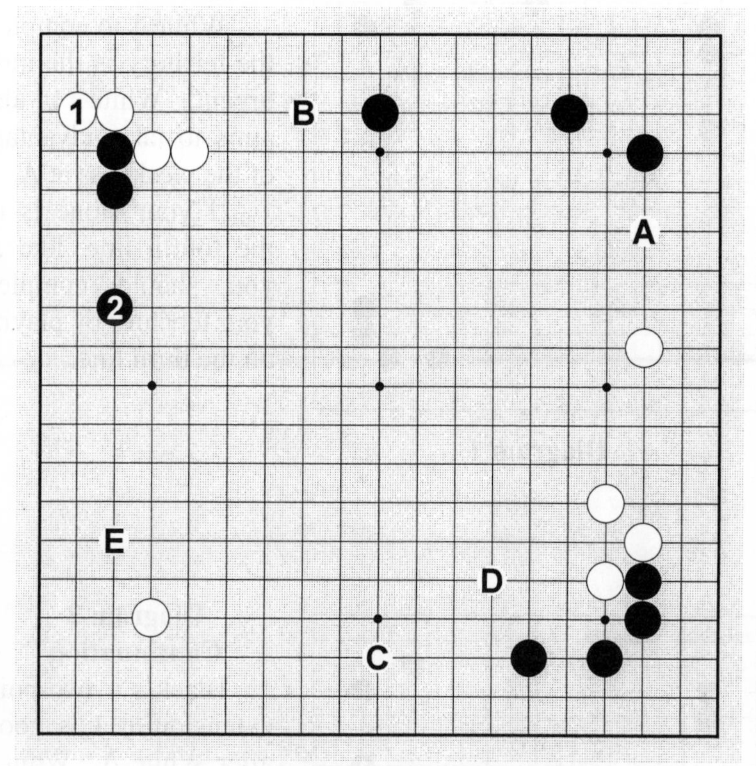

Problem Diagram – White to play

White 1 is big for territory and it also concerns the base of two groups. Black settles the group with the two-point extension at 2. Now you should protect your investment. Choose the correct play from **A** to **E**.

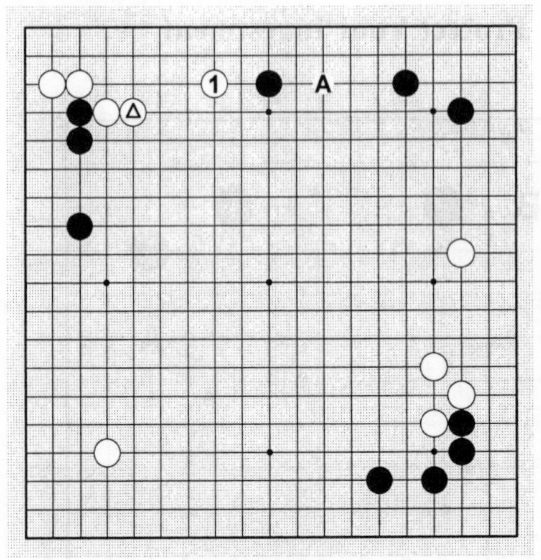

Diagram 1

Diagram 1
Correct Answer

White 1 to complete the territory is the most urgent. White 1 also aims to take advantage of the weakness at **A**.

If your stone is on the fourth line, like Δ, you should complete your territory by playing on the third line.

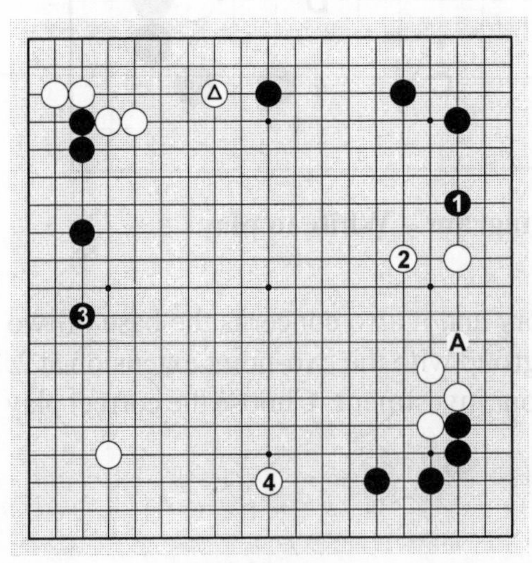

Diagram 2

Diagram 2
Continuation

Black's two-point extension at 1 is good, after White Δ. White's one-point jump at 2 aims to develop further, while protecting the weakness at **A**. Then Black 3 and White 4 are almost *miai*. On the whole, up to White 4, White has the more positive shape.

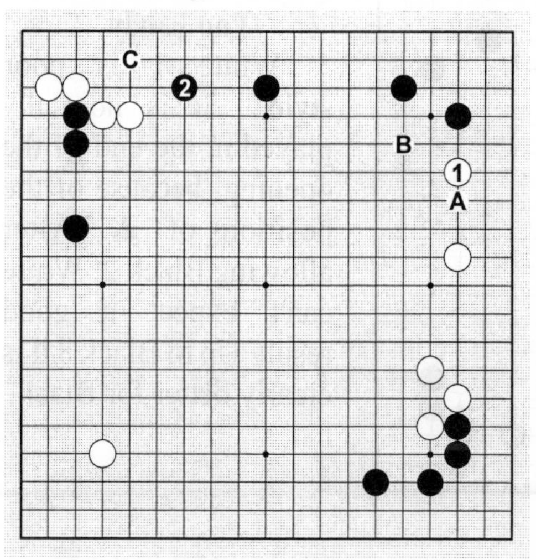

Diagram 3

Diagram 3
Tactical Weakness

White 1 is the second-best play. It prevents Black **A**, and aims at **B** to increase White's influence. But after allowing Black 2, White has a potential weakness at **C**. If White allows Black **C**, White's corner group is immediately in trouble.

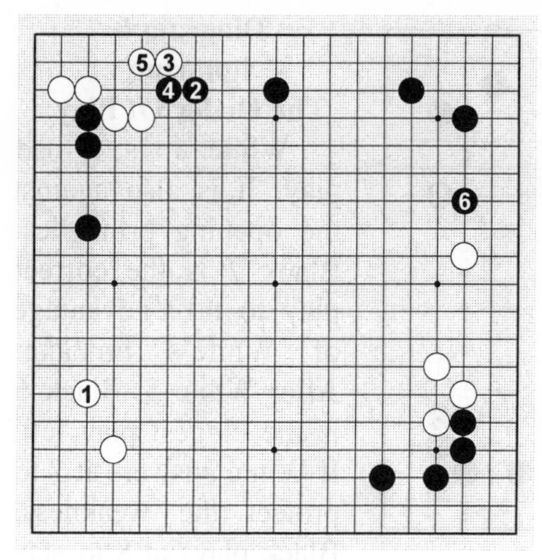

Diagram 4

Diagram 4
Retreat

White's corner enclosure at 1 is too early. Black 2 is very severe on White. Retreat at White 3 and 5 is forced, in order to protect the group. After that Black takes the biggest play left with 6. This result is clearly good for Black.

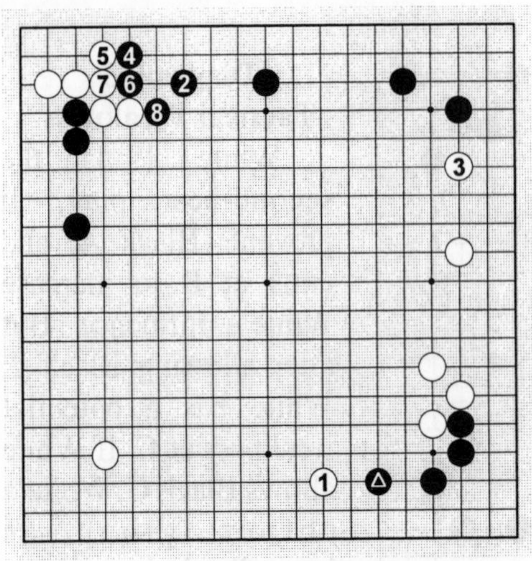

Diagram 5

Diagram 5
Too Early

White 1 is poor style. It is normally played at the end of the opening, because of the position of ▲. After allowing Black 2, White can't expect a good result. Up to Black 8 it is clearly better for Black.

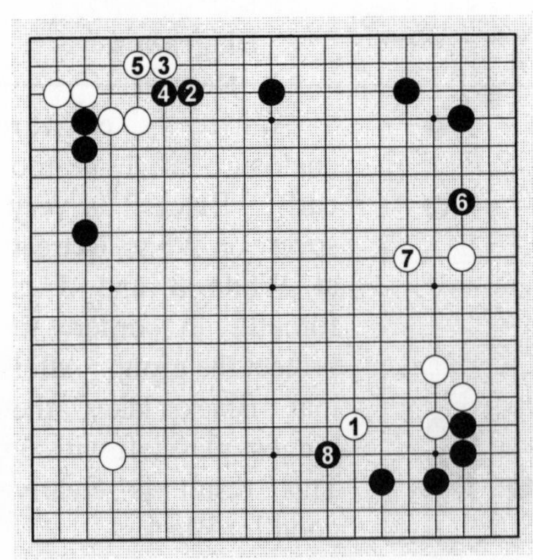

Diagram 6

Diagram 6
Ignoring
The Order Of Play

White 1 is a bad play. It is also against the opening principles. Black 2 is the correct play to take advantage of White's mistake. After White 5, Black 6 is the biggest play left. If White answers at 7 to protect the weakness, Black plays at 8 to stay ahead in the game. This is a good result for Black.